Quizzing America

Quizzing America
Television Game Shows and Popular Culture in the 1950s

MARK DUNN

McFarland & Company, Inc., Publishers
Jefferson, North Carolina

ALSO OF INTEREST

Mark Dunn *and* Mary Dunn
United States Counties
(McFarland, 2003; paperback 2011)

LIBRARY OF CONGRESS CATALOGUING-IN-PUBLICATION DATA

Names: Dunn, Mark, 1956– author.
Title: Quizzing America : television game shows and popular culture in the 1950s / Mark Dunn.
Description: Jefferson, North Carolina : McFarland & Company, Inc., Publishers, 2018. | Includes bibliographical references and index.
Identifiers: LCCN 2017052630 | ISBN 9781476665504 (softcover : acid free paper) ∞
Subjects: LCSH: Television quiz shows—United States—History—20th century. | Television game shows—United States—History—20th century.
Classification: LCC PN1992.8.Q5 D86 2018 | DDC 791.45/6—dc23
LC record available at https://lccn.loc.gov/2017052630

BRITISH LIBRARY CATALOGUING DATA ARE AVAILABLE

ISBN (print) 978-1-4766-6550-4
ISBN (ebook) 978-1-4766-3050-2

© 2018 Mark Dunn. All rights reserved

No part of this book may be reproduced or transmitted in any form or by any means, electronic or mechanical, including photocopying or recording, or by any information storage and retrieval system, without permission in writing from the publisher.

Front cover image of Groucho Marx, with the secret-word duck in *You Bet Your Life* TV series, 1950–1961 (NBC/Photofest)

Printed in the United States of America

McFarland & Company, Inc., Publishers
  Box 611, Jefferson, North Carolina 28640
  www.mcfarlandpub.com

For my wife Mary,
Gary Wetstein and all my fellow
What's My Line? aficionados,
and to the memory of Betsy Palmer,
who taught me to smile

Table of Contents

Introduction   1

1. Radio Daze   9
2. Transition   23
3. All the Little People   29
4. A Nation of Shopkeepers and Worm Farmers   35
5. It's News (or History) to Me   44
6. There Is Nothing Like a Dame   58
7. Sound No Trumpet When Giving Alms   71
8. Welcome to the Big Apple   82
9. Guess Who's Probably Not Coming to Dinner   92
10. A Beautiful Mosaic (Still Under Construction)   105
11. And Now a Mandate from Our Sponsor …   109
12. Walpurgisnacht   124
13. Jackpot!   138
14. What's the Matter with Kids Today?   145
15. The Love That Dare Not Speak Its Name   151
16. All Fall Down   155

17. They Were the Best of Times; They Were the Stupidest of Times	165
18. Future Dark, Future Bright	173
19. A Procession of Game Shows	181
Chapter Notes	183
Bibliography	197
Index	203

Introduction

I spent just three and a half years of my life in the "Fabulous '50s," but I find myself connected to that decade in a number of interesting ways. Long before I contemplated writing this book, I was navigating through the decade with an eye to lending historic authenticity to the ten stories that would make up the 1950s section of my 100-stories-of-the-century opus *American Decameron*. I discovered that the '50s weren't all rock'n'roll and "I Like Ike." Over the course of those ten years, the United States advanced both socially and culturally. Great strides were made in the fields of science, technology, civil rights, governance and the arts.

Conversely, the decade has been deprecated by historians for its many shortcomings and dramatic stumbles.

The 1950s most assuredly had its warts. But it also had "the box."

In its earliest years as a mass medium, TV did a fine job—which radio could only envy—of serving as an enormous picture window for the nation. Its programs reminded us of an astounding number of good things the country had going for it, as well as those things that undermined, even conspired against, its lofty and noble aspirations.

On February 1, 1951, thousands of Los Angeles residents who happened to have access to a television receiver watched the first telecast of an atomic blast—an operation engineered with MacGyver-like resourcefulness by station KTLA.[1] There were live network television broadcasts of both Senator Kefauver's committee to investigate organized crime, and the Army-McCarthy hearings, which shone a bright light on a man who was to some Americans the epitome of redoubtable patriotism, and to a good many others a grandstanding Robespierre-like zealot. Both of the decade's political conventions received extensive TV network coverage—a "you are there" video experience that put the fusty efforts of newspapers, radio and newsreels to shame.

Introduction

I was born at the height of the Baby Boom, when America had a sentimental obsession with love and marriage—which, according to Frank Sinatra, went together like a "horse and carriage." My mom and dad did their duty. Good Protestants, they produced the requisite four Americans-in-miniature. The nation's new moms and dads created a booming market for an eye-popping panoply of products and services related to the birthing, care and feeding of the millions of squirming, cloth-diapered fruits of their unions. They also created a vast market for home entertainment, sponsored by the providers of those products and services.

What's My Line?, the Rolls-Royce of 1950s quiz shows, included as challengers to the show's illustrious bib-and-tuckered panel of occupation guessers, a parade of men and women who made their livings in the thriving and diverse postwar economy. *What's My Line?* booked a surprising number of marriage counselors over the course of its 17-year history. The show also booked a surprising number of girdle models and "lady" wrestlers, too. And there was no shortage of contestants on *What's My Line?* during its first ten seasons—which, first airing on February 2, 1950, came close to spanning the entire decade.

I was friends with the actress Betsy Palmer, who, among her many screen credits, served as a Goodson-Todman game show panelist. Betsy sat for several years behind the *I've Got a Secret* dais. She was generously forthcoming with stories about her work in film (even her turn as Mrs. Voorhees in *Friday the 13th*, which earned her celebrity status at horror movie conventions) and was especially proud of her large body of work from television's "Golden Age" of live drama. Yet Betsy rarely spoke to me about her years as a game show panelist. The best I was able to get was her opinion of fellow *I've Got a Secret* panelist Henry Morgan: his cantankerous reputation was all an act; in reality, Morgan was a "real teddy bear" (at least to her).

I can't say, though, that it was my friendship with Betsy alone that fed my interest in the game shows of TV's formative years. As a high school student, I spent many afterschool half-hours watching Bob Barker and his syndicated version of *Truth or Consequences*. I wondered about the show's network antecedent—the brainchild of veteran game show host and producer Ralph Edwards. Was that earlier network incarnation just as entertaining as the later carnival-Barkered version, or was it even better? My now studied opinion: the original *Truth or Consequences* was better.

I learned while working on this book that my great uncle Tilman once appeared as a contestant on an early 1960s network game show called *Say When*. Uncle Tilman wasn't a winner that day, but he did go home with a couple of not-too-shabby consolation prizes: a Polaroid camera and a set of encyclopedias. And a good friend, Linda Lopez McAlister, revealed that she had appeared on *Twenty-One* but "was *not* one of those who got the answers." Linda, a theater buff, recalled that she used her winnings to buy tickets to every Broadway show on the boards that month.

Game shows offered a certain kind of stimulation that other programming lacked. My great-grandfather, following a series of debilitating strokes in the 1950s, lost all interest in television, with the exception of a single show: *Beat the Clock*. One of the highest-rated audience-participation shows of the decade, *Beat the Clock* was "stunt"-based, subjecting couples, usually husbands and wives, to physical challenges that ranged from silly to outlandish. My great-grandfather's damaged brain was apparently uniquely engaged by the show's shenanigans—he never missed an episode.

My last connection to 1950s game shows comes from my late mother, Mimi Dunn, who, early in my life, acquired such a visceral dislike for a particular show that she banned it from the Dunn family Motorola for all eight years of its broadcast run. Categorized as one of the "agonies" (there were actually several other game shows of this maudlin ilk), *Queen for a Day* is regarded by no small number of broadcast historians as the worst multiple-season series in TV history. (Though, curiously, *TV Guide* lists it among "The Sixty Greatest Game Shows of All Time." Then again, *TV Guide* also includes on its un-explicated list *The $64,000 Question* and *Twenty-One*, two of the biggest offenders in the game-rigging scandal that blackened the eye of the whole industry.[2])

Each weekday, *Queen for a Day* presented four lugubrious-looking women who had become the victims of terrible circumstance. It was the commiserating studio audience's job to select, by the intensity of their applause, one of the four as that day's "queen," complete with crown, robe royal, throne and two-dozen long-stemmed roses. Bestowed upon her highness were prizes that were both specific to her and her family's pressing needs, and absurdly inappropriate. The prize package was especially unhelpful to those women whose challenges were financial in nature, since the lucky winner was expected to pay taxes on everything she'd won, and at the draconian income tax rates of that day.

My mother said that seeing members of her sex humiliated in this manner made her skin crawl. She also happened to have a personal aversion to women who whined in public.

I can't say which of the above connections and memories served as the strongest motivators for my writing this book. Perhaps my inspiration sprung from *all* of the above. ("I'll take *d*, Mr. Cullen: 'All of the above.'")

And I'm certain I'm not the only student of television to recognize that game shows—a fairly recent cultural phenomenon in the history of the world—actually have deep roots in the very development of our species. Man has always enjoyed competing with other men (and with women, and with mastodons). The desire to contend appears to be instinctive; perhaps it's related to the Darwinian drive to survive. Ancient cave drawings seem to indicate that early man had a sporting nature. Mankind has always participated in its programmed extra-curricular pastimes with no small degree of enthusiasm, just as man has demonstrated a commensurate hard-wired propensity for *watching* games being played by others—whether the spectating takes place on hard outdoor bleachers or the soft cushions of one's family room sofa.

Game shows—or "quiz shows," as the format was earlier denominated—didn't descend on us from the blue. (The distinction between game shows and quiz shows is to be taken up later, though I'll be using the terms interchangeably throughout the book.) Game-playing upon the airwaves began in the early days of radio, the quiz show being one of the medium's most successful genres. It took no time at all for television quizzers to fall into a parallel stride. In fact, once network television got up a full head of steam, game shows cluttered the ether. Why? Because TV game shows were *entertaining*.

And in a far different way from, say, Milton Berle, mincing around in drag, or two boxers pummeling each other's faces into cottage cheese. The celebrities who appeared on early TV quiz shows were instantly recognized by viewers from their high-profile careers in radio and movies. At the same time, there was also ample room for participation by *non*-celebrities—average Joes and Janes, people like your own next-door-neighbors (so long as those neighbors lived in a metropolitan area that had a local television station, since large parts of the country couldn't get TV reception until well into the decade). Viewers played along or imagined themselves playing the games, this easy identification with the contestants creating a psychic investment much stronger than that invited by the sitcoms or those body-blocking gals on the roller derby rink.

And early quiz shows were light, genial and disarmingly accessible.

Introduction 5

They were viewer *and* family-friendly, and network censors took special care to keep them that way. The televised quiz shows of the late '40s and early '50s were baggage-free programming that could be welcomed without hesitation into the "safe space" the American living room.

Only later did they become uppity and bigheaded and downright illicit.

But audience appreciation wasn't the only reason for the success of game shows. They were dirt cheap to produce, requiring few or no set changes and usually no demanding costume requirements. (*Masquerade Party* constituted one of the few exceptions. On this show, celebrities wore elaborate makeup and costuming to hide their true identities from the show's panel of celebrity guessers.) Game show concepts were often quite simple to execute—people trying to answer questions, playing charades, listening to a song and attempting to identify it, or balancing various objects on the tops of their heads.

The shows were largely about Americans—with a healthy smattering of friendly "foreigners"—having a good time with one another and frequently being allowed the luxury of just being their own silly selves. Groucho Marx's enormously popular *You Bet Your Life*—popular with both audiences *and* critics[3]—was appreciated more for the lively interchange between host and contestant(s) than for the actual playing of the game. Other game shows tried to emulate this model. *Two for the Money* was first hosted by folksy Hoosier humorist Herb Shriner, then by non–Hoosier humorist Sam Levenson. *Do You Trust Your Wife?* (later: *Who Do You Trust?*) featured the affably glib quizmastering of a young Johnny Carson. In each of these instances, the game became mere pretext for the chat.

Some shows weren't able to make it past their first two or three installments. Those that did have "legs" and got decent ratings contributed to the zeitgeist of the era. Entering the national lexicon were such catchphrases as "I have a lady in the balcony" (uttered by any of several roving assistants with portable microphones on *Dr. I.Q., the Mental Banker*) and "Is it bigger than a breadbox?" (originally asked by *What's My Line?* panelist Steve Allen. And because so many of the shows held coveted prime time slots on the four (later three) national television networks, they propagated millions of next-day water cooler recaps.

The upside was that those who paid the bills—the sponsors—were rewarded with nice profits. And to the benefit of the country at large, those earnings primed the country's economic pump. "So what if the dinner plates of America's titans of commerce were liberally ladled with fresh gravy?" a denizen of the '50s might ask. Wasn't it President Coolidge who famously remarked, "The business of America is business"?

In the 1950s, one could also say, "The business of America is television." Unique among western nations, TV in the U.S. has always been a largely commercial enterprise, just as radio had been. Appropriately, in 1927, American inventor Philo T. Farnsworth[4] broadcast a dollar sign for the first public demonstration of his brand-new electronic television system.[5] *New York Post* editor Stan Opotowsky offered this definition of network television in the U.S., circa 1962: "[Television is] a medium which quite frankly is engaged in the practice of harnessing art to serve the purposes of commerce."[6]

People sold stuff on television. They also offered entertainment. In that order.

For several years in the 1950s, game shows ruled the airwaves. According to the Trendex figures for the week of February 27, 1956, three of the top ten shows were *The $64,000 Question* (#2), *You Bet Your Life* (#7) and *What's My Line?* (#9).[7] In August, quiz shows were faring even better, according to the American Research Bureau, occupying six out of the top ten spots.[8]

1. *The $64,000 Question* (CBS)
2. *The Ed Sullivan Show* (CBS)
3. *The $64,000 Challenge* (CBS)
4. *What's My Line?* (CBS)
5. *I've Got a Secret* (CBS)
6. *General Electric Theater* (CBS)
7. *The Lawrence Welk Show* (ABC)
8. *The Best of Groucho* (NBC)[9]
9. *Do You Trust Your Wife?* (CBS)
10. *Alfred Hitchcock Presents* (CBS)[10]

The shows' collective fortunes declined and their reign ended in the final third of the decade, with the growing popularity of the filmed western, the private eye caper and law-and-order shoot 'em ups.[11] The reputation of game shows as a respectable television programming format was called into question by the quiz show scandals of 1958–59, these leading to a total rewriting of the book on how to put parlor games on the tube. So tainted did the phrase *"quiz* show" become, that it was retired. From 1959 forward, the industry started calling their product *"game* show." So effective was the change, that several decades after the industry took its tumble from grace, the phrase "quiz show" strikes our ears as quaint and anachronistic.

My personal interest in 1950s game shows also stems from my interest in American cultural history, my fascination with the ways that each decade of the 20th century distinguished itself in terms of uniquely illumining and defining the aesthetic and the culture of its period: the music, the clothing, the pastimes, the crazes, the fixations, the prejudices, the ways in which current events got framed and discussed, the ways in which modes of speech and behavior became mainstreamed, the tendency to complaisance and conformity, and the counter-running propensity for incivility and rebellion. As I began to study the quiz shows of the decade of my birth, I discovered that these programs served purposes far beyond their intended ones: sometimes to educate, always to entertain, but most importantly of all: to sell the sponsor's wares. These programs in which people played silly games sometimes quite smartly, and smart games sometimes quite stupidly, for me, reflected for future generations what it was like to be a sometimes silly, sometimes stupid, sometimes savvy American living smack dab in the middle of the last century—the American century.

Fifties America was rife with contradictions. Social advance—that steady progression toward a more civilized, more perfect, more equitable union—was too frequently undercut by the unfortunate legacy of institutional bigotry or by rampant suspicion of perceived insurgents, be they legitimate communist infiltrators or merely nettlesome civil rights activists or fuzzy-chinned Beat poets. The '50s were a decade of undeniable upper mobility, but the country's economic advances weren't evenly distributed among the citizenry. Those citizens with too much melanin in their skin, those who adhered to non–Christian religions, those with "abnormal" sexual identities, those whose choices in music ran counter to the tunes being played on *Name That Tune* and *Stop the Music*, those with aberrant political leanings—anyone who didn't fit the norms endorsed on the 21-inch mahogany-paneled console sitting in one's den—often found themselves with a tough row to hoe in America's mid-century Garden of Eden.

It was a fearful decade, adumbrated by the threat of nuclear annihilation.

And yet ... it was a decade with its moments of great fun and frolic.

Game shows of the 1950s gave the country more than a tiny share of that whimsy and amusement, even as the shows offered hints—and on rare occasions, overt reminders—that all wasn't totally copacetic in Eisenhower's America.

What follows is a look at what Americans loved about their TV game shows and what made them so popular. We of the future will also glean and dissect from the shows' pervasive televised presence, what is worth knowing about Americans in the '50s. As we visit the assorted questions and answers, the cerebral challenges, the scintillating (or completely vacuous) celebrity panel repartee, all the orchestrated tomfoolery, the egg-balancing three-legged races and Jell-O apple-bobbing, the clever attempts at misdirection, the sincere heart-tugging moments of altruism and family togetherness, the manufactured moments of mawk and bathos, a picture will be painted—*à la* the connect-the-dot faces on the ill-fated game show *Dotto* or the incrementally revelatory rebuses of *Concentration*.

A picture of America.

Quizzing America takes the reader on a journey that endeavors to abstain from dry theory and esoteric scholarship, while also attempting to avoid the meringue of pop-culture fluff and tattle—two diametrically opposed approaches to television history that leave a wide, un-furrowed middle ground in the treatment of this subject. Because, in the end, while game show offerings of the 1950s never took themselves *too* seriously, they also rarely took themselves so lightly as to be totally devoid of merit and societal relevance. Quiz show producers struck a delicate balance between ribald raillery (Ralph Edwards' favorite on-camera aside to his audience was "Aren't we devils?") and the sober business of serving the needs of the shows' sponsors, the ad agencies that acted as marriage brokers between program and advertiser-bankroller, the networks and the viewers—without whom, existentially speaking, there would be no show. How to entertain while also uplifting, sometimes edifying and informing, and forever validating the shared cultural phenomenon of living as an American in the fascinating decade of the 1950s ... now *that* was the $64,000 question!

◆ 1 ◆

Radio Daze

> If it weren't for Philo T. Farnsworth, inventor of television, we'd still be eating frozen radio dinners.
> —Johnny Carson[1]

"Before there was television, there was radio."

This statement is problematic. In actuality, radio and television have existed coetaneously since their earliest incarnations. But it was radio that got its first leg up and was soon going like gangbusters, while the video medium was still in its pre-commercial developmental stage. This can be partly attributed to the fact that a lot of time and energy were put into a mechanical form of television, which, if it hadn't been eclipsed by the technically superior electronic version, might have had a generation of Americans watching blurry strobe lights that looked a little like Lucy and Ricky. While Americans weathered both the Great Depression and the "Good War," tuning their table-top radios to FDR's fireside chats or to the diverting amusements of Jack Benny, Bing Crosby and the Lone Ranger, efforts to give the world "radio with pictures" proceeded apace until the war broke out and American technological innovation turned its attention to the far greater imperative of defeating the Nazis and the Japanese.

In the meantime, people listened to network radio—the medium serving as the same kind of lifestyle wallpaper network television would later become.

They listened to situation comedies, variety programs, soap operas, baseball games, crime dramas, homemaker shows, westerns and news summaries. Americans were tuned in when the Hindenburg burst into flames at Lakehurst Naval Air Station. They were listening when Orson Welles played his infamous Halloween prank on America and sent Martians into rural New Jersey. They kept close to their sets during the opening months of the Second World War to hear Edward R. Murrow's spellbinding broadcasts from Blitz-besieged London, and they later followed daily coverage (censored, of course—"loose ears turn Nazi gears") of America's full-piston participation in that historic world conflagration.

But before the war ended and efforts to deliver the miracle of television to America were revived, people turned their dials to a number of radio quiz show favorites—some of which were later reworked as TV programs, others of which lived and died as radio-only offerings. There were, by 1940, more than 50 quiz shows on the air. Ten years later, that number had grown to nearly 200. Their playful names give us a good indication of the mirth and merriment awaiting those who tuned in: *Uncle Jim's Question Bee, Doctor Dollar, Dr. Peter Puzzlewit, The Ask-it Basket, Kay Kyser's Kollege of Musical Knowledge, Doc Rockwell's Brain Trust, Gag Busters* (hosted by Milton Berle), *Crackpot College, Songo, Stillicious Kids Quizeroo, Talk Your Way Out of This One, Stop That Villain, Pick and Pat Time, Try 'n' Find Me, Darts for Dough, Glamour Manor, Time's A'Wastin', What Makes You Tick?, Whiz Quiz, Rate Your Mate, Quixie Doodle* and *What's Doin', Ladies?*[2]

Film director Woody Allen never made a secret of his love of game shows, both radio and TV. In fact, during his successful career as comedy writer and stand-up comic, Allen served several times as a guest celebrity panelist on *What's My Line?*, and was three times the show's mystery guest. Allen also made five appearances on *What's My Line*'s? sister quiz show *I've Got a Secret*. When the comedian became a filmmaker, he used his familiarity with game shows as inspiration for some of the projects he scripted. In one of his earliest works, the satirical comedy *Everything You Always Wanted to Know about Sex* (*But Were Afraid to Ask)*, Allen included a "NSFW" parody of the prototypical celebrity panel show, which he called "What's My Perversion?" In the vignette, filmed to look like an old kinescope, Allen cast veteran game show host Jack Barry as the moderator. (Barry's appearance constituted part of his professional rehabilitation: sixteen years earlier, he and his producing partner Dan Enright had been drummed out of the business for their hand in the quiz show–fixing scandals.) Allen's panel included 1950s game show veteran Robert Q. Lewis, as well as actress Pamela Mason, former wife of James Mason and a contestant on a 1960 broadcast of Groucho Marx's *You Bet Your Life*. With unintended prescience, Allen gave the part of one of the other "What's My Perversion?" panelists to television personality Regis Philbin. Twenty-seven years later, Philbin would serve as host of the American version of *Who Wants to Be a Millionaire*, the first TV game show to award a million dollars, and the show most responsible for ushering in the prime time game show renaissance of the early 2000s.

A more family-friendly demonstration of Allen's fondness for quiz shows is found in his 1987 valentine to the sound medium, *Radio Days*.[3] He includes in this cinematic homage three different scenes pertaining to radio quiz shows. There's also a sly reference to the next chapter in the history of the broadcast game show in the person of Kitty Carlisle. Ms. Carlisle is seen singing into a studio microphone the droll World War II favorite "They're Either Too Young or Too Old." She was a longtime panelist on the TV game show *To Tell the Truth*, both in its prime time network incarnation and then later when it went into syndication. (She's also remembered for playing the female love interest in the Marx Brothers favorite *A Night at the Opera*, and for being married to Broadway playwright Moss Hart.[4])

The film opens with grown-up Joe, the story's narrator (voiced by Woody) telling the story of a burglary at the Needlemans' house in Joe's old neighborhood of Rockaway, Queens, New York. In the midst of the two housebreakers' plundering of the family's front parlor, the phone rings and one of the two men answers. The call is coming from the stage of *Guess That Tune*, a stand-in for the phenomenally popular radio quiz *Stop the Music*. The two burglars correctly guess "Dancing in the Dark," "Chinatown, My Chinatown" and finally, the jackpot tune, "Sailor's Hornpipe." Woody concludes his tale: "That night the Needlemans returned home and were shocked to find a ransacked apartment with $50 and some silverware missing. But the following morning a truck arrived...."

A truck bearing thousands of dollars worth of appliances and furniture.

Music-based radio quiz shows succeeded for a couple of reasons. First, they were perfect fits for the sound medium. Americans listened to an extraordinary amount of music in the '30s and '40s, thanks in part to the ubiquity of radio; there were hundreds of studio musicians who made a very good living playing for variety programs and music-related quiz shows up and down the dial. The other reason was, to put it simply, *money*. The *Guess That Tune*–like quizzes were big give-away shows, and the prizes didn't always go to in-studio contestants. Those lucky enough to be called on the telephone to play *Stop the Music* might find themselves in short order the proud owner of a fully furnished four-room bungalow, recipient of a Hollywood screen test, or even the lucky winner of a two-week uranium-prospecting tour.[5]

One such winner, a Mrs. Julia Hubert of West Philadelphia, was awarded the biggest jackpot in the history of radio give-away shows up that point (March 1949) when she picked up her phone and correctly identified both the preliminary tune and the Mystery Melody to the tune of $35,250, thereby becoming an instant celebrity in her African-American neighborhood. (Racial discrimination on *Stop the Music* was a virtual impossibility given how this part of the game operated.) According to *Life* magazine, which profiled Mrs. Hubert's moment in the national spotlight, she planned to "keep the Kaiser sedan, the $1000 bond, the $1500 for taxes on the Hubert home, the $1500 woman's wardrobe, and the $1500 man's wardrobe." Mrs. Hubert also planned to hang on to the $1000 worth of groceries, the new kitchen, the new paint job for her house, the living room set, the fishing outfits and the year's supply of shaving lotion, roses, candy and haircuts. "On the other hand she intends to sell the piano, the necklace, the two motorcycles, the set of silver, the fireplace set, the Great Dane puppies and the $500 cowboy boots." Ms. Hubert remained undecided about "the $3000 ring, the $2500 watch ... the ermine muff and hat once worn by [actress] Teresa Wright. She will keep the television set because that's the one thing her husband likes. She doesn't. She likes radio better because it doesn't interfere with her crochet work."[6]

Debuting on ABC in March 1948, *Stop the Music* was so successful in drawing in listeners like Julia Hubert (who had finished her dishes early that night so she wouldn't miss the show) that it rose to a rating of 20.0 within only a few months, toppling one of the kings of radio, the wry, Mencken-esque humorist Fred Allen, whose own Hooperating dropped from 28.7 in January 1948 to 11.2 a year later.[7]

But Allen didn't go down without a fight. *The Fred Allen Show* was being ignored by millions of listeners with visions of $20,000–30,000 Bert Parks-bestowed prize packages dancing in their heads, but Allen hail-Mary-ed: he got an insurance company to agree to underwrite any audience member who, by listening to his show, missed their chance to compete on *Stop the Music*. The final jab came courtesy of the radio humorist's famously barbed tongue: "If I were king for one day," he said, "I would make every program a give-away show; when the studios were filled with the people who encourage these atrocities, I would lock the door. With all the morons of America trapped, the rest of the population could go about its business."[8] Though Allen was bested by a game show, his indignation didn't stop him from reluctantly following the old "if you can't beat 'em, join 'em" adage. In the 1953–54 television season, he hosted *Judge for*

Yourself, a talent-quiz show hybrid. Prior to his death on St. Patrick's Day in 1956, Allen had been sitting as weekly panelist on *What's My Line?*, put out by the same producer as his radio nemesis, *Stop the Music*: Mark Goodson.

In *Radio Days*, Woody Allen's second homage to radio quiz shows came in a brief scene that shows Joe and his parents strolling through what looks like the Bronx Zoo. They encounter a 14-year-old mathematical genius, one of the "Whiz Kids," and such a well-known radio celebrity that Joe and his parents know him on sight. The reference here is to one of radio's most popular programs, *Quiz Kids*. The show premiered on June 28, 1940, and continued until July 5, 1953. In its later years, it was running concurrently with its TV version. The "kids"—and there were over 600 of them—were smart, witty and textbook precocious. They gladly answered all manner of questions submitted by listeners to the show, and were more than a little aware of how smart they were, not a single shrinking violet among them.

Although the boy in Allen's film can't help bragging about his 160 I.Q., Ruth Duskin Feldman, who started out as a Quiz Kid herself at age six, remembered that the real Quiz Kids—at least the ones she worked with—might have been eggheads, but they didn't have *big* heads. Most of the children, who ranged in age from six to 15, came from middle-class backgrounds, and in some cases their families might even be deemed lower middle-class. Ms. Feldman recalled almost missing her first appearance on the show, when her father and mother, not able to afford their own car, had trouble hailing a cab in the middle of a rainstorm.[9]

Feldman—who in 1982 wrote *Whatever Happened to the Quiz Kids?*, a book about the different life paths taken by her fellow Quiz Kids—noted that a good many of the juvenile panel members went on to promising careers, sometimes in the very fields in which they'd demonstrated interest on the air. Richard L. Williams, known as the "Human Adding Machine," parlayed his other pursuit, geography, into a career in the Foreign Service, and in 1988 was appointed by President Reagan to be the first U.S. ambassador to the Mongolian People's Republic. Joel Kupperman, another math whiz, became a professor of philosophy and wrote the popular 2006 book *Six Myths About the Good Life: Thinking About What Has Value*. Harve Bennett ended up a successful television and film producer (*The Mod Squad*, *The Six Million Dollar Man* and three *Star Trek* films). Vanessa Brown became a television, film and stage actress; in Broadway's *The Seven Year Itch*, she originated the part played by Marilyn Monroe in the film version. Perhaps the most successful Quiz Kid, James Watson grew up to become a Nobel Prize-winning molecular biologist, best known as one of the co-discoverers—with partner Francis Crick, and Rosalind Franklin—of the structure of DNA.[10]

While they were young, the Quiz Kids captured the hearts of the country. Well-known radio stars Fred Allen, Eddie Cantor, Bing Crosby, and Bob Hope appeared on the broadcasts as guest quizmasters. The children were even invited to the White House by First Lady Eleanor Roosevelt.[11] Parents liked the show because it encouraged their own children to apply themselves in school. In one episode, the kids took turns paying their respects to "the teacher who helped me the most."

In Allen's *Radio Days*, Joe's father wonders aloud why his son "can't be a genius" like the Whiz Kid they just met. He doesn't give Joe a chance to respond: "Because you're too busy listening to the radio all the time!" Later in the film, Joe gets to see a radio broadcast in person. His Aunt Bea and her boyfriend take him into Manhattan and he watches his aunt compete as a quiz show contestant. Bea is asked to identify various stuffed fish presented to her by the emcee. (Woody doesn't seem concerned that, this being radio, the listening audience wouldn't have the benefit of getting to see the various fish as they're brought forward for identification, but no matter; it's just a movie.) Aunt Bea ends up winning the challenge and is awarded 50 silver dollars.

The show on which Bea appears is a takeoff on the popular *Dr. I.Q., the Mental Banker*, which gave the world the snicker-producing double entendre, "I have a lady in the balcony." The lady in the balcony was selected to compete for silver dollars. Because *Dr. I.Q.* was a road show that broadcast from theaters around the country, it was one of only a few national radio quizzers that connected with audiences both personally and locally. And no one who tried to answer the rapid-fire questions parceled throughout the theater audience went away empty-handed. The show's sponsor, the Mars candy bar company, made sure that contestants received, at the very least, samples of their products as consolation prizes. The author of this book can make a good guess as to which of the various Mars candy bars was the preferable parting gift: When he inherited his late father's candy wrapper collection, started when his father was a boy in the late 1930s, there were wrappers from several Mars candy bars of the period. One was called "Dr. I.Q."[12]

Other radio quiz shows had equally large followings. *Information Please*, which ran from 1938 to 1951, gathered together some of the (purportedly) smartest minds in America to take questions from listeners hoping to stump them. Not all of the panelists were academics, though, and each of the members of its waggishly articulate brain trust had their awkward, though amusing, moments of "I haven't the foggiest."

In November 1939, President Roosevelt's Postmaster General James A. Farley came on the show and demonstrated a mortifying unfamiliarity with the American postal system.[13] On another occasion, New York City's Mayor LaGuardia fumbled several questions about Gotham. On the other hand, actress Lillian Gish and writer-actresses Cornelia Otis Skinner and Ruth Gordon, music critic Deems Taylor, playwright Russel Crouse, sportswriter Grantland Rice, novelist James Michener, conservationist Louis Bromfield and cerebral wisecracker Fred Allen demonstrated that they knew things ... a *lot* of things.[14] Listeners also got a taste, given panel participation by several veterans of the storied Algonquin Round Table, of what it might have been like to break bread with that illustrious "Vicious Circle." Franklin P. Adams was a regular, Dorothy Parker, Alexander Woollcott and Harpo Marx also sitting in on occasion. (Harpo, who for obvious reasons hardly ever appeared on the radio, answered his questions in character by whistling and squeezing an old-fashioned auto horn.) When comedienne Gracie Allen came on the show, she put the lie to her on-air caricature of George Burns' ditzy wife by demonstrating a broad grasp of several disparate subjects, including aviation, politics and even pediatrics. In 1940, *The Saturday Review of Books* gave *Information Please* its award for distinguished service to literature. Personal note: The author remembers several years' worth of *Information Please* almanacs on the shelves of his family's den. The annual publication was one of several product spinoffs from the successful show.

Information Please made it acceptable, even respectable, to be a geek. Clifton Fadiman, the show's host (Fadiman was also book editor for *The New Yorker*), remarked that "suddenly, intelligent men and women were looked up to and emulated. And most came across as 'regular guys.'"[15] Such feelings of egalitarian intellectualism were reinforced by the more than two million World War II veterans who had obtained college degrees under the G.I. Bill. They were also embodied in "regular guy" Columbia University Professor Charles Van Doren during his high-profile contestant stint on *Twenty-One*.

Fadiman was happy to add that his show gave the American public new role models beyond those in sports, politics and films.[16] Both *Quiz Kids* and *Information Please* helped to lay the groundwork for the use of quiz shows as adjuncts to the classroom—one of many means by which to "brain up" America, and to remove the stigma of "learning stuff." This enterprise became even more important with the launch of the Soviet Union's Sputnik 1 satellite in October 1957. The need to improve and reform the U.S. education system, to make it more competitive with the U.S.S.R., became a top priority, and game shows—especially those that endorsed, even celebrated, the acquisition of knowledge—played their part. Olaf Hoerschelmann notes in *Rules of the Game: Quiz Shows and American Culture*, "[N]ational debates over the importance of education in the Cold War, and pressures on the networks to incorporate 'enlightenment material,' created shows that emphasized rigid cultural hierarchies of knowledge."[17]

Perhaps the public's appreciation of *Information Please* and its respect for intellect was enough to overlook permanent panelist Oscar Levant's sometimes excessively caustic wit. When the composer, pianist and mordant humorist was asked in one instance to name the author whose autobiography began, "I was born an ugly ducking," he tossed out, "Eleanor Roosevelt." Admirers of the First Lady were not amused. (The correct answer was actress Marie Dressler.)[18]

Information Please was so widely praised that it inevitably inspired a satirical response. It came in the form of another radio show which went on to great success: *It Pays to Be Ignorant.* Not so much a quizzer as a scripted comedy show, it parodied both *Information Please* and *Quiz Kids* and featured a panel of self-styled "experts" who were, in actuality, "dumber than you are and can prove it."

Ralph Edwards' *Truth or Consequences* hit the NBC radio airwaves on March 23, 1940 and was a big hit right out of the chute. Incidentally, it was also the first game show to air on broadcast television, comprising part of New York station WNBT's experimental program schedule on July 1, 1941. Over nine years would pass before *Truth or Consequences* was back on the tube again. In the meantime, its radio version had a knack for involving whole communities—and sometimes, the entire nation—in its stunts, thus demonstrating how successfully a radio show (and later, television show) could energize and mobilize its audience. The house party-like fun and frivolity (also to be found in Art Linkletter's similarly patterned *People Are Funny*[19]—forerunner of a radio and TV show called, naturally, *Art Linkletter's House Party*) sometimes extended far beyond the studio from which it was broadcast; over time, *Truth or Consequences* earned an industry reputation for its enterprise and sheer chutzpah in pulling off elaborate (and oftentimes expensive) remote-broadcast challenges.

Once permanently ensconced on television in 1950, *Truth or Consequences* became the first TV show to use multiple 35mm film cameras shooting simultaneously in front of a live studio audience, a process only later adapted by the makers of *I Love Lucy*, a teleseries long associated with this groundbreaking technique. (It was staff member Al Simon who spearheaded the development of this system for *Truth or Consequences*, which he was then asked to take to *I Love Lucy*.) With the advent of videotape, the show, which was based on the West Coast, also earned the distinction of becoming, in 1957, the first television program to be telecast in all four time zones via pre-recorded tape.[20]

One stunt literally put *Truth or Consequences* on the map, and gave a city in New Mexico a completely new identity. In 1950, in honor of the show's ten years on the air, Ralph Edwards issued a challenge: If a town liked *Truth or Consequences* well enough to take its name as their own, the production crew would pack up and fly out to do their big anniversary broadcast there. It was Edwards' "go-to" idea man Al Simon who proposed this stunt. Edwards signed on without hesitation, although he did inject a couple of stipulations. First, the name couldn't go to a community in the developmental stage—that is, one which hadn't decided yet what to call itself. Second, the town couldn't be Edwards' home town of Merino, Colorado. (Because, you see, it just might upset the sheep for which Merino had been named!)

A number of cities and towns applied, but the honor went to Hot Springs, New Mexico. Hot Springs was Edwards' top choice as well. He appreciated the fact that the city had a strong philanthropic component; Hot Springs, in addition to offering the therapeutic mineral baths for which it was named, was also at the time the home of one of the best children's hospitals in the country, the Carrie Tingley Hospital for Crippled Children. (The institution was supported in some form or fashion by nearly every resident in town.) The selflessness and altruism embodied in the city was, Edwards felt, emblematic of the help-thy-neighbor spirit exuded by the show itself.

When the New Mexico State Tourist Bureau heard about the offer, it quickly informed Hot Springs' Chamber of Commerce. They jumped at the idea, excited about the prospect of all the free advertising and national attention that would come to this heretofore quiet and unpretentious resort town. The members especially liked the chance to end all the confusion with Hot Springs, Arkansas; Hot Springs, California; Hot Springs, Montana; and several other towns with that name.

Hot Springs residents took very little convincing. A vote was held on March 31 and the change was approved by a large margin (1294 to 295). As promised, Edwards, his wife Barbara, the show's production crew and a big press contingent flew to the city to broadcast the tenth anniversary show there the very next day. Across the country, a good many listeners wondered if this was just another example of *Truth or Consequences'* customary mischief and "deviltry," especially given the fact that the broadcast would be on April Fool's Day. (The suspicion was somewhat justified since the broadcast date closest to the actual tenth anniversary would have fallen on Saturday, March 25, not Saturday, April 1.)

But the country would soon learn that it was neither a one-off stunt nor an April Fool's joke. *Truth or Consequences* citizens took so seriously what they had done, they decided to hold a celebration of the name change on the first weekend in May from that point on. The annual fiesta honors both the name change and the memory of honorary citizen Ralph Edwards, who made an effort to be there every year for the next half-century, accompanied by his wife and a cadre of entertainers.[21]

The outlandish stunts created for *Truth or Consequences* often made the papers. In one instance, a player was dispatched from New York City, where the radio program was broadcast, all the way to Holyoke, Massachusetts, for the purpose of digging up 1000 silver dollars that had been buried in a vacant lot there. While the contestant was on his way to unearth his treasure, some 1500 Holyoke residents, outfitted with everything from spoons to a bulldozer, descended on the designated lot at the corner of Prospect and Walnut, eager to dig up the buried cash and claim it for themselves. A 23-year-old carpenter's assistant and his teenage brother-in-law exhumed the bag of coins before anyone else (including the *Truth or Consequences* contestant), and by law had rights to it. Edwards promised to make things right with the show's disappointed treasure hunter, but returning the vacant lot to its former un-pocked state to the satisfaction of town officials was no easy task.[22]

When, late in his life, Edwards was asked to name some of *Truth or Consequences'* most memorable stunts, he recalled with pride getting Hollywood, California, its own postmark, when the U.S. postmaster general, no doubt assuming he'd given the show an insurmountable task, agreed to approve Edwards' request on the condition that he be presented with signatures of one million Americans who agreed with *Truth or Consequences* that Hollywood having its own postmark wasn't such a bad thing. Edwards also remembered shipping a live turkey to Turkey for Thanksgiving and sending a contestant around the world via a pogo stick.

Edwards counted among his favorite stunts those that raised large amounts of money for charity. Indeed, *Truth or Consequences*, as antipodean to the big-money give-away game shows of its day, often found itself the recipient of its audience's munificence, as listeners responded to appeals for donations to various charities as the cost of participating in *Truth or Consequences* challenges. As a result, the show got used to setting itself up as a conduit for audience generosity. The "Mrs. Hush" contest, which asked radio listeners to identify the woman "who did not speak" (her identity guessed after seven weeks: silent screen actress Clara Bow), and the "Walking Man" contest, which riveted the entire country (the footsteps belonged to Jack Benny), raised, respectively, $550,000 for the March of Dimes, and over $1,600,000 to help endow the American Heart Association when it decided to go national.[23] The show also supported the Arthritis Foundation, the American Cancer Society and the Mental Health Foundation.[24]

Truth or Consequences was perhaps the most dedicated of all the radio game shows in its efforts to win the Second World War. Edwards remembered traveling over 100,000 miles on a cross-country bond tour that was responsible for the sale of over half a billion dollars in e-bonds. On one occasion, the show was broadcast from a Linn County, Missouri, high school as a thank-you to its students for collecting 274,000 pounds of newspaper for a wartime paper drive.[25]

In the middle of a wartime copper shortage, Edwards encouraged listeners to take scarce pennies out of home piggy banks and put them into circulation. He did this by asking everyone in his listening audience to send the mother of a 17-year-old Marine—a Mrs. Dennis Mullane, who had been in his studio audience—a copper penny so she could buy a war bond for her son. By day three, the Staten Island woman was inundated at her home by nearly 20,000 letters, containing not only pennies, but money in various other denominations. And the letters kept flooding in; Edwards had to arrange with the post office to have all letters addressed to Mrs. Mullane redirected to NBC offices in New York, where, ultimately, 15 clerks were detailed to open all 130,000 of them. Meanwhile, Mrs. Mullane was busy at home opening packages containing neckties, stickpins, handkerchiefs and other gifts for her son. Nellie Taylor Ross, director of the U.S. Mint, praised the show's campaign and all the people who participated in it for getting the coins into circulation.[26]

With the exception of news broadcasts and radio shows related to news events, no radio program formats were more intrinsically involved in the war effort than were radio quiz and audience participation shows (the two categories distinct but often overlapping). And by the December 7, 1941, Japanese attack on Pearl Harbor, there were a slew of them willing to play their part. One quarter of all the sponsored shows on the radio that year were quiz shows, and most of them stuck around for the duration.[27]

Whereas the writers of soaps, dramas, sitcoms, adventure programs and mysteries crafted stories either about the war or with the conflict heavily threaded through their plotlines, producers of radio quiz shows could bring the war into American homes in ways that were authentic and deeply personal. They enlisted in the cause with intense patriotic fervor, cognizant of their duty to boost morale and encourage community sacrifice, while offering an entertainment escape hatch of disport, laughter and silly fun.[28] Washington quickly recognized the important role the audience participation-quiz shows could play in keeping spirits high and meeting wartime goals and encouraged the shows' involvement—not that the makers of the merriment had to be persuaded.

There were some security concerns which first had to be resolved. The government worried over all the many ways the public was given access to game show microphones. As a result, they prohibited the conducting of interviews from among small groups of people. The shows weren't allowed to draw contestants from studio audiences of fewer than 50, and methods had to be devised wherein contestants were selected from audiences at random, with slots never given to those who asked for them. Once all of this was worked out, game show personnel, just like the crew of *Truth or Consequences*, rolled up their sleeves, packed their bags and trundled themselves off on national bond tours and remote broadcasts from naval bases, Army camps, Air Force fields and military hospitals.[29]

Radio quiz shows contributed to the war effort in three ways. First, they brought attention to war preparations by broadcasting from training camps and other military outposts, and once the shooting war began, they kept up military morale by visiting homeland military bases, and later, when logistics had been worked out, headed overseas. By war's end, Kay Kyser and his *Kollege of Musical Knowledge* had taken his music quiz broadcasts to 500 different troop gatherings and military hospitals.[30] In 1945, he was performing his show throughout Asia, and entertaining nearly one million men and women in uniform. Kyser and his "Kollegians" were in mid-performance in northern Luzon, when word came of the first offer by the Japanese to surrender, news he was delighted to share on the spot with the G.I.s serving there.[31] Even after the war, radio quiz shows continued to do their part for Uncle Sam. *Information Please* removed itself to the American Zone in occupied Germany for the purpose of giving the still-mustered American troops a show that was part USO and part "quiz."[32] One of radio's earliest quiz shows, *Vox Pop*, threw itself hook, line and sinker into winning the war, traveling the country to visit Americans engaged in every facet of the war effort, and transforming itself into less of a quiz show and more of an interview show which sought to introduce listeners to listeners, Americans to Americans.[33]

Another important contribution made by radio quizzers to efforts to win the war was their enthusiastic participation in war bond drives and tours. *Take It or Leave It* host Phil Baker never ended his war-era broadcasts without the reminder, "Bye, bye ... Buy bonds." The Quiz Kids, though too young to take up arms or air hammers, did their bit by periodically hitting the road to sell bonds in a number of large U.S. cities. Over the course of the war, the show's pint-sized panel sold $120 million worth of bonds, a war bond being the price of admission to watch America's "smartest kids in the class" demonstrate their mental prowess.

Another way game shows helped out was by involving servicemen and women in the shows themselves. On *Blind Date*, Arlene Francis, one of broadcasting's first female game show hosts, gave two servicemen the chance to vie for a night on the town with a beautiful young woman. The questions were asked and answered on the telephone, though the participants were actually both on stage at the same time.[34] The idea for the show was recycled in mufti in the 1960s by Chuck Barris and was dubbed *The Dating Game*.

Battle of the Sexes was "guys vs. girls," but with a military theme: Male airplane spotters competed against canteen hostesses, pilots against female factory workers. That same he-vs.-she form of quiz show could be found in *The Better Half*, in which G.I.s competed against those gals who kept the home fires burning.[35] There was *Service with a Smile* (featuring servicemen who could answer questions *and* perform), *Yankee Doodle Quiz* (American history-based), *Battle of the Bureaus* (employees of government agencies pitted against one another) and *Which Is Which*, in which servicemen-contestants tried to guess famous people by their voices. In the latter, the famous folk—Olivia de Havilland, Basil Rathbone, Alfred Hitchcock and others—concealed themselves behind a screen.[36]

At no point in the 1950s did the later television incarnation of the American game show play a role in our national biography as important and as consequential as did those World War II–era radio quizzes and audience participation shows. There were occasional references on television game shows to the Korean Conflict and its fighting men, but nothing approached the determined, all-hands-on-deck effort to win the Second World War put forth by the talent and staff of the radio quizzes. The phrase "all hands on deck" might even be taken literally, when one considers that in one instance, the show *Thanks to the Yanks* took the lead in getting its listeners—in the midst of a severe wartime paper shortage—to send their own decks of playing cards to patients in military hospitals.[37]

◈ 2 ◈

Transition

> Only one thing seems consistently apparent to me, and that is you just have to be twice as good on television as on any other medium.
> —Bing Crosby[1]

There was no clean break between radio and television. In fact, there were a number of years from 1946 until the mid–1950s in which both mediums programmed simultaneously. One of the reasons for this was an FCC-ordered freeze on the assignment of new station licenses, which took effect on September 29, 1948, and wasn't lifted until April 1952. The freeze was necessary to allow the Commission to put into place a master plan for station allocation, since up to that point the process had been haphazard, with the signals of some stations interfering with those of others. The result was that the number of U.S. TV stations increased from 51 in January 1949 to only 108 a few months before the freeze was lifted, this increase reflecting those stations that had already been authorized, and were at various stages of construction when the freeze took place.

The freeze left some cities with only one TV station and many smaller locations around the country without any TV reception at all. Though the sale of TV receivers increased during this period, largely within communities in the Northeast and the industrial Midwest that had one or more stations in operation, by 1950, 21 percent of homes in the country's 25 major metropolitan areas had televisions, while only two percent of American homes located in counties with towns of 35,000 people or fewer had sets.[2] While 25 percent of homes in the Northeast had TVs, only nine percent of those living in the Pacific states were able to turn off their radios and turn on their TVs. The disparity was even more pronounced in Dixie: Only two percent of Southerners had TVs during the freeze, with the rest continuing to rely on radio for their broadcast entertainment. It wasn't until 1955 that television receivers were finally installed in a majority of households in all areas of the country.[3]

Another factor determining who had a television set and who didn't in this early period was the price of receivers. In mid–1948, the average retail price for a TV set was $440, not including installation. That's more than $3000 in 2018 dollars.[4] (The author recalls as a child, looking at advertisements for TV receivers in issues of *National Geographic* from around this time and wondering what would motivate one to spend that much money—even in 1960s dollars—for a television set with such a ridiculously small screen.) The February 26, 1949, issue of *Saturday Review* listed over 40 different table model receivers, ranging in price from $139.50 for the seven-inch-screen Hallicrafters model to the DuMont Stratford, with its comparatively large 15-inch screen, selling for nearly $700.[5] By 1954, the price for a set had fallen to an average of $238 and would drop significantly lower by decade's end. (*And* the screens continued to get larger.)

And what was there in the way of quiz shows to watch on these minuscule screens? Early television game shows fell into two distinct camps:

1. Those shows whose creators deliberately sought to exploit the special properties of the new medium to give movement, animation and visual interest to the art of game telecasting.
2. Those shows whose creators sought to duplicate successful radio formats, resulting to a large degree in repackaged video versions of radio favorites.

In the first group were two of television's first successes among *all* programming formats. *Beat the Clock*, which went on the air on March 23, 1950, was one of the first in a long procession of popular stunt shows. Audience participation game shows like *Beat the Clock, Truth or Consequences, Fun for the Money, It Could Be You, Midway, County Fair, Try and Do It* and *Dollar a Second* were comprised of funny physical business that could be enjoyed without benefit of any sound at all. *Pantomime Quiz* had its own large and dedicated following, and was the first game show to win an Emmy. The show was basically charades played by movie stars. It was soon joined by *Say It with Acting*, which was basically charades played by Broadway actors.[6]

On the other hand, the early popularity of television panel shows like *What's My Line?* and *I've Got a Secret* demonstrated that viewers didn't necessarily need physical stunts or clever miming to be entertained. While some popular radio quizzers like *Information Please* fizzled when they transitioned to television, others either kept or expanded their audience in their new incarnation, due to reasons that weren't always easy to pin down. However, the reason for the success of the TV version of *You Bet Your Life* could be summed up in a single word: Groucho.

You Bet Your Life producer John Guedel made the accurate call in not mucking around with the show's radio format; Guedel predicted that those who liked listening to Groucho Marx in the radio version of the show, would naturally be just as happy seeing him on their television screens. It wasn't necessary to impose on *You Bet Your Life* all the glitter and glitz of, say, Milton Berle's "vaudeo" juggernaut *Texaco Star Theater*.[7] It would simply be Groucho, having fun with his contestants. Guedel's job of convincing others that "less is just fine" wasn't easy. According to the show's director Robert Dwan, "television experts" worried that the program was "squandering a great resource." Television was a visual medium, these folks argued, and as such, viewers would be looking for "Dr. Hackenbush with painted eyebrows and mustache, frock coat and loping walk." In other words, burlesque was in, or weren't Guedel and Marx paying any attention to the preferences of that legion of fans commanded by Uncle Miltie?

Both men stuck to their guns, Groucho even more so than his producer. There would be no Dr. Hackenbush and no weekly entrance into the studio upon a sedan chair (although this entrance was tried once on a lark in the last season of the show's long run). The only accommodation Groucho was willing to make had to do with the mustache. Yes, he'd have one. But instead of painting it on as he'd done for all the Marx Brothers movies, he simply let nature take its course.[8]

Writer Goodman Ace came to the defense of Marx and Guedel in his column for *The Saturday Review of Literature*, published after the first TV broadcast of *You Bet Your Life* in the fall of 1950:

> Ben Gross, in his column in the *Daily News* ... was displeased with the Marx show. "This is not TV," he said.... "This is radio." Later in the week, this same opinion on sight and sound appeared ... in *Variety*.... This essay does not advocate the abolishment of action in television.... [But] there are shows which can be just as entertaining if a man sits there quietly smoking a cigar and leering through his mustache.... Oh, yes, he gave them action. He moved his lips, and bright, adult sounds came out.[9]

On the other hand, there were early television quiz shows that failed to effectively marry medium to mission (that is, the mission of entertaining). *The Art Ford Show* pitted three radio disc jockeys from around the country against one another. The game: to identify composers, vocalists and orchestras from the various records played for them by a beautiful hostess. The show, which aired in the summer of 1951, also injected a live musical performance into the game. But the idea of watching three radio D.J.s mostly just sitting around and listening to records could not be extolled as TV at its finest. The program was cancelled after only seven weeks.

The television game show's potential to present games in a variety of different ways led, over time, to such latter-day video competitions as the blowout 1970s stunt extravaganza *Almost Anything Goes, American Gladiators* (1989–1997) and the explosion of competitive reality shows of the early 21st century, ranging from *The Amazing Race* to *Fear Factor* to *Dog Eats Dog*. On the other side of the ledger were popular simple-play games like *Password*, based on the almost ascetic concept of single word association. Yet it is now considered one of TV's classics.

Whereas radio quizzes were limited to question-and-answer formats (augmented by engagingly witty colloquy and commentary), or the process of listening to and identifying snippets of popular songs, television game shows of the late '40s and 1950s fell into a wide range of categories of play. Jason Mittell in his book *Television and American Culture* breaks these down by program type and subgenre. He bases them on the mechanics of the game, its competition features, and on the specific areas of pleasure derived by viewers:

> **Factual Quiz Shows**. These are built on a series of contests based on questions of knowledge. They reward contestants for their mastery of trivia and/or for their retention and command of facts. Examples: *The $64,000 Question, Twenty-One.*
> **Stunt Game Shows**. When questions and answers are used, they serve only to segue into different physical stunts and challenges. Examples: *Truth or Consequences, Beat the Clock.*
> **Panel Shows**. These shows focus on the interaction between celebrities and contestants as the celebrity panel endeavors to correctly guess something about the contestant that is germane to the purview of the show. Comedic banter often serves as the shows' primary appeal. Examples: *What's My Line?, I've Got a Secret.*
> **Games of Skill**. These use well-known parlor games and other

forms of competitive challenges that do not generally include a simple regurgitation of facts and trivia. Example: *Concentration, Down You Go.*

Specialty Knowledge Games. These shows highlight the contestants' use of knowledge within a specified subject realm, such as sports, music and consumer pricing. Examples: *Name That Tune, The Price Is Right.*

Social Games. These are built around interpersonal relationships. Examples: *Blind Date, With This Ring.*

Games of Chance. No special skills or knowledge or ability needed here, though a knack for assessing odds is helpful. Drama is created from uncertainty; success is largely attributed to luck. Example: *Treasure Hunt.*[10]

It was the game show in all its forms and formats that played a major role in ushering in the era of American television after years of fits and starts—though World War II did throw its own gorilla-sized monkey wrench into the works for five interruptive years.[11] Commercial television was born on July 1, 1941 (five months before the attack on Pearl Harbor), when two stations signed on: WNBT (Channel 1) and WCBW (Channel 2), both in New York City. On that day, NBC/WNBT telecast a quizzer, *Uncle Jim's Question Bee,* and a stunter, Ralph Edwards' *Truth or Consequences.* The next day, CBS/WCBW answered its competitor's one-off broadcasts with *The CBS Television Quiz,* TV's first regularly scheduled quiz show. Amazingly, this primitive, early iteration of a TV game show—broadcast from CBS's television studios above Grand Central Terminal—ran for over a year.

Several months after VJ Day, the spunky DuMont Television Network—otherwise known as "the little network that could ... and then didn't"—began broadcasting on a regular basis in New York City and Washington, D.C. Its two-station network started beaming into a few thousand households and neighborhood taverns in April 1946. And within two months of its kick-off, DuMont was putting its first game show on the air. *Cash and Carry* used the tried-and-true Q&A format, but it added a soup-can of verisimilitude by playing its game on a set made to look like a supermarket. It was hosted by a man who became one of the most familiar faces in 1950s television, Dennis James. From 1944 to 1946, CBS used the grocery store backdrop for real, with *Missus Goes-A-Shopping* broadcast from actual Manhattan grocery stores. (At the time,

CBS hadn't yet become a full-fledged television network, limiting its broadcasts to receivers in New York City.)

In television's earliest days, when game shows, beloved on radio, were just getting their bearings in the new medium, there was a desire on the part of the shows' creators to connect with average viewers in venues that were comfortable and familiar to them; for example, the place where they purchased the food that would wind up on the family dinner table. On one of the first game shows to be broadcast in the daytime, NBC's *It's in the Bag*, contestants filled their "bags" with actual cans of food. Collecting enough cans entitled them to play for the grand prize, a major appliance.

Attempts to win over a curious television audience were made easier by the fact that Americans were already game lovers and had been watching game-playing in a variety of other contexts for years. Unlike radio, which restricted itself to that which could be apprehended by the ear, television offered a vast array of possibilities for entertaining audiences with broadcast game play. And in the course of doing this, audiences got a good look in the national mirror. What they noticed first, in fact, was themselves.

◆ 3 ◆

All the Little People

> It turns out that all of our respondents prefer the contestants to be average people. They say: "It is expected of college people that they know everything. I would not want to compete with them. I prefer the people on the program to be people like myself."
> —Herta Herzog, "Professor Quiz—A Gratification Study"[1]

Without an audience, there is no show. And there are more things for a quiz show to do with its audience than simply request that they tune in, or climb down from the bleachers to enter the lists themselves.

Quiz show creators have acknowledged the importance of their audience since the early days of radio. One of the very first audience participation shows was launched by KTRH in Houston, Texas. *Vox Pop*, which went on the air in 1932, was built around a simple concept: lowering a microphone from the window of the KTRH studio above the Rice Hotel and then asking questions of passersby (especially those curious enough to stop and wonder why a microphone was hanging out of a hotel window). Those who answered the questions correctly were awarded a dollar. (The first of the jackpot give-away shows!) *Vox Pop* was created by a couple of local Texas good ol' boys, Parks Johnson and Jerry Belcher. It remained on the air for 16 years.[2]

Another radio quiz show which took full advantage of the loyalty of its listeners was one of the early big money game shows, NBC's *Pot o' Gold*. The program was, among other things, an anthropological study in mass mania. Within four weeks of its September 26, 1939, debut, it was pulling in huge ratings. Why? Because it gave away money. Lots of money. And just for answering your telephone. According to the show's host, bandleader Horace Heidt, *Pot o' Gold* was the first program to extend prizes beyond a studio audience to people listening in their homes. Throughout the country.[3]

The prize: a whopping $1000. That was a lot of money for people still trying to lift themselves up financially after ten years of historic economic depression.

As a result of this gimmick, people stopped everything they were doing to tune in each week, situating themselves within easy grabbing distance of their telephone receivers. Each listener waited with a lottery player's unrealistic hope that he or she would beat the astronomical odds: The show's giant spinning wheel would pick *their* city's phone directory, the wheel would then select the page in the book on which *their* listing appeared, and then the wheel would miraculously target the line on which *their* name and phone number appeared, thus placing the listener and his or her family at the end of the rainbow. One of the results of this national obsession was plummeting attendance at movie theaters on Tuesday nights.[4] Telephone usage also dropped that night from 8:30 to 9:00 EST, to keep the phone lines clear.[5] (And woe to those unfortunate enough to share a party line—especially if those other parties weren't interested in listening to the show!) Havoc was raised by aggrieved near-winners when a phone call got dropped, a long distance telephone operator screwed up, or when someone moved and it was their *old* number that got picked. (All three of these things actually sent the injured parties to their lawyers.)

In 1940, as *Pot o' Gold* fever swept through the land, anti-lottery activists went to the FCC and pushed the agency to obtain a ruling from the Justice Department on whether the show and its growing list of imitators constituted illegal lotteries. In the end, Justice declined to prosecute under the anti-lottery statutes.

A dodged bullet. The big money shows would find themselves back in the government crosshairs a few years later.

Throughout the 1950s, television game shows reached out to their audiences not only for the purpose of soliciting their participation as on-camera contestants, but also to give them opportunities to play the game at home. In some cases, lucky home audience members didn't have to lift a finger (after submitting a postcard); there would be on-air contestants (often celebrities) who were happy to play the game on their behalf and reward the home players accordingly. In other cases, more was required from viewers. The shows solicited trivia questions as well as suggestions for stunts and challenges. If an audience member's submission made it on air, the person was paid in either cash or merchandise.

3. All the Little People

From the earliest days of television, networks reached out to viewers, soliciting their involvement as an incentive not only to get them to watch but, of more immediate importance, to get them to buy televisions. There had been so few TV sets purchased in New York City at the time DuMont's game show *Cash and Carry* went on the air (it ran from June 20, 1946, to July 1, 1947) that a Manhattan viewer named Harry Dubin won the prize nearly every week for phoning in his guess as to what was hidden under a barrel. Within a few short months, all of this would change.[6]

When *The Price Is Right* premiered in November 1956, its producers could not have predicted the degree to which its viewers would involve themselves in the show. And it took no time at all before those producers found themselves in a real fix over the show's "showcase feature." In addition to on-stage contestant play in which four men and women bid against one another in an attempt to come closest to naming the list prices of particular merchandise items, there was also a showcase of prizes simply there for the snatching by some price-savvy home viewer. One of the show's producers, Bob Stewart, recalled a period during which *The Price Is Right* was receiving an average of forty million postcards a month. When the very first mail-in game was played, three and a half million viewers flooded the show's offices with cards. Goodson-Todman resorted to hiring a special mail service to deal with the entries, and the mail service resorted to hiring hundreds of Queens housewives to go through the mail (and make a little extra money for their families in the process).

Even as the postcards were eventually leveling off to about a million a week, there were other problems. Retail stores across the country were complaining that their phone lines were being tied up by showcase players calling to check the prices of certain items. Brooklyn viewer Gerard Mignone tried to bribe the show's mailroom staff to the tune of $2000 to let his postcard win. Police were summoned and when Mignone refused to surrender, he was chased down and shot.[7]

The Price Is Right was tailor-made for the American proletariat—the first TV game show anyone could play. There were no questions to answer, no stunts requiring special forms of dexterity to be performed. On *The Price Is Right*, as its decades of popularity in various incarnations would attest, a contestant need only come closest to guessing the list price of a certain item (without going over) to take that prize home. The democratization of the TV game show had elitists, intellectuals and quiz show purists up in arms. To them, *The Price Is Right* presented Americans as meretricious and greedily materialistic. But the show did have its defenders.

In *TV Guide*, psychologist Allan Fromme commended the series for not making people feel inferior, as quiz shows sometimes did—especially those quizzers that dealt in intellectual esoterica.[8]

Two 1950s quiz shows with similar names found unique ways to involve their audiences even more deeply in all the fun. *Anybody Can Win* employed a blatant gambling feature, which gave members of its studio audience the chance to guess before the show went on the air which of its four celebrity panelists would correctly answer the most questions. Those audience members who chose the winner became winners themselves: They got to split $2000. (Not a bad way to pull in a full studio audience every week!) *Anybody Can Play* gave home viewers the opportunity to compete for large cash and merchandise prizes by predicting the order in which the show's four studio contestants would finish, as well as guessing other things about the contestants that were easily quantifiable, such as their ages and weights.[9]

The 1953 ABC prime time auction game show *What's Your Bid* didn't reward its contestants with cash or prizes. It actually had those members of the studio audience who'd been picked to play the game bidding *with their own money* for merchandise. The proceeds taken in from the winning bidders for the various auction items were donated to a different charity each week.[10]

It was the "little people" appearing on *You Bet Your Life* who helped to make this popular show even more appealing to audiences. Early television was somewhat schizophrenic. On the one hand, there were video-vaudeville programs like Milton Berle's *Texaco Star Theater*, whose producers were pleased as punch to be offering its viewers the chance to actually *see* performers performing: dancing, juggling, walking about the stage on stilts, clowning and lampooning in full costume.

Radio for the eyes.

And Americans couldn't get enough of it.

Conversely, there was another large contingent of viewers who didn't want to be transported to the Palace Theatre every night. These people first listened to, and then watched, shows like Groucho's for the chance to enjoy comical exchanges with interesting guests. Before playing the game, they talked. They talked about things with which audiences could easily identify: spouses (especially the often humorous circumstances under which couples met), kids, jobs, how men felt about women, how women felt about men. Obviously, everything was milked for a laugh, but in the process of the give-and-take, viewers never lost sight of the genuineness of the show's real-life contestants, and they enjoyed being made privy to the conversation. There were veterans of World War II, now in the process of integrating themselves back into American society. Sometimes they stood next to their blushing war brides, many of whom were still in the process of learning English. There were beauty queens and country preachers from the South, and elevator operators ("car jockeys") and homebuilders from the North. There was even the wife of a Connecticut tobacco farmer (back when Connecticut shade tobacco was a major agricultural engine for the region). There were those bachelors and bachelorettes of a certain advanced age who had no interest in marrying, and young singles who couldn't wait to find the right mate. And Groucho was always happy to do a little on-camera matchmaking to help that latter group of contestants along.

But with each of the contestant-pairs, there was always something that made what might initially seem ordinary, actually a little *extra*ordinary. Robert Dwan, director of *You Bet Your Life*, put it this way:

> Our basic contestant was a normal citizen with an ordinary occupation—plumber, baker, post office worker—a mother, grandmother, a Girl Scout, or a set of newlyweds. But we also looked for the offbeat and unusual in the background. A couple about to be married turned out to be an Army nurse and a man who had been one of her patients.[11]

As late as 1967, game show producers were still looking for common folks with uncommon abilities or accomplishments. Maxene Fabe's *TV Game Shows* highlights one such show, *One in a Million*, packaged by Merv Griffin Productions. Fabe blames the show's short run—it lasted only ten weeks—on its running out of "95-year-old grandmothers who could chin themselves" and "lumberjacks from the Bronx who could play the violin while standing on their head *and* reciting *Hamlet*." More than likely, the swift demise of *One in a Million* can be attributed to the very simple fact that in an era in which all of America was being encouraged to "do your own thing," the idea of average Americans doing unusual things had lost most of its currency. What had been excitingly non-conformist in the very conformist 1950s, had become fairly run of the mill in the midst of all the ferment and foment of 1960s individualism.[12]

Game shows had a habit of turning little people into big people—or, rather, unknowns into well-knowns. "The contestants became the forerunners of Andy Warhol's idea of instant fame," writes David Halberstam in *The Fifties*. "People plucked out of total anonymity and beamed into the homes of millions of their fellow Americans."[13] And sometimes the fame lasted for much longer than a Warholian 15 minutes. In addition to Dr. Joyce Brothers and child actress Patty Duke, both of whom competed on *The $64,000 Question* and went on to national celebrity in their careers, a man attempting to pass himself off as a Saudi Arabian prince on a February 9, 1961, broadcast of *You Bet Your Life* also found fame and fortune not too far down his life's road. Although Groucho quickly saw through his ruse (Marx got suspicious when he learned that the "prince" was a friend of the show's announcer, George Fenneman), the gentleman split a cash prize of $10,800 with his female partner. After winning the jackpot (by identifying the authors of several famous quotations), the contestant was casually asked by Groucho what he planned to do with his half of the take. "It's going to finance me to finish my next book," he replied. The fake prince's name was William Peter Blatty, and the book he was referring to was *The Exorcist*.

◆ 4 ◆

A Nation of Shopkeepers and Worm Farmers

> Do you work for a profit-making organization? Do you wear a special uniform or costume in your work? Do you touch people when dealing with them? Do you touch them above the waist? Could your product be found in the home? Is your work more physical than mental? Do people come to you for your services? Are people better off after using your services?
> —Questions frequently posed by *What's My Line?* panelists

In the '50s, *What's My Line?* wasn't the only TV quiz show to highlight what Americans did for a living in that transitional decade, but it probably did the best job of it. Through the weekly procession of people who, to borrow from Donna Summer, worked hard for their money, we who now study that era have been given a very good idea what our mid-century ancestors did to earn their paychecks. We've learned about all the many things they made, all the various remunerated services they performed for their fellow Americans, and all the places where they were employed doing things that sometimes still get done, but just as often, in this far more technologically sophisticated age, just might be gone with the wind.

To begin with, once upon a time in this great land, Americans actually did make things.

Manufacturing had yet to be outsourced to foreign countries, and automation, though it was starting to impact the American worker, still hadn't totally transformed American factories and left millions of workers scrambling for other forms of employment. With only six percent of the world's population in the 1950s, the U.S. produced almost half of the world's manufactured goods. Controlling only seven percent of the world's landmass, the U.S. contained within its borders 75 percent of all the cars in the world. Add to that, 60 percent of all the world's telephones and 30 percent of its TVs and radios.[1] The U.S. didn't just *make* things. It also *consumed* a whole lot of the things it made.

Weekly "challengers" to the *What's My Line?* panel were involved in the machine-manufacture or hand-crafting of false teeth, bedsprings, mousetraps, garbage cans, handcuffs, fireworks, false eyelashes, cellophane hula skirts, hula hoops, pogo sticks, bathtubs (porcelain-coated cast iron, not today's fiberglass and thermoformed acrylic), safety pins, park benches, ladies' hairnets, bird baths, heating pads, boxing gloves, dog houses, sleeping bags and ladies stockings … to name only a fraction of the products that got guessed (or didn't get guessed!) on the show. All the men and women who created these items of everyday American life (if, that is, the average American was given to wearing false eyelashes and cellophane hula skirts) came on *What's My Line?* for the purpose of stumping the panel and, on a good day, winning a top cash prize of $50 for their trouble. (Inflation was never acknowledged on *What's My Line?*. The maximum payout never budged from its original 1950 ceiling.)

What's My Line? contestant bookers did repeat a few "lines" over the course of the show's long 17-year prime-time network run. There were, for example, a few Atlantic City Steel Pier horse divers (four, actually) and way too many worm farmers and marriage counselors. And because panelists' queries had a better chance of eliciting audience giggles and guffaws when there was some question as to whether a contestant's line involved man or beast, there was an over-abundance of challengers in canine-related professions: dog catcher; a salesman of dog meds; the owner of a "dog washing service"; a dog psychologist; a manufacturer of doggie blankets; makers of dog biscuits, dog collars, dog muzzles, dog cosmetics; a seller of dog soap; a poodle clipper; the manager of a beauty school for bowsers; even a woman who sold canine life insurance. (Ms. Irene M. Peterson most assuredly did *not* insure cats!)

Many of those things that got made and then sold, and many of the services rendered in the work-a-day world of enterprising America in the '50s, were related to the Baby Boom.

But before there was a Baby Boom, there was a marriage boom. One of the groups of challengers most often seen on the show were those in the marriage-related trades: matchmakers, teachers of classes in "marriage," bridal consultants, makers of bridal garters, county clerks (who issued marriage licenses), wedding ring manufacturers and a rice salesman—*perfumed* rice, to be thrown at weddings. One of the challengers on the July 1, 1956, episode was his honor Seymour Rabinowitz, the judge who married Marilyn Monroe to her third husband, playwright Arthur Miller.

To Tell the Truth, taking its own occasional ride on the marriage-go-round, brought on as "real claimants" husband-and-wife professional wrestlers, a husband-and-wife steeplejack team, and a husband and wife whose twins were also married to one another. *You Bet Your Life* frequently featured married contestants, and had a special affinity for newlyweds in particular. And *You Bet Your Life* wasn't alone. In fact, long before Chuck Barris added *The Newlywed Game* to ABC's daytime lineup, there were game shows and audience participation shows that focused on the just- or recently married: *The Bill Gwinn Show* (called at various times *It Could Happen to You, It Could Be You, This Could Be You* and *This Is My Song*), *It Pays to Be Married* and *Two in Love*. There were also matchmaking shows like *Blind Date,* later called *Your Big Moment* (and hosted by Melvyn Douglas), and those shows which, like *Love Story,* gave young lovers a chance to "tell their story" and then answer questions for cash and fun *stuff*. On *With This Ring,* recently engaged couples were asked their opinions about how to handle situations that might come up in a marriage. A couple of married celebrity judges picked the winning couple and awarded them a special honeymoon trip.

ABC's *Chance for Romance,* a daytime offering in the fall of 1958, left nothing to chance for its contestants. Players with romantic potential were picked by a board of experts in human relations: a psychologist, a sociologist and a marriage counselor (a far more scientific approach than Groucho's propensity for throwing total strangers at each other and then all but calling for a preacher).

The radio, and later television, program *Bride and Groom* married an impressive 2350 couples during its first nine years on the air. It also acquired a little notoriety in connection with a peripheral viewer, definitely not a fan. A husband—not in league with those happily married couples feted on the show—expressed his displeasure that his wife was such a devoted fan of the program by pulling out a .38 revolver and shooting their TV. Upon incarceration at San Quentin, (in the state of California in the 1950s, one could apparently be sent up the river for murdering a television), he was faced with a bit of poetic irony: a recent poll of his fellow inmates revealed that *Bride and Groom* was one of *their* favorite daytime shows, too.[2]

The most famous person ever to have been married on *Bride and*

Groom, Dick Van Dyke mentioned on *I've Got a Secret* that when he and his first wife Margie were wed on the show on February 12, 1948, they received bookcases, an electric iron, some silverware and a honeymoon stay at a lodge in Mt. Hood, Oregon. Van Dyke is probably the only groom to appear on *Bride and Groom* who went on to host a couple of game shows of his own: *Mother's Day* and *Laugh Line*. Neither lasted for more than three months.

A Martian hacking into the broadcasting signals emitted by American game shows of the 1950s would be left with the impression that the United States of America did nothing in that decade but marry and have babies—*lots* of babies. Most of the game shows of the decade seemed to acknowledge in some form or fashion the propensity of Americans for being fruitful and multiplying. *Truth or Consequences* staged baby races. Married female contestants often felt the need to name their children, and give their respective ages, as part of their meet-and-greet with the emcee. But it was *What's My Line?* that took the cake—the baby shower cake, that is—for bringing on a myriad of those in the American baby business: makers of baby high chairs, baby carriages, baby bibs, teething rings, baby bottles; the owners of diaper services; a woman who wove the cloth for diapers; sellers of rubber pants, basinets and, of course, maternity clothes.

That last *What's My Line?* contender was engaged for the purpose of having some fun with a very pregnant Dorothy Kilgallen on the February 21, 1954, episode. Since the word "pregnancy" was verboten in that day, fellow panelist Arlene Francis was forced to choose her words carefully when seeking to know if the product the contestant sold had to do with "motherhood." Euphemistic phrases like "with child" and "in a family way" were also employed. (Thirteen months earlier, writers of *I Love Lucy* had the same problem describing Lucille Ball's own real-life-imitates-art [and vice versa] condition.)

Quite a few of the professions and plain ol' day jobs that received the *What's My Line?* treatment were those which have either largely been made obsolete by advances in technology or have disappeared due to changes in societal tastes and mores. Are there still Turkish baths? Hat-check girls who actually check hats and not just coats? Is the manufacture of men's spats still a viable profession? Are there still door-to-door Fuller brush salesmen? Gone are the managers of burlesque theaters, the boys who reset the pins in bowling alleys, and the installers of TV antennas atop the roofs of America. Do people still eat Limburger cheese, or is it culturally relegated to malodorous hijinks in old Three Stooges and Our Gang shorts? Are there still a few men left who wax their mustaches? One of the *What's My Line?* challengers actually made a living wrapping mustache wax.

Similarly, how many occupations have become taboo (or are at least generally frowned upon) due to modern-day political correctness and current social sensitivity? A viewer would be unlikely to see on a revival of *What's My Line?* today the following animal-related occupational challengers: bullfighters of both genders; big game hunters, also of both genders, including one who proudly limits his slaughter to gorillas only; a man who sells horsemeat; and a woman who raises mink (and not for the purpose of cuddling them in a ferretine manner). All of the individuals mentioned above appeared on the show during its 1950s heyday, and there do not appear to have been complaints from either audience or on-air panelists about what they did for a living.

And *What's My Line?* wasn't unique in presenting occupations which in the twenty-teens would be frowned upon. On a March 1955 *You Bet Your Life*, a gentleman named Joe Weinstein let it be known that he made his living as a feather merchant, buying and selling feathers plucked from the world's most exotic avian species. To which, according to the show's director Robert Dwan, there came not a single negative peep or chirp from the studio audience, nor were there any angry letters, to Dwan's recollection, received from bird lovers.[3] In the 1950s, Rachel Carson's groundbreaking book on pesticides, *Silent Spring*, was still seven years away, the ecological and pro-environment movement still in its muted infancy.

As late as March 4, 1951, there were still men delivering ice for those who had yet to take Betty Furness's advice and get themselves a Westinghouse refrigerator. Actually, it wasn't an iceman who cameth on *What's My Line?*, but an ice*woman*—a sly wink at guest panelist Furness. (Panelist Louis Untermeyer referenced the obsolescent profession by quipping that the deliverywoman had a "*nice* job if you could get it.") Appearing on the show over the years were also a snuff salesman, a corset salesman and a man who bottled cod liver oil—back in the day when health-conscious Americans drank a lot of cod liver oil. There were also manufacturers of Pullman berths, steam cabinets, monocles and Murphy beds.

And as late as the 1950s, people were still carving cigar store Indians.

No discussion of the varied professions guessed and dissected on *What's My Line?* would be complete without mischievous mention of those times when the show's occupation bookers got a little mischievous. These are actual jobs that kept people employed in the 1950s, and which in a good many instances left Ms. Francis, Ms. Kilgallen and Mr. Cerf completely baffled:

> A concocter of nostrums for "raising hair on bald heads"
> An alligator wrestler
> A saleswoman of pistols for women (in assorted colors)
> A skunk trapper
> A salesman of exploding cigars
> A jellybean polisher
> The inventor of whiskey-flavored toothpaste
> A snail farmer
> The manager of a flea circus
> A donkey farmer
> A bubble gum tester
> A seller of the little paper hats that, once upon a time, were affixed to the bones of rib roasts

And, because the show had an affinity for those who worked in zoos: a hippo keeper, an elephant keeper, a snake keeper, an ape keeper, and a penguin keeper.

All of these people came on the show. And all of them went away infinitesimally richer and gladdened in the knowledge that in the U.S. of A. in the middle of the twentieth century, a kid could grow up to be just about anything.

As for occupation-related contestants on other '50s game shows, *To Tell the Truth* had a special claim on those whose résumés were distinguished by extraordinary personal achievement. Muriel Agnelli's "truth," for example, was that she had been editor for Dorothy Dix (Elizabeth Meriwether Gilmer), who earlier in the century had been America's highest-paid, most-read female journalist. Dix's marital advice column appeared in 273 newspapers throughout the world and was read by an estimated 60 million people.[4]

One of *I've Got a Secret*'s occupational interests was professional athletes, and the show prided itself in bringing on a number of sports greats. *I've Got a Secret* hit a home run with its September 28, 1955, broadcast, which coincided with the first game of that year's "Subway" World Series between the New York Yankees and the Brooklyn Dodgers. There were six different World Series match-ups between the two powerhouse teams

4. A Nation of Shopkeepers and Worm Farmers 41

from 1947 to 1956; 1955's was, coincidentally, the only one won by the Dodgers. In honor of the legendary series, *I've Got a Secret* welcomed three legendary record-holders of the game, dubbing them "Mr. A," "Mr. B" and "Mr. C." The baseball fans on the panel, Bill Cullen and Henry Morgan, were blindfolded for these challenges; for their female counterparts Jayne Meadows and Kitty Carlisle, who weren't well-versed in the game, the blindfolds weren't necessary.

Mr. "A" was Leon Cadore, whose secret was, "I pitched the longest major league game in history." The game, which took place on May 1, 1920, went 26 innings and would have gone longer if it hadn't been called for darkness. What isn't mentioned in this segment is the fact that Cadore shares this record (which still stands as of the writing of this book) with opposing pitcher Joe Oeschger of the Boston Braves.

Another record that has yet to be bested is held by Mr. "B": Cincinnati Reds pitcher Johnny Vander Meer threw two no-hit games in a row in 1938, the first against the Boston Braves on June 11, the second against the Brooklyn Dodgers on June 15. (Coincidentally, this was the first game ever played at Ebbets Field at night.)

Mr. "C" was none other than Ty Cobb who, during his lifetime, held 90 Major League Baseball records. Host Garry Moore confessed to viewers that it was difficult to single out just one of his records for Cobb's "secret." As luck would have it, the record that was selected is one which still stands today: Mr. "C"'s secret was "I have the highest lifetime batting average in baseball" (367). Although many of Cobb's records have fallen since his retirement as a player following the 1928 season, he still holds the career record for stealing home (54 times) and for stealing second base, third base and home in succession (five times). Cobb was also the youngest player ever to reach 4000 hits and to score 2000 runs. (Other sports legends welcomed on 1950s game shows are profiled in Chapters 5 and 8.)

There were a couple of related professions that received only an occasional mention on the panel game shows, except in the context of the shows' relevant sponsorships: the makers and peddlers of pharmaceutical products. Perhaps this was due to the fact that drug companies received sufficient exposure by virtue of being big game show advertisers. Geritol, the tonic for "iron-poor, tired blood," sold over $25,000,000 worth of bottles when it bankrolled *Twenty-One*.[5] Net profits for the product jumped to $14 million in 1957 from $10.5 million the previous year (before sponsorship of *Twenty-One*).[6] Pharmaceuticals, Inc., producer of the tonic, was also a long-time sponsor of *To Tell the Truth*. On each of the episodes, emcee Bud Collyer was required to open the show by holding up a bottle and saying, "*To Tell the Truth* is brought to you each Tuesday night by Geritol, America's #1 tonic—the high potency tonic that helps you feel stronger fast."

Quiz and other audience participation shows of the 1950s often changed sponsorships or took on a second sponsor ("our alternate sponsor"). Late in the 1950s, *To Tell the Truth* ended its association with Pharmaceuticals, Inc., and began a partnership with an advertiser not nearly so health-minded: Marlboro cigarettes.

On *Twenty-One*, quizmaster Jack Barry was required to hold up a bottle of Geritol, and each week, just like his *To Tell the Truth* counterpart, make the same sloganized claim. But there was a fly in the ointment—or rather, the tonic: the slogan wasn't all that truthful. The subject of several years of investigation by the Federal Trade Commission, Pharmaceuticals, Inc., was ordered in 1965 to radically alter its Geritol pitch. From that point forward, the makers of Geritol were enjoined to state that their product was efficacious only in persons who were sufferers of iron deficiency anemia. Unfortunately for Pharmaceuticals, Inc., most people who are tired aren't tired because they're anemic. The FTC went so far as to accuse the company of gross negligence "bordering on recklessness" in making their misleading contention; and Pharmaceuticals, Inc., was later asked to pay the largest FTC fine up to that point (1973), $812,000.[7]

Pharmaceuticals, Inc., was also responsible for an over-the-counter drug called Zarumin, another *To Tell the Truth* sponsor. Its catchphrase was "The most important new advance for relief of common rheumatic and arthritic-like pain." Note: "arthritic-*like* pain." And the panel show over the years was also sponsored by a product from a different drug company, J.B. Williams: Serutan, a "natural" laxative (read the letters backwards), leaving one to wonder about the age of the show's demographic. (Serutan was also advertised on *The Lawrence Welk Show* and *The Original Amateur Hour*.)

A popular over-the-counter drug of the 1950s, advertised all over the tube (including on the early 1950s talent show *Chance of a Lifetime*), was Bromo-Seltzer. As quintessentially mid-century American as Tupperware parties and Burma-Shave road poetry, "Bromo" was promoted as a delightfully effervescent antacid that not only relieved heartburn and upset stomach, but also possessed analgesic properties (those properties first being attributed to acetanilide, later found to cause liver and kidney damage). In addition, Bromo-Seltzer, because of its "special ingredient," sodium bromide, acted as a mild sedative and was a popular hangover remedy. As a class of tranquilizers, bromides were taken off the U.S. market in 1975 because of their toxicity.

One of the challengers on a November 1, 1956, *What's My Line?* was a woman who "packages reducing pills." Am Plus, a prescription-only drug sold by the Charles Pfizer company, reportedly worked miracles in helping its users drop the pounds. It did this because Am Plus was actually speed. In their 2013 *Wall Street Journal* piece "A Nation of Kids on Speed," Pieter Cohen and Nicolas Rasmussen spent some time recounting the early history of amphetamine addiction in the U.S. By the '50s, amphetamine use for dieting and depression was rising to the level of epidemic, aided and abetted by drug companies like the one for which Mrs. Elsie Lawrence worked.

Meanwhile, back at home, amphetamines were heralded as the first antidepressant, and shortly thereafter as an ideal weight-loss pill. One 1955 advertisement for Am Plus amphetamine tablets assured users that they would be "beachable by summer."[8]

When the panel found out that the full-figured pill packager had lost 40 pounds while taking her employer's product, she was asked by panelist Bennett Cerf how long she intended to *keep* taking the diet pills. "Until I lose 55 more pounds," Mrs. Lawrence freely admitted.

Game shows weren't the only TV vehicle for sponsorship by American drug companies. In his 1962 book *The Great Time Killer*, Harold Mehling listed 50 different pharmaceutical companies advertising on TV at the time, and he included their addresses so viewers could contact them to complain about the quality of the programming they were sponsoring. Given the length of this list, one isn't quite sure if Americans in the 1950s and early 1960s weren't the sickest or, with such easy access to so many meds, the *healthiest* people on Earth.[9]

Perhaps a tabulation of all the sick days taken off from the thousands of different jobs they performed throughout the decade would tell the story.

◈ 5 ◈

It's News (or History) to Me

> TV exposes people to news, to information, to knowledge, to entertainment. How is it bad?
> —Tom Clancy[1]

Denizens of the 1950s sought their news in places very different from where today's news consumers get their daily fix. Newspapers were the primary source for news throughout the decade. Without online versions of the papers, Americans actually had to go out to their front yards and retrieve their morning editions from the shrubbery or off a lawn still wet with dew. City folk stopped at the corner newsstand or got their afternoon edition from a teenage newsy with a satchel.

Radio, magazines and movie newsreels did their part in informing Americans about the big news events of the day (or week). But TV started to make inroads from the very beginning. In addition to nightly news broadcasts (originally 15 minutes in length), public affairs programming like Edward R. Murrow's *See it Now* and stand-alone documentaries, the networks also brought Americans live coverage of special newsworthy events like political conventions and Congressional hearings—impressive undertakings given the unwieldiness of the videosaurus television equipment of that day.

Because a majority of game shows were live in the 1950s, their participants often found themselves in the unique position of commenting either intentionally or tangentially about what was going on the world, exercising a topicality in their discourse that set them apart from the growing number of filmed programs or dramatic and musical offerings that afforded little or no opportunity to discuss contemporaneous events and current newsmakers. Indeed, a number of panel shows brought people in the news directly onto their shows for the purpose of integrating their recent activities and experiences into the games themselves.

The programs' hosts, panelists and guests were expected to present themselves conversant in the news events of the day and thoroughly *au courant* via tossed-off allusions to all the buzz and grapevine. Whatever was being discussed at America's water coolers, construction sites and Wednesday afternoon bridge club meetings was also being chatted up (or at least given passing mention) in the context of video game-playing. NBC president Pat Weaver may not have realized he was making a case for the live broadcast of the decade's popular panel shows when he claimed, "It is this ability to surpass all expectations in a live performance that will always bring a high degree of excitement to the panoply of forces arrayed when a curtain goes up in the theater or in television.... The unexpected, the spontaneous are always there—the topical, the todayishness, the current and most talked-about—these too are there in live television."[2] Mark Goodson, impresario nonpareil of live 1950s panel shows, remembered them with a special fondness. Interviewed in 1984, he compared live TV to a "car without brakes, a pencil without an eraser. Tape is easier, but you lose something that those earlier shows had."[3]

Spontaneity, topicality, "todayishness."

And there were game shows that were actually about the news itself: *It's News to Me, Quizzing the News, What Happened?, What's the Story?* and the long-running *Who Said That?*

Many of the panel shows also had newsmen and newswomen as weekly contributors. The shows' producers liked the fact that journalists and columnists like *What's My Line?*'s Dorothy Kilgallen, *To Tell the Truth*'s Hy Gardner and *Who Said That?*'s H.V. Kaltenborn and Bob Considine were up on current events and for this reason better able to play their program's games, which were often related to stories and personages turning up in the headlines. It didn't hurt that newspaper owners planted themselves at the front of the line when the FCC began to assign television licenses around the country. Among the first stations to broadcast in several cities were those owned by dailies: the *Atlanta Journal, Chicago Tribune, Memphis Commercial Appeal, Milwaukee Journal, Philadelphia Inquirer, St. Louis Post-Dispatch* and *Washington Star*.[4]

Obviously, one could not get all the news that was fit to be aired by watching *Who Said That?* or *What's the Story?*, just as today's boast that "I get all the news I need from *Bill Maher* and *The Daily Show*" doesn't hold much water either. But as a barometer of what was going on around the country and throughout the world, live television game shows didn't do so terrible a job of intimating what might be worth paying attention to.

Just three months after the outbreak of the Korean War, *New York Times* television columnist Jack Gould, who rarely gave TV quiz shows a thumbs-up, aimed his poison pen at the most big-hearted show on the tube, *Truth or Consequences*, for having the audacity to televise a mother's reunion with her injured soldier son:

> Television reached a new low in taste last night. It came on the "Truth or Consequences" program, which inexcusably exploited a mother's understandable shock when she unexpectedly saw her son, a Korean combat casualty, on the stage of the Ralph Edwards program.

Gould carped that this "intensely personal private moment" was one which no outsider had the right to share.[5] Of course, the reunion had been purposefully engineered by Ralph Edwards and his staff to share with the show's audience the joy of a son returning from war to the arms of his mother—something that *Truth or Consequences* had, by 1950, gotten very good at facilitating. If it hadn't been for the show, there would have been no reunion for Gould to snark about.

I've Got a Secret put a personal face on the Korean War with its Christmas week broadcast in 1953 by bringing on a Korean War orphan, adopted by a U.S. naval officer, to receive gifts from Santa. *What's My Line?* featured as its July 26, 1953, mystery guest General James A. Van Fleet, who replaced Matthew B. Ridgway as commander of the U.S. Eighth Army and United Nations forces in Korea. (Ridgway had taken over for General MacArthur when he was recalled to the United States by Truman.[6]) General Mark Wayne Clark, who also served as top officer in the United Nations Command, appeared as a *What's My Line?* mystery guest challenger on February 19, 1956.

A genial, crewcut-wearing young man by the name of James Buck had fun with the *What's My Line?* panel on the show's March 29, 1953, broadcast. An army paratrooper, he agreed to come on the show on the very night before he was to be shipped out to Korea.

The October 5, 1955, *You Bet Your Life*, featured an appearance by Anthony Herbert, the most decorated veteran of the Korean War and also, several years later, one of the most controversial officers serving in Vietnam, following claims made by the lieutenant colonel that he'd witnessed war crimes, which his commanding officer refused to investigate. Though dozens of official Army Criminal Investigation Division documents substantiated Herbert's charges, and he passed more than one voluntary polygraph test, the Army contended that Herbert had "a propensity to lie or exaggerate." Herbert blamed General William Westmoreland in particular for "doing everything he possibly could to keep my case covered up because of the heat being placed on the Army from the My Lai case."[7] Herbert's lawsuit against CBS, over bias allegedly exercised by *60 Minutes* in its reporting of his charges, ended up on the doorstep of the Supreme Court on a question of First Amendment protections, although his original suit was dismissed in the U.S. Court of Appeals in 2005.

In 1957, *I've Got a Secret*, remaining true to its reputation as the most free-form and heterodox TV panel show, decided to break all the rules for a worthy cause. Noting the unacceptable number of traffic deaths and injuries occurring during holiday weekends, it devoted a whole show—the episode broadcast prior to Labor Day weekend—to demonstrations, statistics and driving tips, intended to keep American motorists safer on the road. In this pre-seatbelt, pre-airbag era of American motoring (the bare minimum—two-point lap belts—weren't required in American passenger vehicles until 1968), it all came down to defensive driving, caution and alertness. Panelists Faye Emerson and Henry Morgan took a simulated driving test (for which neither got perfect scores), while on a more sober note, one of the show's cameras panned rows of empty seats in the studio, representative of the 420 Americans estimated to lose their lives in traffic accidents over the weekend.[8] The most chilling moment of the telecast came when the curtain opened on a crumpled carcass of a car. A man came out and gravely whispered his secret into Garry Moore's ear: "My son was killed in this automobile."[9]

I've Got a Secret's job was made more difficult by the fact that Americans in the 1950s—despite the fact that 40,000 of them were dying on the country's roadways each year—didn't express that much interest in having safe cars; and the car manufacturers, in response, saw little need to press the need.[10] In light of this, what *I've Got a Secret* did was commendable. Most television shows that either had car makers for sponsors or might possibly have them on board in the future were scared of losing lucrative automobile advertising contracts if they drove home too doggedly the necessity of auto safety features, which today seem commonsensible. The word from Detroit—an actual slogan of the period—was that "safety doesn't sell." In the end, it was all about keeping the customer happy, even if that customer ended up as one of the 100,000 Americans each year gurneyed away from a bad accident with a permanent disability.

With the greatest war in the history of the world a relatively recent memory for Americans as the 1950s rolled in, it was inevitable that so many game show contestants, both by fortuity or design, would have been either active participants in that war or among those many noncombatants who otherwise were strongly connected to the conflict.

In January 1957, *To Tell the Truth* featured in one of its identity-guessing segments the military historian and investigative journalist Ladislas Faragó, whose books on General George Patton and the Japanese attack on Pearl Harbor became the basis for the acclaimed films *Patton* and *Tora! Tora! Tora!* As was often the case with accomplished Americans who appeared on these shows at an early stage in their career, some of their more impressive accomplishments were achieved *after* their participation. (And then there is the opposite: those who, like Anthony Herbert above, appeared on a game show early in their career and then later went on to controversy and even notoriety.) Faragó spent the latter part of his life investigating controversial claims that Hitler's personal secretary Martin Bormann had been living into the 1970s in exile in Argentina—claims which, whether true or not (there are strong advocates on both sides), helped to confirm a postwar Nazi presence in South America.

Pappy Boyington, famed commander of the U.S. Marine Corps fighter squadron VMF-214 (nicknamed the "Black Sheep" squadron), appeared on *To Tell the Truth* in July 1957. During the military conflict between China and Japan, he had been a P-40 Warhawk fighter pilot with the 1st American Volunteer Group, colloquially known as the Flying Tigers. The next year, Air Force Brigadier General Robert Lee Scott Jr., another Flying Tiger, and author of the bestseller *God Is My Co-Pilot* written about his experience, made an appearance on the show.

In between the two, on August 20, *To Tell the Truth* panelists had a chance to guess which of three claimants was the real Frank E. Toscani. Toscani was the real-life inspiration for the character of American Army General Victor Joppolo in John Hersey's Pulitzer Prize-winning novel *A Bell for Adano*. The book told the story of a temporary Allied-occupied town administrator, who helps a small town (in Toscani's case, the Sicilian port town of Licata) find a replacement for its 700-year-old bell, which Mussolini ordered melted down for war weaponry. In civilian life, Toscani was a handy *To Tell the Truth* contestant to bring on: He worked as a clerk in New York City's Department of Sanitation.

The show also featured as challengers Eric Ericson, an American-born World War II spy working for the O.S.S. out of his adopted country of Sweden; and Gil C. Alroy, who, as a teenager, escaped from a Nazi concentration camp by impersonating a German soldier (with the help of a friendly German officer) and in 1959 achieved the highest GPA of any student in the 112-year history of City College of New York.

The May 18, 1955, *I've Got a Secret* included the secret, "I helped raise the U.S. flag at Iwo Jima." The keeper of this brief confidence was U.S. Marine Corporal Rene Gagnon, who in the iconic photograph associated with the flag-raising on Mount Suribachi, is the second infantryman from the right. He also appeared on a special Armed Services Week broadcast of *I've Got a Secret* on May 14, 1958.[11]

On Veterans Day 1953, *I've Got a Secret* gave its viewing audience a chance to meet Elliot White Springs, whose "secret" was, "I shot down 12 enemy planes in World War I." In actuality, Captain Springs, who flew with the Number 85 Squadron of the Royal Air Force, was either personally responsible, or shared credit, for bringing down *16* enemy aircraft.[12]

Ann Brusselmans, who—of course!—hailed from Brussels, Belgium, came on *I've Got a Secret* on December 10, 1958, along with four of the 175 American airmen shot down over Europe whom she harbored from the Nazis during the war.

What's My Line? had as mystery guests the commander of the Third Fleet, Admiral William F. "Bull" Halsey, and artist George Petty, whose "Petty Girls" were copied by military artists onto the front fuselages of a good many World War II warplanes, including the legendary *Memphis Belle*.

Two of the most emotionally moving moments in 1950s game show history took place on the Ralph Edwards-produced series *It Could Be You*, which ran from 1956 to 1961; both were related to the Holocaust. In one episode of the show, which was well known for its reunions, host Bill Leyden reunited a blind 19-year-old man named Mordechai Zarchi, living in Israel, with his foster mother Ethel Kline, who lived in Los Angeles. Mrs. Kline had befriended the young man on a visit to Israel, after he'd lost both parents in the war.

The largest number of fan letters ever received by *It Could Be You* came as a result of a different reunion, this one dubbed "the concentration camp miracle." Twelve years earlier, a camp survivor, Ilona Sasse, was informed that her two young daughters, Renate and Ursula, had been killed during the final months of the war. After living for years in denial, which involved a long futile search, Mrs. Sasse came to accept what she thought was the truth about her daughters' fate.

But Mrs. Sasse was wrong.

Leyden found out through the Red Cross that the two girls had in fact survived the war, and were then living in Germany. The show flew them over. Mrs. Sasse was tricked into coming to the studio, and when Renate and Ursula were escorted out, one can only imagine the sobs of joy that ensued.[13]

I've Got a Secret and *To Tell the Truth* both did a good job of staying on top of the news stories of the day. In the case of the latter, however, its efforts were somewhat undermined by the show's format. On *To Tell the Truth*, viewers were as much in the dark as to which member of the trio of contestants was the real deal as the show's panelists. As a result, any viewer without an especially retentive memory would lose the sense of which were the true facts related to a particular news story and which were imposter-spouted fabrications. (Indeed, as the author was preparing this book and watching episodes of *To Tell the Truth*, it was necessary for him to determine, first, who was the real McCoy and who were the fakers, lest a bit of false testimony find its way by mistake onto these pages!)

The Cold War was given a human face when Warren Hair, an American hitchhiker, discovered that he and his friend had unknowingly crossed into Hungary. They were subsequently captured by communist soldiers and held prisoner for 13 days behind the Iron Curtain. Hair appeared as a contestant on *To Tell the Truth*.

The Hungarian Uprising of 1956 was referenced several times on American game shows. Two escapees from the revolution appeared on *Break the Bank* in a special category called "Fight for Freedom." A contestant on the January 22, 1958, *I've Got a Secret* had an equally timely secret: "I led 25 Hungarians through the Iron Curtain to freedom." The confider wasn't able to actually speak those words because, being a German Shepherd, Rex could only bark.

The national obsession with the Soviet launch of Sputnik 1 was quite in evidence on the October 30, 1957, *I've Got a Secret*. The "secret" of an unhappy Schenectady, New York, man named Anthony J. Renaldi was actually an anti–Russian complaint: "My garage door opened every time Sputnik flew over." (President Eisenhower also had reason to complain about the satellite: His poll numbers dropped 22 points in the wake of Sputnik's taunting launch.)

On November 5, 1959, a few weeks after USSR premier Nikita Khrushchev and his wife's visit to the United States, *To Tell The Truth* featured as one of its challengers Soviet defector Peter Deriabin, the author of several books on the KGB.

A number of sports legends appeared on '50s game shows, with special attention given to them by the panel shows. Don "Midnight" Miller was one of the first celebrated competitors on *To Tell the Truth*; he appeared on the February 5, 1957, episode. Miller, who was inducted into the College Football Hall of Fame in 1970, was best known as one of Knute Rockne's "Four Horsemen"—the four members of Notre Dame's legendary 1924 backfield. Quarterback Harry Stuhldreyer had made his own panel show appearance on the October 7, 1953, *I've Got a Secret*. His induction into the Hall of Fame came later, in 1958. ("Small world" factoid: Fellow "Horseman" halfback Jim Crowley went on to become the coach of the Fordham Rams, whose September 30, 1939, gridiron face-off with the Waynesburg Yellow Jackets in New York City was the first American football game ever televised. Fordham won, 34–7.)

To Tell the Truth also brought on George Mikan, a.k.a. "Mr. Basketball," a pioneer of the sport best known as inventor of the "Mikan Drill," which he designed to help forwards and centers develop rhythm, perfect their timing when rebounding, and improve their scoring in the paint.

Other athletes who challenged the *To Tell the Truth* panelists were Olympic sprinters Bobby Morrow and Wilma Rudolph, Dodger pitcher Don Drysdale (who also appeared on *You Bet Your Life* with his first wife Ginger) and Jack Kelly, Olympic rowing champion and older brother of actress Grace Kelly. *To Tell the Truth* specialized in bringing on athletes who weren't necessarily recognizable on sight, since the play format, unlike *What's My Line?*, didn't permit blindfolds. (But in spite of the producers' attempts to fool the panel, every now and then a panelist would be wise to a particular player and have to disqualify himself.) As a result, contestants came on the show as representatives from a wide array of different sports. There was Montreal Canadien hockey player Jean Béliveau; Olympic medalist high diver Dr. Sammy Lee; polo champion Herb Pannell; cricket player Abdul Hatwz Kardar; Formula One race car driver Stirling Moss; ski-jumping champion Ansten Samuelsten; Olympic figure skater Hays Jenkins; champion bowler Marion Ladewig; young waterskiing champion Victoria Van Hook; and fencing champion Maria del Pilar Rodan. There was a badminton player, an archer, a skeet shooter and even the winner of the 1957 Soap Box Derby. On one occasion, the panelists had to identify the Major League baseball pitcher who was also a professional basketball player. His name was Gene Conley. He played for both the Boston Braves and the Boston Celtics and is one of only two professional athletes (the other, Otto Graham) to win championships in two of America's four major sports.

For its January 15, 1957, broadcast, *To Tell the Truth* invited on a musician by the name of Manny Balestrero, who was the subject of Alfred Hitchcock's only docudrama, *The Wrong Man*. Balestrero had been falsely accused of robbing an insurance company, and the movie documents the long nightmare he and his wife went through before he was exonerated. Hitchcock's film, with Henry Fonda as Manny, had been released less than a month before the broadcast and might still have been playing in theaters when real-life Manny took his place in the *To Tell the Truth* lineup.

On the February 20, 1957, *I've Got a Secret*, 30-year-old Michigan Congressman John Dingell confided to the audience that he was the youngest member of the U.S. House of Representatives. Dingell went on to serve in the House of Representatives for over 59 years. Upon his retirement on January 3, 2015, he'd racked up the longest Congressional tenure in U.S. history.

On occasion, the panel shows got ahead of the news. John Schisler appeared on *To Tell the Truth* on July 22, 1958, to relate his story of being taken hostage a month earlier by Cuban rebels. Schisler was supervisor of the Moa Bay Mining Company and his kidnappers were led by the future president of Cuba, Raúl Castro, brother of Fidel. Schisler was held for ten days as a protest against the United States government. By the end of the year, President Batista had fled the country and Raúl's brother Fidel was in charge.

In conjunction with Alaska and Hawaii becoming the 49th and 50th states in 1959, several politicians affiliated with the territories-states were given berths on panel shows late in the decade. A year before Hawaii joined the union, *What's My Line?* introduced viewers to territorial governor William F. Quinn, who was later elected the state's first governor. The next year, one of the state's first two Senators, Oren E. Long, took his seat next to John Charles Daly, the show's moderator. *To Tell the Truth* had the privilege of presenting to the country the first Congressman from the new state of Alaska, Ralph J. Rivers. *What's My Line?* brought on Alaskan territorial governor Mike Stepovich a year before statehood. Stepovich spent most of his term advocating for Alaskan statehood, which included this visit to the popular panel show.

On the July 9, 1958, *I've Got a Secret*, host Garry Moore and panelist Henry Morgan got their polio shots. Very soon after Salk's vaccine was licensed in 1955, a major children's vaccination campaign was launched, most Americans hastening to safeguard themselves and their families from an illness which had struck fear in the hearts of Americans for decades.

As recently as 1950, the National Foundation for Infantile Paralysis reported 31,989 cases after the previous year's record of 41,442 cases.[14] The disease had crippled an American president, Franklin D. Roosevelt, and even made an impact on the radio and television industry: Bill Cullen, regarded as the dean of game show hosts, after a five-decade career in radio and television, almost lost a hosting gig on *Give and Take* in 1952 because the producers were uneasy about his noticeable limp, which he had acquired from both a bad traffic accident and a childhood bout with poliomyelitis.[15] In the same way in which FDR was rarely photographed struggling to accommodate himself to his disability, Cullen's many producers limited instances in which the limp would be obvious to viewers. This is the reason the perpetually congenial quizmaster and celebrity panelist would often take his seat behind a podium and panel after only a short step from behind a curtain.

Senator Estes Kefauver, already a national celebrity following televised hearings of his Senate special committee to investigate crime in 1951, appeared on *What's My Line?* one month before the release of the committee's final report. Hearings were held in 14 major cities and more than 600 witnesses were questioned; an estimated 30 million Americans were watching the broadcasts around the time of Kefauver's *What's My Line?* appearance. The committee's findings led to major changes in how organized crime was fought on both a national and local level; the Racketeer Influenced and Corrupt Organizations Act (affectionately known as RICO) was a direct response to Committee recommendations. Another outcome of the hearings, thanks to the medium of television, was the raising of Kefauver's profile, this helping to put him on the Democratic national ticket in 1956 as Adlai Stevenson's running mate.

Even the Suez Crisis of 1956 found its way into the world of the American TV game show, in the person of a pilot, Al Beale, who lost his job with the French-run Suez Canal Company when Egypt's General Nasser nationalized the canal. Just five weeks after Beale's *What's My Line?* appearance, Egypt was invaded, first by Israel and then by Great Britain and France, in a concerted effort to regain Western control of the canal and remove the general from power.

Because so many of the most important news events of the 1950s were referenced, sometimes made corporeal and given immediacy and relevance by the appearance of game show participants with a stake in those stories, and because copies of so few of the tens of thousands of individual broadcasts have been preserved, one can only assume that the examples noted above comprise only a small representation of that frequent intersection between news-making and televised game-playing.

Granted, there were roadblocks to that intersection. There were things that could not be discussed on '50s TV shows for reasons of prevailing standards of decency (it wasn't until late in the decade that game shows were finally permitted to advertise laxatives) and ever-present was the heavily censorious hand of network Standards and Practices. Local stations could lose their licenses if they broadcast material found objectionable to "family viewers." The embargo on the word "pregnant" represented only one of a great many words and phrases that weren't permitted on the air. Likewise, there were news stories that, because of their potential for giving offense in some quarter or another, could not be discussed. And there were restrictions related to the dispensing of proprietary information. Remember that this was a period during which advertisers weren't allowed to mention a competing brand by anything but the comically euphemistic "Brand X."

But one marvels at how many things actually did get discussed and given passing reference, so willing were game show participants to deliver that "todayness" of which Pat Weaver was so fond.

And it wasn't just *current* events that got brought up on these broadcasts. Game shows of the decade frequently dug deep into the vaults of history, not only in creating new play-formats with strong historical trivia components, but also as vehicles for bringing forward individuals who had personal connections to important historical events.

Garry Moore's first contestant on the February 8, 1956, *I've Got a Secret* was a 96-year-old gentleman by the name of Samuel L. Seymour. Mr. Seymour's secret was one of the show's most remarkable, though it was somewhat inaccurately stated: "I saw John Wilkes Booth shoot Abraham Lincoln." Young Sammy was at Ford's Theatre on the night of April 14, 1865, and watched as Booth dropped to the stage from the president's box after firing the fatal shot, but he hadn't actually seen Booth shoot Lincoln. Still, Seymour was the last living witness to events of that night. As a side note, Moore didn't offer Seymour the customary parting gift of a carton of Winston cigarettes because the old man had mentioned earlier that he didn't smoke cigarettes; however, since he did smoke a pipe, Seymour left the studio with a different R.J. Reynolds product in hand—a can of Prince Albert pipe tobacco.

To Tell the Truth brought on Wrong Way Corrigan, who, as the legend goes, "accidentally" flew from Brooklyn, New York, to County Dublin,

Ireland, on July 17–18, 1938, when he was supposed to be heading to Long Beach, California. It has been estimated that more people attended his ticker tape parade down Broadway than turned out to see Charles Lindbergh 11 years earlier. (Such a claim is difficult to quantify.)

I've Got a Secret introduced the country to Curt Hamill on September 2, 1959. His secret: "I drilled the first oil gusher in history (1901)." Curt and his two brothers Jim and Al started drilling into the Spindletop salt dome oil field, located south of Beaumont, Texas, on October 27, 1900, and the gusher hit on January 10 of the next year, thus kicking off the Texas oil boom of history and legend.[16]

Melvin Purvis challenged the panel to pick him out of the lineup on *To Tell the Truth*'s October 1, 1957, broadcast. Purvis was the "G" man who led the John Dillinger manhunt. He's less remembered for doing something that had even greater historic importance: As an Army intelligence officer, he helped to compile evidence used against Nazi leaders in the Nuremberg Trials.

On April 11, 1956, the tenth anniversary of the commissioning of the aircraft carrier USS *Leyte* (CV-32), *I've Got a Secret* opened its stage to the officers and crew of the ship, who crowded together, their celebration underscored by a brass band. Amidst cheers of "Hip-hip-hooray!" the sailors tossed their hats high in the air, a giant birthday cake commanding center stage. What wasn't mentioned in this moment of spirited remembrance is the tragedy that had struck the ship less than three years before: On October 16, 1953, while *Leyte* was being converted to antisubmarine carrier, there was an explosion caused by the accidental ignition of hydraulic fluid in her port catapult machinery room. Thirty-seven men died and another 28 were injured. This tenth anniversary celebration points up the fact that game shows like *I've Got a Secret*, while often shining a sobering light on events of both past and present, still maintained control of the narrative. The narrative on this particular April 11, 1956, broadcast was joyful celebration, not a memorializing of those whom the ship had lost—the loss made especially tragic by the fact that the deaths weren't attributed to wartime torpedoing, but to peacetime carelessness.

Other individuals of historical accomplishment who appeared on 1950s game shows, mostly as challengers to celebrity panelists, were Jack Bursey, who explored the Antarctic under the command of Richard E. Byrd (*To Tell the Truth*); A.H. Waite, who participated in all three expeditions to rescue Admiral Byrd who, stationed alone at a South Pole meteorological station, came close to death from carbon monoxide poisoning

(*I've Got a Secret*); Benjamin Minge Duggar, who in 1945 discovered Aureomycin (trade name for the antibiotic chlortetracycline), the first tetracycline to be identified (*I've Got a Secret*); George Schuster, who won the 1908 New York-to-Paris auto race; : Sir Edmund Hillary, who with Tenzing Norgay, became the first two climbers to reach the summit of Mount Everest in 1953 (*To Tell the Truth*) (Norgay appeared on *To Tell the Truth* on July 27, 1964); Parker Christian, the great-great grandson of *Bounty* mutineer Fletcher Christian; Elmo M. Pickerell, whose "secret" on *I've Got a Secret* was that he had been taught by the Wright Brothers to fly, back in 1910; and John Thomas Scopes, whose trial for illegally teaching evolution in Dayton, Tennessee, in 1925 brought together two of the most famous men of the twentieth century, William Jennings Bryan and Clarence Darrow, in a Modernist vs. Fundamentalist courtroom match-up that still resonates today (*To Tell the Truth*).

Featured on *I've Got a Secret*'s special May 14, 1958, Armed Services Week broadcast were Gus Lambert, who received a Congressional medal for participating in Walter Reed's Yellow Fever experiments in 1900[17]; Dick Shanafelt, one of Teddy Roosevelt's Rough Riders[18]; Air Force Lt. Colonel James Jabara, the first U.S. jet ace[19]; Commander Frank Kaine, one of the first frogmen; Major General Lee Wade, pilot of the first round-the-world flight (in 1924); and a pigeon named G.I. Joe, who delivered a message over enemy lines, which, according to Garry Moore, saved the lives of 1000 Allied soldiers. G.I. Joe was decorated by the Lord Mayor of London for his heroism, this fact prompting Moore to quip, "This is the first time a *pigeon* has been decorated by a *person*." The show was kicked off by a drill demonstration of members of all four branches of the U.S. armed forces, operating as a single unit (a television first).

Astronomer Clyde Tombaugh's secret whispered to Garry Moore on the October 24, 1956, *I've Got a Secret* was, "I discovered the planet Pluto." Tombaugh holds the very odd distinction of being the only game show contestant (indeed, the only human) to have some of his ashes sent outside the solar system: A portion of his remains were placed on the New Horizons space probe, which, on October 25, 2016, completed its fly-by of the planet (later downgraded to dwarf planet) Pluto. Tombaugh, in keeping with a fine tradition practiced by residents and visitors to his adopted state of New Mexico, made a well-documented sighting of multiple UFOs outside of Las Cruces, New Mexico, on August 20, 1949. Although he never concluded that it was a collection of extraterrestrial craft he'd been looking at that night, it's nonetheless interesting to note that his observation came on the cusp of the most flying saucer-obsessed decade in history, an obsession buttressed by other claims of visitation by space aliens to the "Land of Enchantment."

On March 5, 1957, television audiences tuning in to *To Tell the Truth* got to meet a man with an important title, but with not much to do: Steve Martini, barber to one of America's baldest presidents, Dwight D. Eisenhower. Ike's senior helicopter pilot, the official White House Santa Claus and the White House's head chef also played the game. Eisenhower's golf caddy made a *What's My Line?* appearance in the summer of 1959, when Ike was playing a lot of golf.

President Eisenhower loved playing golf. Just as much as he loved watching game shows. President and Mrs. Eisenhower's favorite was *You Bet Your Life*.[20] According to Gil Fates, executive producer of *What's My Line?*, they were big fans of this show as well, seldom missing an episode.[21] Like most Americans, the Eisenhowers actually enjoyed a lot of different programs, including *I Love Lucy* and *Arthur Godfrey's Talent Scouts*. Mamie watched the soaps and romantic movies and musicals, while Ike was drawn to westerns.[22]

But there still had to have been something very special about seeing your own barber on national television.

❖ 6 ❖

There Is Nothing Like a Dame

> In 1956, there were 100 women for every 98.6 men in America. Men had an average of 9.9 years of formal education, women 10.7. Women comprised almost one-third of the U.S. work force. The median annual wage for men was $3552, for women, $1363.
>
> —*Life* magazine, December 24, 1956[1]

When it comes to television's role in the advancement of civil rights for women in the late 1940s and throughout the 1950s, there is much to be said for the gains that were made, just as one cannot avoid admitting that much work on the feminist front lines still lay ahead. In the plus column were panel shows like *What's My Line?* and *To Tell the Truth*, which offered a cavalcade of accomplished women whom young female viewers could admire and aspire to emulate. Game shows like the *G.E. College Bowl* (the "Varsity Sport of the Mind") and *Quiz Kids* also proved, beyond doubt, that women (and girls) could be every bit as smart as men (and boys).

Some of the biggest winners on high-stakes video quizzers like *The $64,000 Question,* its spin-off *The $64,000 Challenge, Dotto* and *Twenty-One* were women. Though an unfortunate number of these bright females got branded as game-rigging accomplices (just like a lot of the men), later-life celebrity psychologist Dr. Joyce Brothers refused to accept any "special" help from the *$64,000 Question* producers when it came to answering questions in her specialty area: boxing. When attempts were made to kick her off the show, she refused to stay down for the count. According to David Halberstam, efforts to deep-six her were fairly brutal, the questions she was asked made unusually difficult.[2] Dr. Brothers was even asked the names of referees for certain historic matches. But in the end she prevailed, undaunted and untainted, and became the second person on the show to score its top prize. Moreover, the bright 28-year-old psychologist had the chance to demonstrate that there were women out there who knew a hell of a lot about prizefighting. (Maybe that's why she was such a scrappy competitor herself.)

All told, more female challengers appeared on *What's My Line?* than male. Granted, this was due in part to the fact that the show's producers loved to book women who were working in male-dominated professions as a challenge to the panelists' traditional conceptions about women and the ways they should be bringing home the bacon. ("Lady" wrestlers, female cops, high-heeled private eyes and winsome matadors were especially popular with the show's contestant procurers.) Initially engaged as occupational curiosities, these professional women soon took a firm grip on the narrative and ran with it. American women actually *could* do more with their lives than just be helpmates and mothers, and who knows but maybe Rosie the Riveter just might like to keep right on riveting. And yes, there were even statistics to prove it—stats that put a big dent in the prevailing mythology that Harriet Homemaker was quite content, thank-you-very-much, with half an apple pie. In 1950, there were 15.5 million women working outside the home. By the end of 1956, that figure had grown to 22 million, which comprised almost a third of the labor force.[3] Granted, homemakers of the 1950s were a large enough demographic that TV programmers found the need to target them with shows presumed to be of interest to stay-at-home moms. But the true picture of what women were doing with their lives in that decade is far more complicated than conventionally suggested.

Women appearing in 1950s game shows were largely referred to as "girls." There were whistles from the studio audience when a particularly pulchritudinous contestant stepped out in front of the cameras (something that *What's My Line?* moderator John Charles Daly jocularly attributed to "our drafty TV studio"). And for every Dr. Joyce Brothers, there was a Dagmar. For a period of time in the '50s, the busty actress was all over the dial and getting whistles that gave even Marilyn Monroe—her big screen correlative—a run for her money.

Television censors kept their clamps firmly in place, and Daly elicited a roar of laughter from his audience when he found an opportunity to use the word "damn"—or at least its homophone—when referring to a U.S. Army Corps of Engineers' fish counter at Dow and Utila Dams: "That's a lot of dam fish!" But game shows allowed for a little more leeway when it came to gaga over gams and glands. And leave it to the Brits to sum it all up so pithily. In the 1963 comedy *It's a Mad, Mad, Mad, Mad World*, Terry-Thomas'[4] Lt. Colonel J. Algernon Hawthorne inflicts the following observation on Milton Berle's J. Russell Finch. It relates to the collective national hobby of American men:

> In all my time in this wretched, God-forsaken country, the one thing that has appalled me most of all is this preposterous preoccupation with bosoms! Don't you realize they have become the dominant theme in American culture, in literature, advertising, in all this entertainment—in everything! I wager you anything you like that if American women stop wearing brassieres, your whole national economy would collapse overnight.

Those bosoms were in ample supply on the uncomfortably sexist March 2, 1955, *I've Got a Secret* featuring Jackie Gleason: Pretending to be unhappy with the show's celebrity panel, he kiddingly brings out a panel of his own to replace it. He introduces, one at a time, four beautiful, well-formed young women. As he mentions their impressive *faux*-vocations, there are howls of laughter from the audience (as well as titters from Moore and the show's real panelists). The humor lies in the incongruity of four gorgeous women having the smarts to be, respectively: an atomic physicist, *The New York Times'* chief editorial writer, the editor of *The Encyclopædia Britannica*, and the former president of the University of Chicago.

In the end, a good, chauvinistic time was had by all.

While there were legions of male game show hosts, 1950s television offered up only a handful of female emcees (a.k.a. "femcees" and, with tongue deposited in cheek, "emshees").[5] Arlene Francis switched from soldiers to collegians when her matchmaking game show *Blind Date* moved from radio to television. Other females who hosted game shows in TV's first dozen years were Denise Darcel (*Gamble on Love*, 1954), Gypsy Rose Lee (*Think Fast*, 1949), Vera Vague (*Follow the Leader*, 1953) and Kathy Godfrey (Arthur's sister), who co-hosted *On Your Way* with John Reed King. But as late as the 1970s, game show producers were squeamish about handing over quizmaster responsibilities to women. Mark Goodson explained it to game show chronicler Maxene Fabe, with no apparent inkling his remarks might be interpreted as sexist:

> Finding the right woman to host a game show is very difficult for societal reasons. So far it's been tough to get a woman who has the necessary control, who can say, "All *right*, that's enough fun, let's *play*!" without sounding like a third-grade teacher or a gym coach. Often, if you can get a woman who's soft and pretty and feminine, she comes over as mousy or saccharine or like a B-girl. And when you consider a woman celebrity to host a show, most of them are actresses. Acting is not good preparation for hosting, since it's all ad lib, without a script in sight.[6]

6. There Is Nothing Like a Dame

One wonders if Goodson might have changed his opinion had he lived long enough to experience the whip-cracking bad-assedness of that schoolmarm from Hell, *Weakest Link's* Anne Robinson.

In reality, the majority of women who appeared on game shows in the 1950s did so as either contestants or assistants (or "hostesses" as they were often called). This didn't mean there wasn't the occasional break-out personality—some '50s version of *Wheel of Fortune*'s Vanna White—who was able to build up her own fan base among viewers. Perhaps the best known of such TV personalities was a stunningly beautiful blond fashion model who, though born Dolores Rosedale, went by the stand-alone name of Roxanne. As Bud Collyer's *Beat the Clock* assistant, she became a veritable superstar among 1950s TV performers, ending up on the covers of *People Today*, *TV Guide* and *Life* magazines. There was even a doll made in her likeness, complete with the camera she used to photograph the contestants on *Beat the Clock*, whose sponsor was Sylvania, maker of radios, TVs and camera flashbulbs. (Roxanne wasn't the only person employed by the *Beat the Clock* producers who was using the show as a springboard to national popularity: Among its stunt conceivers were the Pulitzer Prize–winning playwright Neil Simon and his big brother Danny. James Dean, early in his television career, served as a stunt tester.)

There was never a consensus of opinion on how the American woman should be used, portrayed, valued and exploited by the TV game show. The producers of some of the first TV quiz and audience participation shows were most comfortable simply contextualizing women in terms of their limited roles of housewives and mothers. Game shows from the late 1940s and 1950s went by such names as *Do You Trust Your Wife?*, *Feather Your Nest*, *Glamour Girl*, *Ladies Be Seated*, *Missus Goes-A-Shopping*, *Mother's Day*, *Queen for a Day*, *This Is the Missus* and *Okay, Mother*.

Freedom Rings was typical. It gave telephone contestants the chance to answer questions and possibly win one of the sponsor's products: kitchen appliances from Westinghouse. Studio audience members, all homemakers, also had a chance to compete for prizes. They were brought on the stage and presented with various challenges related to household chores. The show's name is a puzzler. Is the "ring" the ring of a telephone, carrying with it the enticing possibility of a homemaker winning more freedom for herself through the acquisition of an energy-saving Westinghouse appliance? Or is the "ring"—more cynically—a wedding ring, and the housewife's "freedom" that devolved from it nothing but cruel jest?

Similarly, the show *Mother's Day* put homemakers to the test. Three mothers, selected from letters of support written by their husbands, children and family friends, were subjected to four rounds of play, which gave the moms the chance to demonstrate, for example, their ability to tell a hard-boiled egg from an un-boiled one, or choose a four-pound steak from among six variously weighted slabs of beef. This being the fur-loving '50s, the winner received a mink coat or something similarly "mother-appropriate."

Conversely, there were those producers and show packagers who resolved in the late '40s and throughout the '50s—at least in theory—to place the female sex on an equal footing with men, their shows featuring celebrity panels composed whenever possible of as many gals as guys. The following is a nearly exhaustive list of such network shows—along with their play-hooks—in which real live women were actually placed before television cameras and given leave to cogitate and render opinions (just like men!). The list also gives the reader a good idea of the breadth and scope of the mid-century TV panel game show, since there were few programs of this format whose celebrity panels *weren't* mixed-gender in makeup.

> *Americana* (American history and folklore)
> *Answer Yes or No* (hypothetical situations)
> *Anyone Can Win* (celebrities answering questions)
> *Ask Me Another* (sports personalities)
> *Down You Go* (Hangman)
> *Droodles* (captions for Droodle Picture Drawings)[7]
> *Guess What?* (film clips)
> *It's About Time* (historic events)
> *It's News to Me* (news events)
> *I've Got a Secret* (secrets)
> *Keep Talking* (ad libbing stories)
> *Laugh Line* (creating captions for "living" cartoons)
> *Let's See* (what did a contestant previously see?)
> *Make the Connection* (connections between contestants)
> *Masquerade Party* (guessing the identity of disguised celebrities)
> *The Name's the Same* (ordinary people with famous names)
> *One Minute Please* (extemporaneous speaking)
> *Personality Puzzle* (identifying celebrities by their personal possessions)

QED (telling mystery stories)
Quick on the Draw (cartoons)
Quizzing the News (news events)
Super Ghost (Hangman and Ghost)
Take a Good Look (news events)
Take a Guess (identifying mystery objects)
Think Fast (out-talking one another)
To Tell the Truth (distinguishing the real McCoy from imposters)
Twenty Questions (animal, vegetable, or mineral?)
We Take Your Word (definitions of words)
What Happened? (news events)
What's Going On? (guessing odd things celebrities are doing)
What's in a Word? (rhyming word association)
What's It For? (inventions)
What's My Line? (guessing people's professions)
What's the Story? (news stories)
Where Was I? (photographs)
Who Pays? (guess the celebrity by his/her employee)
Who Said That? (identifying recent quotes in the news)
Who's There? (guessing celebrities by their stuff)
Who's Whose? (matching women to their spouses)
Who's the Boss? (what well-known person does this secretary work for?)
Why? (guessing the fifth "W" of the five Ws)
and the infamous *You're in the Picture* (see Chapter 17).

Still, Betty Friedan, writing in *TV Guide* in 1964, took the medium to task for rampant institutional sexism. Brushing aside the exceptions to her thesis as embodied in the strides in gender equality made in such shows as those listed above, she wrote in blanket dismissal:

> Why is there no image at all on television of the millions and millions of self-respecting American women who are not only capable of cleaning a sink, without help, but of acting to solve more complex problems of their own lives and their society? That moronic housewife image denies the 24,000,000 women who work today outside the home, in every industry and skilled profession, most of them wives who take care of homes and children too. That image also insults the millions of real American housewives, with more and more education, who shape U.S. culture, politics, art and education, by their actions in PTA, League of Women Voters and local political parties, and who help to build libraries, art galleries and theaters, from Detroit to Seattle, and even strike for peace.[8]

Ms. Friedan was at her most critical when it came to young homemakers, whom she called

> the growth-stunted young mothers who quit school to marry and became mothers before they grow out of bobby socks themselves.... They may writhe forever in that tedious limbo between the kitchen sink and the television game show, living out their century-long life ahead, in a complex world which requires human purposes, commitment and efforts they never ever glimpsed.[9]

Here were two extremities of thought on how women were regarded both as participants on television and consumers thereof; while the truth about how the world of television game shows dealt with the distaff half of the American populace—with apologies to the impassioned Ms. Friedan—clearly lay somewhere in the middle.

One wonders how Ms. Friedan would have dealt with a gentleman (actually, he was *no* gentleman) by the name of H.G. Morton, a management consultant whose claim to fame was founding "The Society for the Domination of Women." Morton, whose appearance on *You Bet Your Life* on February 12, 1959, seemed a transparent effort by the show to invigorate the battle of the sexes, especially given his provocatively extremist positions (which he was happy and proud to bruit on national television). Morton not only wanted to disenfranchise American women, bring back dowries and raise entry requirements for young women who wished to go to college (while lowering the requirements for men), he believed that because the country was veering close to matriarchal imperium, men should rise up and first re-establish control of the purse strings in their families. Amidst groans and boos from females in the audience, Morton pressed his case that even the women themselves weren't comfortable with their newfound predominance over men:

> GROUCHO: In your opinion, why have women gotten in such a sad shape?
> MORTON: They've been placed in this freedom that physiologically and psychologically they're not capable of handling. They're like a parakeet that's out of the cage, and they can't wait to get back in the cage.
> GROUCHO: I need to ask you one final question: are you stewed?

As idiosyncratic as Mr. Morton might have seemed when it came to his views of women, there were those sociologists and social historians of the day who argued as Morton had (perhaps with slightly more elegance and erudition) that women were psychologically damaged and disordered—especially in their relationships with men—when they attempted to assert themselves outside their domesticated pigeonholes. Ferdinand Lundberg and Dr. Marynia F. Farnum's 1947 treatise on postwar American women,

Modern Woman: The Lost Sex, was a bestseller in its day. David Halberstam writes of its chilling indictment of career women, and gives us an inkling as to the complicated environment in which American women were forced to negotiate their place in society during the decade—the chore being made even more onerous by the conflicting depictions and participation of women on the numerous television game shows being broadcast through the '50s:

> Feminism itself, in their words, "was a deep illness." "The psychosocial rule that takes form, then, is this: the more educated a woman is, the greater chance there is, of sexual disorder, more or less severe. The greater the disordered sexuality in a given group of women, the fewer children they have," they wrote. They also suggested that the federal government give rewards to women for each child they bore after the first.[10]

Game shows of the 1950s were both the best of times and the worst of times when it came to the regard with which American women were held, how they were employed on the broadcasts, what the shows had to say about a woman's place in American society, and even how women were treated once they found themselves on camera. And it was hard not to pay attention, even in real time. Media studies and feminist scholar Marsha F. Cassidy, writing about daytime TV in the 1950s, points out that "for the first time, the intimacy of the television camera permitted an unprecedented close-up look at postwar femininity, and millions of women around the nation tuned in to watch."[11]

There were game show hosts like Art Linkletter and Garry Moore, who were known for their gentle touch with women and only the occasional wink-wink, nudge-nudge required of red-blooded 1950s males. On the other end of the spectrum was a Groucho Marx, who so burlesqued the notion of skirt-chasing through double entendre, leering eyebrow raises and feline *mrrrrows*, that the act became more a mockery of the wolf than an attack upon its female prey. On the other hand, there were those game show hosts like Johnny Carson of ABC's *Who Do You Trust?*, whose hot-blooded American maleness might have brought the blood of no small number of women to the point of simmer back in the day. *Who Do You Trust?*, originally called *Do You Trust Your Wife?*, featured married contestants answering questions for cash. Rather than simply ask the same question of both in the manner of Groucho Marx (and have the contestants put their heads together and come up with an answer together), or take turns asking questions, first of one spouse and then the other, it was required by the rules of the game that the husband make the decision as to which of them would answer. If he thought he'd do better, he'd take the question himself; if he thought his wife might know, he'd pass it to her. The men's better halves had no say in the matter.

Not only were the *Who Do You Trust?* wives subordinated by the rules of the game, Carson frequently ignored the women altogether in his attempts at effecting same-gender camaraderie with the husbands. And Carson took frequent opportunity to make jokes that fleeringly objectified the women who came on his show, including those who served as on-camera eye-candy assistants. On one broadcast, in the course of a husband's demonstration of his ability to "sales-pitch" a kitchen potato "stretcher," the contestant tossed off the observation that "that's a real nice potato, isn't it, John?" To which Carson, turning to ogle his on-camera assistant Cindy, delivered roguishly, "Yes, it certainly is." Such innuendo, superficially tame by today's standards, also seemed to confirm a sense in the male-dominated game show culture of the decade that "women are to be seen, even eyeballed lustily, but not heard."

One show that did allow women to be heard (in addition to the purposefully gender-balanced panel shows) was *The Big Payoff*, which was broadcast through almost the entire decade before being yanked off air in October 1959, when NBC swept out its door all of its big money shows in the middle of the quiz show mess. The woman who was privileged to speak, although limited in that speech to describing a wealth of big-ticket prizes tailored exclusively for women, was Bess Myerson. Bess had a voice, but Bess was also an American beauty, having won the title of Miss America 1945.

The Big Payoff was famous (or notorious) for its plethora of prizes (some $2,000,000 worth in its first two seasons),[12] awarded to women lucky enough to have husbands who could stand before a television camera and place their significant others as high upon the feminine pedestal of husbandly admiration as words could take them. The husbands and wives were selected from letters in which hubby made a solid case for why his wife deserved a mink coat (*The Big Payoff* gave away 104 of them in just its first three seasons), a trip to Paris, a new car or any number of other items of sumptuous magnificence.[13] Explains Cassidy in her book *What Women Watched: Daytime Television in the 1950s*, "In the constituent terms of *Payoff*'s formula, men endeavored to compensate women for the insufficiencies in their lives by attaining for them all the luxuries of feminine embellishments."[14]

Each episode presented silent, tenterhooked women waiting to see what prizes their smart husbands would snag for them (four correct answers entitled the wife to the "big" prize). There was also a fashion show segment in which shapely female models paraded across the stage clad in the latest haute couture. And then there was Myerson, the country's first "thinking" Miss America, dressed in mink, who, even as she was vocally girdled during her eight years on the show, appeared as a voluble celebrity panelist on *The Name's the Same*, and then later made 219 appearances as a regular on *I've Got a Secret*. Myerson was arguably among the most articulate and learned members of the interchangeable celebrity panel fraternity (and sorority) active throughout the '50s and the first half of the '60s. (Myerson, the only Jewish Miss America, was also the victim of anti–Semitism, a hurdle not only for her, but for a number of other Jews affiliated with TV game shows. This sad verity is taken up in Chapter 8.)

But it was the panel game shows that gave American women hope for the future of their sex. Contestants on these shows included a large number of women (*What's My Line?* being more representative of the rule rather than the exception here). Though the presentation of women of achievement—or simply those females who had broken down occupational barriers—might be attributed to tokenism and isolated anecdote, it was nonetheless refreshing and encouraging to women viewers to see members of their sex making proud claims to accomplishment, even if it didn't necessarily advance the cause of women's rights by earth-shaking bounds.

On the other hand, while *What's My Line?* was booking female contestants who were cab drivers, plumbers, dentists, gas station attendants, nightclub bouncers, steam shovel operators, jazz drummers, gold miners, steeplejacks, garbage truck drivers and billiards players, both *What's My Line?* and its sister panel shows also got a big kick out of bringing on winners of Miss America, Miss World, Miss Universe, the Miss U.S.A. *entrant* in the Miss Universe Pageant and, on *What's My Line?*'s May 22, 1955, broadcast, the winner of *Mrs.* America (no relation to the latter-day competition by that name), a Mrs. Ramona Deitemeyer. The Mrs. America pageant was created in 1936 by public relations executive Bert Nevins to promote Palisades Amusement Park. It was deliberately emulative of the Miss America pageant, its participants judged on attractiveness, poise and personality. But, unlike its companion pageant, contestants were also graded on family psychology, and such homemaking skills as cooking, sewing, ironing and party planning.

For her "line," Mrs. Deitemeyer was described as "housewife." It was the last time a self-described housewife would appear on *What's My Line?* Only a few years before, the word had been so commonplace that it had reached shibboleth status on a radio quizzer called *Second Honeymoon*. This New Jersey–based show was hosted by Bert Parks (before being deposited on the Atlantic City boardwalk). Parks rallied his audience of Garden State homemakers with the sprightly show-opener, "Who's the pillar of American society?" The answer, dutifully shouted back with aproned pride: "The housewife!"[15]

To Tell the Truth had a special interest in winners of beauty pageants, which seemingly bordered on obsession. During the four years it was broadcast in the 1950s, *To Tell the Truth* featured Miss America 1957, Miss Universe 1957, Miss Indian America 1957, Miss America 1958, Miss Hawaii, the traveling companion to Miss America, the 1958 Miss Young America in 4-H, Miss World 1959, the Pan American Coffee Queen, Queen of the U.S. Armed Forces, the 1959 Hot Dog Queen, a "former Miss Universe," Miss Youth Fitness, the 1960 National College Queen, and Jacque Mercer, Miss America 1949, who was also noted for having written a book called *How to Win a Beauty Contest*.

In addition to female butchers bakers, and candlestick makers (there actually was an episode—the May 8, 1960, broadcast—in which all three of these professions were represented just for fun), *What's My Line?* did what few other game shows were doing at the time: introducing women of unique accomplishment to American viewing audiences. There were female politicians like Senator Margaret Chase Smith and Red Bank, New Jersey, mayor Katherine E. White. First Daughter Margaret Truman appeared more than once. There was political hostess Perle Mesta (the inspiration for Sally Adams in Irving Berlin's *Call Me Madam*); pioneer in physical therapy Sister Elizabeth Kenny; world-famous Italian fashion designer Elsa Schiaparelli; French resistance fighter and Indo-China-based reporter Brigette Friang; foreign correspondent Marguerite Higgins; Mary Lou Milligan, head of the Women's Air Corps; professional golf champion Patty Berg; and record-breaking open-water long distance swimmer Florence Chadwick. "Rosie the Riveter" was never booked, but instead, the producers found a "Carol the Riveter," a.k.a. Mrs. Carol Foley.

The show also featured Delores Lee, pitcher for the Rockford Peaches (1952–1954) in the All-American Girls Professional League. The Peaches were the team featured in *A League of Their Own*, the 1992 film about players in the league during World War II. Bonnie Baker, another player in the league, who played catcher during the war, and appeared on the show on August 17, 1952, inspired Geena Davis's character Dottie Hinson in the film. Ms. Baker's appearance also educed a long sequence of questions from panelist Hal Block, who thought Ms. Baker a bubble dancer and asked questions along those lines. This sent the audience into hysterics and, one imagines, pleased Mr. Goodman and Mr. Todman to no end.

The longest serving female treasurer of the United States also appeared. (The treasurer's signature appears on all federal reserve notes.) Ivy Baker Priest, appointed by President Eisenhower, was the second female treasurer after her predecessor, Truman appointee Georgia Neese Clark. Every treasurer since then has also been a woman.

To Tell the Truth, like *What's My Line?*, featured during its 1950s seasons a number of diverse professional women as contestants: an air traffic controller, a taxi driver, an IRS agent, a veterinarian, a lobster fisherman, a stunt pilot, a big game hunter, a men's basketball referee, a roulette dealer, a forecaster for the U.S. Weather Bureau, and the director of the U.S. Passport Office, among others.

In 1957, "American Mother of the Year" Hazel Abel appeared. Apart from, apparently, being a paragon of motherhood, she had the historical distinction of being the first woman to succeed another woman in the U.S. Senate. After the April 1954 death of Nebraska Senator Palmer Griswold, rancher Eva Bowring was appointed and, because of a quirk in Nebraska law, she was required to step down on Election Day and turn the seat over to the winner of a special election. Ms. Abel defeated 18 other candidates for a term which ultimately lasted only seven weeks. Her most important claim to fame is voting to censure fellow Republican Joseph McCarthy, who had made things difficult for so many members of the TV and film industry.

Colonel Julia E. Hamblett, Director of Women Marines; architect Natalie DeBlois (best known as the designer of the Union Carbide Building [now 270 Park Avenue], familiar to fans of the film *How to Succeed in Business Without Really Trying* as the headquarters of the World Wide Wicket Company); Dorothy Stratton, executive director of the Girl Scouts (and director of the United States Coast Guard Women's Reserve, SPARS during World War II); and ecologist Anne LaBastille also made *To Tell the Truth* appearances.

On the December 31, 1959, broadcast of the current events panel show *Take a Good Look*, Women's News Service reporter Elaine Shepard discussed being the only female reporter to accompany Eisenhower on his recently completed 11-nation tour. Shepard is best known for her

Vietnam War coverage. *The Doom Pussy*, her semi-fictional account of aviation during the early part of the war, was published in 1967.

What viewers learned from the integration of these women's stories into the framework of television's more politically, culturally and socially relevant quiz shows, was that there were smart women of drive and consequence throughout the world, who stood out among men not just because of their sex but because of the things they did that helped to make the world a better place.

◈ 7 ◈

Sound No Trumpet When Giving Alms

> When the developers of TV were tinkering in their laboratories, they had visions of the medium bringing opera, concerts and lectures into the home. They had the foresight to produce the cathode tube but not the foresight to predict *Queen for a Day*.
>
> —Stan Opotowsky[1]

One of the strangest and, at times, the most controversial, category of 1950s game show was the "misery" or "agony" series, *Glamour Girl*, *Queen for a Day* and *Strike It Rich* being the best-known examples. Agony shows weren't about contestants getting cash and merchandise for correctly answering questions or performing nonsensical stunts. They were more akin to contemporary, emotive reality shows like *Extreme Makeover*, *Extreme Makeover: Home Edition*, *The Swan* and *The Biggest Loser*. As 1950s forerunners to the 21st century warm-and-fuzzies, they built within their competition-based framework an opportunity for viewers to empathize with the shows' contestants and to commiserate with their life challenges and hardships. But collaterally, audiences also found themselves—with varying degrees of personal discomfort—pitying the shows' participants. Since the winners of most of these contests were determined by audience applause, studio audiences (and, vicariously, those watching at home) had the chance to, in the words of Marsha F. Cassidy, "listen every day to the [participants'] stories of struggle and discontent, and to evaluate, adjudicate and even ameliorate their lives of quiet desperation."[2]

Of course, amelioration only went so far.

Strike It Rich, like *Queen for a Day*, started out as a popular radio show, before retooling itself for daytime TV (and also as a weekly evening version during part of its video life). It was based on a simple concept, one shared by all of the "sob" shows. (The uncomplimentary descriptors for this kind of program made full use of Roget's.) The concept was this: that there were a great many Americans dealing with a great many serious problems—bad health, physical disabilities, personal tragedy, lousy relationships, financial woes. A lucky few, proportionally speaking, might be interested in making a full, public unbosoming of their troubles in exchange for the opportunity to win cash, consumer goods or even a beauty makeover, as was conferred on winners of NBC's short-lived *Glamour Girl*.

There were other game shows similarly concocted to tug at viewers' heartstrings: *High Finance, The Big Payoff, Welcome Travelers, Place the Face* and *On Your Account. Balance Your Budget* lent a helping hand to those contestants who had allowed their household budgets to "slip into the red." In exchange for the bailout, the contestant was required to answer personal questions related to how they got into such a fix. Even more broad-spectrum audience participation shows like *Truth or Consequences* and Art Linkletter's *House Party* and *People Are Funny* had segments that invited audience empathy for its contestants. *Have a Heart* was set up to give prevailing teams the chance to donate their winnings to needy groups in their home towns.

Most of these shows escaped criticism, given that they were either totally non-exploitive or only marginally so. But programs like *Strike It Rich* and *Glamour Girl* didn't get off so easy. The ethics-based dustups in which these shows' purveyors found themselves frequently received unflattering media attention.

A good many people, including viewers, network executives, TV critics and even politicians were uncomfortable with the tendency on the part of the programs' producers to parade the drab and the dreary before the cameras for the purpose of exposing (some would say capitalizing on) their misery to help sell the sponsors' wares (even *if* the contestant ended up with a year's supply of whatever those wares were). Others were troubled by the perceived admission by these shows that postwar optimism was being oversold, that not every American was happy, prosperous and well-adjusted, wasn't safely and securely nestled in society's various social safety nets—that, in fact, a good many citizens of the most affluent, most flourishing, most proudly capitalistic country on Earth had among its citizenry, folks who were being allowed to tumble away at the margins.

7. Sound No Trumpet When Giving Alms

The potential for anti–American propaganda by the Soviet bloc was painfully apparent. Those under-citizens who clung to the dangling threads of American prosperity exposed shortcomings that postwar-era movers and shakers didn't want on nationally linked coaxial cables.

Strike It Rich producer Walt Framer had high hopes for his show when it first aired on radio in 1947. The son of a Russian immigrant, he watched his family rise from poverty, thanks to the opportunities offered by a country in which upward mobility was made possible by hard work *and* a helping hand extended by others. It was the "helping hand from others" part that spurred him to create a "quiz show with a heart."[3] Framer told *Newsweek* in 1953 that his show wasn't just another "give-away," but much more.[4] By "much more," he must have meant that if his down-on-their-luck contestants expected to be helped by the show, they were first going to have to sing a little for their supper (or for the brand new Magic Chef gas range on which it might be cooked) by answering some questions in traditional quiz-show fashion.

It wasn't question-answering that was required of the women who gathered each weekday morning outside the Moulin Rouge, the theater-restaurant on Sunset Boulevard in Hollywood where *Queen for a Day* was produced; it was the public recounting of their sad life stories, concluding with the imparting of their present-day needs. Four life-oppressed women were asked under bright lights and before a large and frighteningly attentive studio audience to lay bare their souls in exchange for the chance to be crowned "Queen for a Day." (They tried not to think about the tens of millions of viewers watching at home.)

Likewise, the sometimes homely, sometimes stout young women who appeared on *Glamour Girl* had troubles of their own to disclose. But these contestants weren't asking to be draped in ermine and pated with a crown; it was a "glamorous" life-altering makeover they coveted. Or, in the words of the show's executive producer Jack McCoy, a transformation "into an exciting, thrilling, brand-spankin' new personality."[5] The right person to oversee this ugly duckling-to-swan cosmological and fashion miracle was Mary Webb Davis, described as "consultant to the stars" (this show was also broadcast from Hollywood) and the "finest glamour expert in America."[6]

Each of these agony shows was savaged both individually and collectively by the editorial press. *New York Times* TV critic Jack Gould called out *Strike It Rich* in particular for its "blatant capitalization of raw human emotions." Although each of Gould's denunciations led, according to

Framer, to a reactive improvement in the show's ratings, the columnist did not relent in his crusade of castigation.[7]

In Gould's November 9, 1951, column, for example, he denounced a *Strike It Rich* segment featuring a frightened young woman whose husband took flight when she became pregnant. The wife told host Warren Hull that she would have to give her baby up for adoption if she couldn't get financial help.[8]

Not a problem. We're here to help. Now if you'll just answer the following trivia questions.... Which the young woman did and, as a result, she went home with $500 *and* a pledge of a $40-a-month stipend (to carry her along until she remarried), telephoned in by a deep-pocketed Good Samaritan viewer, courtesy of the show's "Heartline" donation apparatus. Gould found the whole thing "warped beyond belief."[9] Especially offensive to the critic was the segment's jarring proximity to the TV commercial which followed: an ad for an underarm deodorant, pitched by a glamorous movie star dressed only in negligent negligee. For Gould, the show "[hit] the jackpot in bad taste."[10]

By the summer of 1953, and with the addition of *Glamour Girl* to the mix, the whole country found itself in a heated debate over whether such shows were just simple, innocent fun (as most 1950s game shows tended to be), or if they did indeed represent something quite sinister: exploitive vehicles which called into question the ability of supposedly self-respecting Americans to take care of the least among themselves. A scathing August 17 indictment of the genre by *Life* magazine's editors elicited a barrage of reader responses. In the provocative editorial, titled "Charity Vaunteth Not Itself," Gould's concerns were ratified through reference to a roller skate manufacturer "moved by the plight of a paraplegic" appearing on the frequently feel-good "Don't I know you?" game show *Place the Face*. "Why," asked *Life*, "doesn't [the manufacturer] buy him a wheelchair, instead of smothering him with brand-name roller skates?" (This prickly matter of sponsor-advertiser control over game shows is more closely examined in Chapter 11.) The editorial referred to a "would-be suicide confronted with the man who rescued him," and then mused hypothetical about a convicted murderer coming face to face with the dug-up corpse of his victim. The $500, the editors mordantly surmise, "could be split between the executioner and the exhumers."[11]

Over the next three weeks, *Life* received a torrent of letters expressing both support and opposition to the magazine's editorial stance on misery shows and those who trafficked in them. Robert Harris, a director of the

Prom Cosmetics company which sponsored *Place the Face*, took issue with the program being described as a "give-away show," a true slur given that *Place the Face*, Harris explained, "features reunions of persons who have played a role in one another's lives. We consider the small gifts awarded as completely incidental to the entertainment value of the meetings."[12]

Mr. Harris had something there. This particular agony show *was* less about abject despair and more geared to those lump-throated feel-good moments when do-gooders meet on-camera the recipients of their generosity, or longtime enemies are given the opportunity to forgive and make amends.

On the other hand, the Reverend Koenig from Yonkers, New York, directing his ire at *Strike It Rich* in particular, described it as "horrid." The reverend was pleased that somebody (read: the editors of *Life*) "would strike a blow for decency and humanity, [and] yes for morality, by protesting.... Gentleman, we are in your debt."[13]

The clergy seemed uniformly exercised over *Strike It Rich*, *Queen for a Day* and similar shows. They were especially incensed by the fact that the programs were being heralded in some circles for their (without question) irreligious displays of altruism and video philanthropy. In his article for the conservative Catholic publication *America*, the Reverend Alfred J. Barrett, S.J., a professor of theology at Fordham University, contended that such misery programs were a "total violation of the letter and spirit of Christian charity."[14] He went on to remind his readers of instructions found in Matthew 6:2 of the King James version of the Bible regarding charitable giving: "Therefore, when thou givest alms, do not sound a trumpet before thee, as the hypocrites do...."[15]

Few trumpets blared as loudly as the big brass band called network television.

Father Barrett was also troubled by the degree to which the sob shows served as "communist propaganda."[16] He wasn't alone in fearing that the shows were sending the wrong message overseas to countries caught up in the crossfire of the ongoing Cold War battle for the hearts and minds of the world. The implication that the U.S. government was failing to provide basic services to its citizens irritated even television's most well-behaved proponent, *TV Guide*, which in January and March of 1954 raised objections to "stupid publicity material" put out by the producers of *Strike It Rich*, and deemed the show "a desperate travesty on the very nature of charity" and a boon to "Red propagandists."[17]

(Father Barrett's widely cast net of excoriation caught a few questionable fishes. The priest, for some inexplicable reason, included in his hit-list of shows which purportedly served communistic ends, the wholesome and even inspirational *This Is Your Life*, a weekly 30-minute "capsule biography" of the life of a particular American—both the well-known and the previously unsung. *This Is Your Life* shone a bright studio light on the positive contributions individuals made to the lives of others. The show could be thought communist only if one gave undue importance to the color of the book Ralph Edwards carried tucked under his arm throughout the broadcast: It was *red*.[18])

Strike It Rich, to its additional misfortune, came under other forms of scrutiny. When a sympathetic contestant named George C. Poper appeared in 1954 and won $165, the publicity surrounding his appearance resulted in his apprehension by police in upstate New York. As it turned out, Poper might have come off as a nice guy, but he was also a fugitive from the law and, in fact, had recently been indicted for theft and embezzlement. As a result, the show's screening process came under fire.[19]

This New York City–based program was also called out by the city's welfare commissioner for inadvertently encouraging potential contestants to come to the Big Apple in hopes of getting on the show. When their efforts failed (and they inevitably did), the would-be contestants ended up as burdens to the city's already overtaxed Travelers' Aid Society.[20] In some cases—these being those in which the individuals (sometimes accompanied by spouses and children) chose not to return to the places whence they came—they got added to the city's equally overburdened welfare rolls.

Strike It Rich and other give-away game shows, especially those that awarded generous prizes, found themselves in the FCC's bull's-eye in 1949 (when *Strike It Rich* was still a radio-only offering), when the commission decided once again to take a bat at the sticky wicket of whether or not big-prize radio and TV game shows should be outlawed. Did they or did they not violate the U.S. criminal code's prohibition against lotteries? It wasn't until 1954, when the case finally made its way to the Supreme Court, that the FCC's ruling was definitively smacked down. The nation's highest court made the unanimous decision that big-money game shows were *not* lotteries, because simply listening to or watching them did not constitute the consideration necessary to establish that munificent quiz shows bore any practicable resemblance to high-stakes bookmaking. Although SCOTUS expressed tangential concerns about the societal value of the programs, it could not permit the FCC to remedy the problem through its own administrative muscle. The decision was important because it cleared a path to the astronomically large monetary jackpots that would soon be awarded by shows like *Twenty-One* and *The $64,000 Question*.[21]

Glamour Girl had problems of its own. Although the accusations made against the other misery shows—that they exploited human misery for commercial gain—could be leveled here, the show was particularly irksome in that its problem-solution construction bore no resemblance whatsoever to stark reality. The show offered, via the prying TV camera, a close-up look at women who, as Marsha F. Cassidy reminds us, bore the mark of "social misfortune, inadequacy or abuse" in the form of an "unattractive body"—a body that needed making over. It was a remedy for social displacement that was both facile and troubling.[22] Executive producer Jack McCoy couched *Glamour Girl*'s mission in terms that, in spite of his perceived sincerity, might seem laughable to those possessed of more evolved 21st century sensibilities: "I think almost every lady is basically very glamorous. [It just takes] outside touching around" to draw out the glamour that lives inside.[23] In more than one instance, a contestant sought glamorization for the sole purpose of winning back her husband, whose eye had begun to rove as some of the bloom dropped from his once-precious uxorial rose. The fact that this rationale for makeovers was found unconvincing even to a good many viewers also helped to limit the run of this controversial misery game show to a mere six months.

Queen for a Day lasted far longer. It began as a Mutual Network radio show in 1945 and continued in this medium into June 1957. Mutual broadcast it as a local TV show in greater Los Angeles beginning in February 1952. After briefly playing on several West Coast ABC affiliates, *Queen for a Day* landed in the peacock pen on January 3, 1956, before moving back to ABC in 1960. Its last queen was crowned on October 2, 1964.

Everybody wanted a piece of this smash afternoon hit. The show elevated NBC's sagging daytime ratings by 44 percent, attracting more viewers than 20 of ABC's *prime time* programs.[24] It was the highest-rated daytime program in 1957, averaging a 12.3 rating for the year.[25] *Look* magazine gushed, "Mops are dropped and diapers ditched from coast to coast every day at 4:00 p.m. when NBC-TV presents *Queen for a Day*."[26]

And nobody at NBC saw any disconnect between cancelling a *Glamour Girl* while keeping the postmeridian queens securely on their thrones, in spite of the fact that *Queen for a Day*, with a formula that traded just as wincingly in human misery, was as roundly censured as all the other game shows in this category.

The difference: ratings. *Queen for a Day* caught fire. It became a guilty pleasure, the *ne plus ultra* of TV kitsch.

No one knew this better than Howard Blake, the show's longtime producer. And though the show remained popular throughout its long network-hopscotching run, Blake still felt it necessary to deliver his postmortem mea culpa in the appropriately titled tell-all "An Apologia from the Man Who Produced the Worst Program in TV History." In it, he confessed that his association with the show left him with a troubled conscience. "The losers were deliberately ignored," Blake admitted. "Their disappointment and tears [were] never shown on camera." Blake revealed that the show's pre-screening process rejected scores of women whose life stories weren't sufficiently enthralling, whose problems weren't adequately tear-rendering, or, more importantly, weren't soluble by means of the products and services offered by potential sponsors.[27]

By contrast, the show's folksy host, Jack Bailey, remained to the end of the broadcast run, irrepressibly buoyant (when he didn't come off commiserative to the point of creepy mawkishness), remarking with rose-colored earnestness upon the occasion of *Queen for a Day*'s 15th anniversary in 1960:

> It's like giving real, sincere good help without being a Pollyanna. It's not so much the wish as the why of the wish. Many women put on their cards that they'd like an ironer to make their work lighter. Who wouldn't? But the woman who wants an ironer so she can take in ironing to help the family finances, that's a different story.[28]

In the spirit of full disclosure, Bailey admitted that the show had to adhere to certain rules governing who got on and who didn't. "No blind people and no cripples—no crutches," he told an interviewer. Bailey knew his audience. "If you allow them on, you might just as well throw away the other contestants. They would always win. So in fairness, we don't pick them."[29]

Regarding those "losers" whose treatment Blake decried, program assistant and on-camera fashion commentator Jeanne Cagney had no problem putting on her own pair of roseate eyeglasses, telling the *Los Angeles Times* writer of a piece about the show, "It's a heartwarming experience … but I often think of the runners-up and hope that maybe it helps them just to come on the show to tell someone about their problem."[30]

Howard Blake didn't agree. He knew that it was torture for many of

7. Sound No Trumpet When Giving Alms 79

these women to come on the show. He felt especially guilty over the fact that *Queen for a Day* put forth the fiction that the winner would be healed of whatever ailed her by the very products the sponsors were—by fortunate coincidence—able to shower upon her. "A candidate had to want something we could plug," he wrote. "A stove, a carpet, a plane trip, an artificial leg." (Yes, companies that made human prosthetics could use a little TV advertising too.) Alas, those potential contestants who required the services of doctors and lawyers were out of luck, since the producers of agony shows could never find any medical and legal professionals willing to work for an on-air plug.[31]

On any given *Queen for a Day* telecast, a viewer was likely to hear four hard-luck stories that may or may not have borne resemblance to those told by the following women, whose requests have been documented from the handful of show recordings still in existence:

- A mother of seven who needs diaper service for her infant triplets.
- A caregiver of two special-needs children, husband and parents, all of whom have now passed away, who'd like a vacation trip to decompress.
- A mother of two who needs help taking care of four additional children, whose father has just walked out on his family.
- A wife and mother of an asthmatic husband and son in need of a dehumidifier to help them breathe.
- The mother of a brain-damaged boy who needs special education aids; she would also like to give her boy a pet collie.
- A mother who'd like to pay for a hole in the floor of her upstairs children's bedroom, "to get some heat up there."
- The mother of a son in a body cast who'd like a hospital gurney as well as a transistor radio ("a shortwave radio would be nice too") to help the young man pass the time.
- A widow who'd like money to go to beauty school so she could support her children.
- The co-owner (with her husband) of a small, struggling grocery store, who needs the store's bare shelves restocked.

And in the credibility-straining category of wish-listing:

- The owner of a motel who believes she has talent as a singer if only someone would give her an audition.

- A booster of her local fire station, who would like five electric blankets for "five cold firemen."
- A car owner whose vehicle needs a motor overhaul because "my old jalopy's about all in."
- The wife of a hunter who'd like to prove herself useful to her husband by getting a muskrat trap and taxidermy set.

The slightly less cringe-worthy *High Finance* was largely concerned with making financial dreams come true. Its shelf life was less than six months, appearing and then disappearing in the latter half of 1956. *High Finance* is best remembered for extending the hand of charity to former heavyweight champion Joe Louis and his wife who, having fallen on hard times (the couple owed over a million dollars in back taxes), made eight weekly appearances as special contestants. Every penny of the $41,000 they won went to Uncle Sam.[32]

What all of these shows said about Americans—and, more specifically, about American women of the 1950s—is telling. In spite of growing prosperity, postwar America had yet to put a Ford Thunderbird in every garage and two chickens in every pot. There were great numbers in the heartland—and female citizens in particular—who had yet to achieve the American dream. Millions of American women—single mothers, divorcées, widows, and abused wives—had few options and very few resources for addressing their unfortunate, and sometimes even dire, economic and domestic circumstances. In the middle of the land of milk and honey, people still got sick and couldn't pay their medical bills. Men still walked out on wives they'd grown bored with, even when that also meant walking out on their children. On top of it all, there remained a long-harbored distrust of Americans who weren't white and weren't Christian and didn't remotely resemble the Wonder Bread families depicted in TV sitcoms and photographed for magazine ads. That suspicion and discomfiture only exacerbated the struggles by certain groups of marginalized citizens—struggles that sometimes manifested themselves in hail-Mary bids for redemption and respect, offered by the most unlikely of benefactors: the TV game show.

On the other hand, there were a good number of unhappy housewives who, in spite of their largely un-articulated feelings of isolation and discontent with the stultifying constraints of suburban marriage and motherhood, could at least take pleasure in watching *Queen for a Day* and *Glamour Girl* contestants, who seemed far worse off than themselves.

7. Sound No Trumpet When Giving Alms

The shows invited these women to measure their own lives of quiet suburban desperation against the Debbie Downers weeping on cue before the cameras. They could sit in convenient judgment (just as the audiences at the Moulin Rouge were asked to register their opinions via *Queen for a Day's* trusty Applause-o-Meter), and say to themselves with cold comfort, "There but for the grace of God..."

Perhaps, one might even theorize, the sad-sack regal hopefuls on *Queen for a Day* weren't representative of Real America at all, and were merely the exception that made the rule.

Take *that*, Premier Khrushchev!

◆ 8 ◆

Welcome to the Big Apple

> As for New York City, it is a place apart. There is not its match in any other country in the world.
> —Pearl S. Buck[1]

In the years before network television, Americans learned about the nation's biggest and brassiest city by reading the papers, watching newsreels and listening to radio programs that originated there. They watched movies, some of which portrayed Gotham, especially during the Depression, as a collection of skyscraping penthouses, where the "best" people, sporting gay apparel, sang and danced and worked their witty way through pesky relationship problems in Art Deco splendor.

Conversely, there were those films that showed the bruised side of the Big Apple, depicting an asphalt jungle of grit and grime and poverty and crime. A place where just setting foot outside one's brownstone might put one in the crossfire of a gangster turf war. The city became even more forbidding to the non–New Yorker with the arrival of the urban *film noir* crime dramas of the late '40s.

The real New York City lay somewhere between those extremes. And it was early television that gave Americans the far more accurate picture: Molly Goldberg gossiping with her neighbors out her apartment window; live TV dramas by Paddy Chayefsky about Marty the butcher[2] and Agnes Hurley, who wanted a "catered affair" for her daughter's Bronx wedding. And the quiz shows—the majority of which emanated from New York.

TV in the '50s showed Americans a New York City that was even more real than Chayefsky could limn. This was due to the medium's early marriage of convenience with the city. Television was born in New York, and to the degree that it served as both the centripetal and centrifugal fulcrum of the nation, the city gave TV-watching families from Springfield and Paducah and Cedar Rapids a taste of what it was like to live there, to walk with a Manhattan strut and speak with a Brooklyn brogue.

New York City's dominance of the TV industry didn't last long: TV production began its shift to the West Coast quite early in the 1950s. By the end of the decade, the exodus to Southern California was in full swing, as the movie studios stopped fearing and loathing "the box" and found profitable ways to partner with networks and producers and packagers of TV programming. The move was led by ABC, which sought to improve its last place network standing (after the demise of DuMont in the summer of 1955) by creating an abundance of filmed television series shot in and around Los Angeles. By 1960, there were only a handful of live New York City–based TV shows still on the network schedules.

And yet, whereas the television game show had been live when almost all of television had been live (this being one of the reasons so many TV quiz shows premiered in the summer; they were off-season replacements for shows that couldn't be re-run), a few remained live, even into the 1960s.

And live, more often than not, meant New York.

Most of the contestants on the Manhattan-based game shows hailed from the tri-state area. National viewers of the decade's quizzes and audience participation programs got very familiar with the geography of the New York metropolitan area and with the neighborhoods of the borough of Manhattan in particular.

Celebrity regulars on the various New York panel shows made frequent references to events taking place around town, to current openings on Broadway, to who was last seen at the El Morocco or 21. A viewer of these shows always knew when the Ringling Brothers and Barnum and Bailey had pitched their tent at Madison Square Garden, because *What's My Line?* and *I've Got a Secret* had a habit of welcoming into their studios contestants who were knife throwers, embroiderers of circus elephant blankets, fire eaters, sword swallowers, tiger trainers and "human cannonballs." (These shows were especially fond of "human cannonballs.") *What's My Line?* panelists would often prep themselves for a broadcast by reading *Variety*. Here they'd find out which entertainers might happen to be in town that week, as an assist to their guesswork on that Sunday night's show. Bennett Cerf was especially diligent in noting everyone he'd read and heard about who was in New York at the time of the broadcast. Executive producer Gil Fates remembered that each Sunday night, Cerf would "come to the studio with a scribbled list of the suspects he knew to be in town. Just before the program took to the air he would stand alone backstage with his glasses pushed up onto his forehead and a scrap of paper held close to his nose, squinting at their names in the dimmish light."³

New York "characters" frequently made themselves available to the celebrity-based panel show circuit. *Masquerade Party* was a special gathering spot for New York luminaries. The show was nearly unique in bringing on notables from entertainment, sports, politics and industry, who would be known not only to the ratiocinative celebrity panelists but also to the home viewer. *Masquerade Party* panelists were asked to identify a famous (or semi-famous) person in spite of heavy makeup and costuming (chosen to provide a clue as to their identity). As a result, it was one of the very few TV game shows of the decade in which *non*-celebrities—that is, the American rabble—played no role at all.

Incidentally, *Masquerade Party* holds the distinction of being the only game show to be telecast on three different networks on the same day, as broadcast vehicle for the September 22, 1954, national appeal on behalf of the United Community Campaigns of America. The broadcast included a message by Vice-President Richard Nixon and was aired live by CBS and NBC in the afternoon and then on ABC in the evening by means of kinescopic filming. (Kinescopes, TV's earliest way of recording its telecasts, were made by pointing a film camera at a video monitor.) The special broadcast was only one of many instances in which TV quiz shows—like radio's *Truth or Consequences*—partnered with charitable organizations to raise money for worthy causes.

What's My Line? introduced viewers to Sherman Billingsley, former bootlegger and colorful owner of the Stork Club. Personal sidebar: The East 53rd Street restaurant closed in 1965, its building sold to CBS (*What's My Line?*'s long-affiliated network). CBS president William S. Paley had the structure torn down. In its place, he installed a private park, named for his father. For many years its next-door neighbor was the Museum of Broadcasting—later the Museum of Television and Radio—where this author once worked. Without knowing it at the time, I brown-bagged where, formerly, New York's haut monde had hobnobbed and tablehopped under Billingsley's solicitous gaze.

What's My Line? gave viewers the chance to meet Toots Shor, owner of the eponymous saloon and restaurant. Shor was friend and confidant to a great many of the city's best-known citizens, and very good friends with *What's My Line?* moderator John Charles Daly.

Others who filled the show's weekly mystery guest spot were New

York–based stage and TV performers. The show was also welcoming to several local sports figures with national reputations: the manager of the Brooklyn Dodgers, Chuck Dressen; Yankee Joe DiMaggio; Brooklyn Dodger catcher Roy Campanella; New York Giants center fielder Willie Mays; Brooklyn Dodger Duke Snider; Yankees center fielder and homerun king Mickey Mantle; pitcher for the Giants, Dodgers, *and* Yankees Sal Maglie; and Branch Rickey, best known—when general manager for the Brooklyn Dodgers—for breaking the Major League's color barrier by signing Jackie Robinson. Although Robinson never appeared on the original *What's My Line?*, he did pay a visit to the syndicated series that succeeded it (see Chapter 9).

Fans of the show had the chance to watch its panel try to guess the occupation of a bagel baker and a matzo ball maker, an Ebbets Field hotdog vender, a Metropolitan Opera wig-fitter, a Penn Station train announcer, a Macy's Santa and a Macy's complaint adjuster, a Christmas shopper for men at Saks Fifth Avenue, a dresser of showgirls at the famed Latin Quarter nightclub (originally owned by Barbara Walters' father Lou), a high-kicking Rockette, the manager of Grant's Tomb, a Rheingold beer salesman[4] and *New York Daily Mirror* celebrity gossip columnist Walter Winchell.

I've Got a Secret viewers got a taste of the famed 21 Club on December 2, 1953, when actor George Raft delivered gravy with truffles, prepared in 21's kitchen. Host Garry Moore proceeded to use the gravy to paint a spot on Raft's tie; detecting the resultant smudge constituted the panel's challenge for this round.[5]

I've Got a Secret also introduced the country to a New Yorker named Joseph Papp, who, in 1954, established the Public Theatre and founded the New York Shakespeare Festival. His love of the Bard was quite in evidence on *I've Got a Secret*'s fifth anniversary show (June 19, 1957) when a youthful-looking, nearly 36-year-old Papp performed Marc Antony's "But yesterday the word of Caesar might have stood against the world" soliloquy from *Julius Caesar*. Papp got the chance to perform this Shakespeare cutting thanks to his day job. He was the show's stage manager, and anniversary broadcasts gave staffers a chance to show off some of their other talents.

A good example of what a New York–centric show *What's My Line?* was (in addition to the fact that its celebrity panelists were always dressed to the nines for its weekly broadcast) was Julie Andrews' mystery guest appearance on February 7, 1960. Having completed her long run as Eliza

Doolittle in the smash stage hit *My Fair Lady*, and while preparing to originate the role of Queen Guinevere in *Camelot* (which would also take Broadway by storm), Andrews was becoming a familiar name to New Yorkers, and was much beloved by the show's Broadway-savvy panel (Arlene Francis and her husband Martin Gabel, a frequent panelist, were stage veterans, and Dorothy Kilgallen's column was called "Voice of Broadway"). When it was time to film the big screen version of Lerner and Loewe's Shavian classic, Jack Warner, head of the Warner Brothers studio, didn't think the country knew Andrews well enough to put her in the role with which she had been most closely identified and, instead, gave the part of Eliza to Audrey Hepburn. Was Andrews only a "New York" phenomenon, and was *What's My Line?*, because of its strong New York identity, not, therefore, culturally translatable to the country at large? *What's My Line?*'s consistently good ratings and Andrews' Oscar for *Mary Poppins* (produced the same year as *My Fair Lady*) provided easy answers to both questions.

Whereas Hollywood had always held Americans in thrall, with the magic, glamour and glitz of its imagination factories, New York offered a different kind of appeal. It was smart and urbane, at times a little too big for its britches, but always standing tall, with both feet securely planted on terra pavement. When watching a live game show broadcast from New York, one sometimes heard fire engines or police cars blasting their sirens outside the studio. When the weather was snowy or slushy, celebrity panelists might make casual mention of it on the broadcast. Labor strikes and other municipal happenings also received on-air reference. On two occasions, *What's My Line?* was interrupted by the appearance of an unwanted guest. One intruder simply wanted to wish everyone a happy Mother's Day.

The quiz shows, panel shows and other audience-participation shows broadcast from New York were good for the local economy. In 1954 alone, 1.5 million people attended the profusion of TV broadcasts that originated from specially built studios and retrofitted theaters throughout Manhattan. Of that number, two-thirds resided either in the city or in one of its suburbs. This left a half-million people in attendance who had come to New York from someplace else, and no small number of them ventured to the city just to make the rounds of the live-audience TV shows. In the 1950s, game show telecasts were one of the top visitor attractions in the city, and certainly one of the cheapest.[6]

New York's quiz shows made household names of people who weren't traditional entertainers. In his autobiography *At Random: The Reminiscences of Bennett Cerf*, the Random House publisher, largely unknown outside publishing and New York society circles prior to becoming a *What's My Line?* panelist, told the story of flying down to Oxford, Mississippi, with his business partner Donald Klopfer and author William Styron to attend the funeral of one of Random House's (and America's) most acclaimed authors, William Faulkner. Cerf, who wasn't recognized at first, wrote about encountering curious, even hostile stares from townspeople and those gathered at the Faulkner home. The three were read as outsiders, "interlopers," as Cerf put it. But then ...

> When Donald and I went down to get something to eat [after paying respects to Faulkner's wife and daughter], all the food was just sitting there, untouched. Suddenly, one woman—I don't know who she was—said, "Aren't you that fellow we see on TV every Sunday night on *What's My Line??*" I said, "Yes, I am." Well, immediately they all came crowding around me and began asking me about the show. The hostility was gone. I was now one of the people who came to their house every week; I was an old friend. It was incredible to watch the change the minute they recognized me.[7]

New York game shows of the 1950s also reminded Americans of the fact that although still characterized as predominantly Protestant, the United States had for a number of decades also been home to a growing number of people of non–Protestant, even non–Christian faiths. The most religiously pluralistic city in America in the 1950s was New York, which, in addition to its strong Roman Catholic character, had long been home to a majority of America's Jews. With a mass migration to the United States taking place in the last decades of the 19th century, there were by 1900 1.5 million adherents of the Jewish faith residing in the U.S., the third most of any nation (after Russia and Austria-Hungary). By 1942, that number had climbed to over four million, and during the 1950s, the number of Jews in New York City alone had reached two million, or roughly one quarter of the city's population.[8]

A great many Jewish New Yorkers found themselves in that decade either working in the city's booming TV industry or appearing in *front* of its cameras as contestants and studio audience members on quiz shows and other forms of audience participation programming. For this reason, viewers in other parts of the country—especially those residing in homogenous Christian communities—were reminded on a daily basis that the U.S. was indeed an ethnic and religious melting pot—its sieve located in the city of immigrants.

This was illustrated by the July 23, 1958, *I've Got a Secret*, which featured memory expert Harry Lorayne. His secret was that after having met one-on-one a good portion of the show's audience members (roughly 500 of them by host Garry Moore's estimate), he'd committed to memory every one of their names. When it came time for Lorayne to demonstrate his special skill, he was able to recite row by row a good 20 of those names without difficulty. (The rows were selected randomly by emcee Moore and panelist Betsy Palmer, Moore also picking audience members at random by tossing tennis balls into the audience.) As a result of this stunt, viewers of this broadcast got the chance to meet average New Yorkers—straphangers and area commuters alike—with such surnames as Saar, Finkelstein, Harpin, Stern, Pearlstein, Rosenberg, Friedman, Zeisler and Ackerman (mixed in with a few presumed gentiles with the names Rutherford, Watney and Duggins).

While so many vaudevillians were getting work on the flurry of live variety shows of the early and mid–50s, thus exposing Americans to a wide diversity of ethnicities and religions, several game shows featured as their emcees and celebrity panels Jewish comedians—veterans of the Borscht Belt comedy circuit of the Catskills. The most successful of these was Jan Murray (born Janofsky), who hosted eight different game shows from 1950 to 1960. Some of them lasted only a few weeks, but *Dollar a Second* and *Treasure Hunt* ran for multiple seasons. Not only did Murray serve as emcee for *Treasure Hunt*, granddaddy to *Deal or No Deal* (and kissing cousin to another latter-day popular game of chance, *Let's Make a Deal*), he was also the show's creator and producer.

Another Jewish comedian who found his way to New York TV rarely worked alone because of his friendship with a wooden boy named Jerry Mahoney. Paul Winchell (born Wilchinsky) and his buddy Jerry had their own variety show from 1950 to 1954, *The Paul Winchell-Jerry Mahoney Show*, which included a quiz segment called "What's My Name?" In addition to his talent as a ventriloquist and actor, Winchell had several claims to fame among game show professionals: He was a trained acupuncturist and medical hypnotist, as well as the inventor of several medical devices. Winchell shared the patent with Dr. Henry Heimlich (yes, *that* Dr. Heimlich) on an artificial heart, which the doctor claimed was identical to the Jarvik-7, successfully implanted in Barney Clark in 1982. Winchell also invented and patented a blood plasma defroster, a disposable razor, flameless cigarette lighter and battery-heated gloves. In the 1980s, his concerns about the African food supply motivated him to cultivate tilapia fish for tribal villages and other small African communities. Not since Hedy Lamarr and her invention, with composer George Antheil, of a radio guidance system for torpedoes has an entertainer made such an important contribution to the world in the way of scientific invention.

Joey Adams, who literally wrote the book on the Borscht Belt—titled, appropriately, *Borscht Belt* (1966)—was quizmaster for *Back That Fact*. Morey Amsterdam hosted the game show-talent contest *Battle of the Ages*, and comedy Renaissance man Carl Reiner (who was more Broadway than Catskillian in his early career) helmed the 1958 ad lib–based *Keep Talking*.

The introduction of Jewish performers into American living rooms didn't end homegrown anti–Semitism, but it did move the country incrementally toward acceptance of those American citizens who didn't happen to be Anglo/Northern European Christians. But in the 1950s, there was a price to be paid for the employment of so many followers of the Hebrew faith. The Red Scare and its attendant blacklists targeted Jews with precision, hanging their smear campaigns on the contention that because Jews—and especially those working at high-profile jobs in the New York City and Southern California–based entertainment industry—were largely left-leaning in their political views, they must also either be communists or communist sympathizers. Over time, "New York" became, in some right wing circles, synonymous with "Jewish," and by, extension with "anti–Americanism."

New Yorker Bess Myerson, who served as "hostess" on *The Big Payoff* and as panelist on *I've Got a Secret*, had a difficult time being accepted in the public arena because of her Jewish identity. As the first woman of her faith to be crowned Miss America, it was in her nature to be outspoken, and her intellect and eloquence only got her into trouble with those who felt that pageant winners could be smart, but it also helped if they knew how to keep their mouths shut. Myerson recalled being openly insulted by anti–Semites, turned away from "restricted" clubs, and turned down for jobs with companies that weren't comfortable with her "Jewish" name. Although she hid her resentment from public display, she admitted to feeling "a rage that has never left me.... I was trapped in the disguise I myself had agreed to wear."[9] She nonetheless continued to speak out against bigotry, taking public stands in person and on the radio, such positions putting her on the wrong side of the beauty pageant that had originally facilitated her celebrity. Pageant director Lenora Slaughter worried publicly that Myerson was being influenced by "Jewish communists from New York's Garment District."[10] Myerson ignored the criticism and ramped up her attacks on racism and prejudice. In one speech, she proclaimed that

> ... you can't be beautiful and hate. Miss America represents all America. It makes no difference who she is, or who her parents are. Side by side, Catholic, Protestant and Jew stand together.... [I]f we want a strong, united America pushing on toward its unlimited horizons, there can be no place for prejudice in our nation ... or in our hearts.[11]

Although it was Myerson's candor and pluck that got her tapped for *The Big Payoff*, producer Walt Framer, fearing repercussions in an environment of communist-obsession, robbed her of any chance to use his game show as a soapbox, relegating his hostess to the sanitized role of "that beautiful lady in mink." Despite the point Framer was also making in hiring Myerson: that television needed people of every ethnic and religious stripe, she became, in the end, just another objectified female clotheshorse. Randy Merriman, the show's emcee, succinctly summed up Myerson's status on the show when, on one particular broadcast, he remarked, "Ladies love fashions ... [and you men like] such beautiful things as Bess Myerson."

Luckily, through her long tenure on *I've Got a Secret*, Myerson was able to demonstrate to viewers that, in addition to her Miss America good looks, she also had a sharp mind and good sense of fun.

Because New York City was also the undisputed capital of America's publishing industry, its quiz show casting personnel often found themselves drawing from the local literati for celebrity participants. Laura Hobson, author of the novel *Gentleman's Agreement*, served as panelist on several early episodes of *I've Got a Secret*. Gore Vidal did similar duty in 1960 and 1964 on *What's My Line?* James Michener was a *What's My Line?* panelist in 1957 and 1959, and Herman Wouk in 1955 and 1956. Playwright and novelist Jean Kerr (*Please Don't Eat the Daisies*) served as panelist on *Down You Go* in 1951.

Jacqueline Susann was the best-known author to work on a game show *before* the publication of her first novel—in Susann's case, the bestseller *Valley of the Dolls*, which came out in 1966. Susann served as hostess for a 1952 swapping game called *Your Surprise Store*. After becoming famous, she appeared multiple times on *Match Game* and *Hollywood Squares*.

Bennett Cerf took advantage of his permanent-panelist status on *What's My Line?* to promote Random House, its authors and its new titles, whenever opportunities presented themselves. No one seemed to object to this free form of advertising for the big New York house, even in the era of "payola"—the "pay-to-play," under-the-table system of record promotion that was sullying the reputations of radio disc jockeys across the country.[12] Perhaps allowing Cerf his weekly off-the-books form of book-boosting was viewed as the cost of getting Random House authors (among them many of America's finest writers) on the show and, after all, wasn't permanent panelist Dorothy Kilgallen's syndicated newspaper column also getting a weekly shout-out, and the Broadway plays her husband Richard Kollmar produced receiving generous on-air mention as well? Likewise, regular panelist Arlene Francis was forever talking up her own Broadway stage roles throughout the decade, as well as those of her stage actor husband (and frequent panel fill-in) Martin Gabel.

In 1953, Cerf had no qualms about explaining to *New York Times* writer Bernard Kalb how all of this worked: "I talk about my books. I get in little plugs for my firm and my authors—like Faulkner, Shaw, O'Hara, Schulberg…. It all blends in."[13]

Veteran actor and game show mainstay Orson Bean summed up New York City in the 1950s better than most, pointing up the paradox that was New York:

> It was *Leave It to Beaver*. There were certain things about the 1950s. If you fell asleep in New York on a hot night in Central Park, you just slept there. There was no street crime to speak of. There was a drug store every other block where you could buy a rubber or something. I would go to 52nd Street to the jazz joints and they were going to three or four in the morning. The subway was a nickel. That aspect of it was nice. Then there was the other side. If you touched Pearl Bailey's arm on television, the show [camera] would cut away.[14]

Which leads one to wonder …

◆ 9 ◆

Guess Who's Probably Not Coming to Dinner

Madison Avenue is afraid of the dark.—Nat King Cole[1]

In Ralph Ellison's celebrated 1952 novel *Invisible Man*, a nameless black man searches for his identity in a hostile, compartmentalizing world. His personal struggle, described by Ellison with irony and wit, reflects Black America's efforts during this period to define itself in the context of the black-white racial dichotomy of the day, while giving name and form to every man's journey of personal discovery.

African-Americans sought a far more valued and self-affirming berth for themselves in mid–20th century America: The process threaded through the courts, with stops along the way at lunch counters, the front seats of public conveyances, and desks in formerly all-white high school classrooms. They hungered for greater visibility in the various American media, and especially a fairer and more just, let alone less discriminatory, representation in the developing medium of television.

Like Ellison's protagonist, black Americans remained largely invisible on TV screens in the 1950s, and those infrequent times they did by chance find their way onto the airways, their appearances were usually either severely circumscribed or came with a price. In 1952, Georgia Governor Herman Talmadge attacked network television for racially integrating its programming. Editorializing in his newspaper *The Statesman*, he expressed his strong objection to black entertainers dancing with "scantily clad white females." He was especially offended by programs that had the audacity to show blacks and whites talking together "on a purely equal social status."[2]

If one were to take his accusation literally, then one wonders if Talmadge gave the sitcom *Beulah* a pass. When the radio *Beulah* became the

TV *Beulah* in 1950, its eponymous lead character, played on the radio by a white man, and on television by three accomplished black actresses—Hattie McDaniel, Louise Beavers and Ethel Waters—was still a black maid working for a white family, and for that reason most definitely not "on a purely equal social status." The television version of the popular *Amos 'n' Andy* might also have been exempted by the governor, since its entire dramatis personae was comprised of men and women of color (not interacting with whites at all!). But the show was so steeped in derogatory, racially stereotyped characterizations that it came under intense fire from the NAACP. As a result, it was pulled from the air after two seasons.[3]

While *Beulah* offended only to the extent that it upheld a long, tiresome tradition of casting black actors as characters subservient to whites, the cloud of controversy surrounding *Amos 'n' Andy* helped to kill further network attempts at creating sitcoms that dealt, however disingenuously, with black America. For this reason, situation comedies joined other television program genres in leaving to black actors only the same kinds of demeaning walk-on roles they'd been assigned in movies since the days of the silents.

In the late '50s when the airways were crowded with "horse oaters," the American West depicted in these series was far from historically accurate. No character on any western television series was ever known to have said, "Go west, young black man."

Nor was contemporary Los Angeles—the city in which more and more television shows were being filmed as the decade wore on—a place of shining racial diversity in its own video depictions. It wasn't until 1956 that the popular L.A.-based police procedural *Dragnet* cast its first black actor. A black viewer spoke for many when he complained that the show's writers "believe Los Angeles [has] no Negro policemen, no Negro criminals, no Negro citizens who are victims of crime or witnesses or innocent bystanders."[4]

And things were no different in New York City. Odell Clark, speaking on behalf of the NAACP and the Coordinating Council for Negro Performers and the Urban League, told J.P. Shanley of *The New York Times*, "In a typical New York scene on television, not a single Negro is found. If television shows a subway scene, there is not a single Negro in that subway."[5]

Ethel Winant, casting director for CBS's live television drama, remembered those early days of lily white TV programming. "There were no [black] porters," she recalled in amazement. "It was a *white* conductor who put your bags on the train. It was so stupid and so terrible. It drove me crazy that I couldn't use them on television." She also remembered the difficulties Sidney Poitier faced when he was, by some miracle, allowed to appear in Robert Alan Aurthur's "A Man Is Ten Feet Tall," a *Philco Television Playhouse* episode: "He was questioned about his politics and his sex life by a committee from the [advertising] agency. He was willing to do it to make a point. The show won some awards, but the sponsors hated it so much, they wouldn't accept it."[6] Perhaps one of the reasons Philco hated the teleplay was due to the fact that several Southern television and radio dealers stopped handling Philcos because of it. A petition from Jackson, Mississippi, signed by 10,000 white sons and daughters of Dixie, threatened to boycott all Philco products if such a transgression occurred again.[7]

Singer-actress Eartha Kitt recalled playing Salome in an *Omnibus* broadcast. CBS's *Omnibus* was billed as an educational arts program, and before professional sports took over Sunday afternoons, this broadcasting slot was generally known as that place to which TV shows were dispatched for which ratings didn't matter ("who watches television on Sunday afternoon anyway?" being the rationale). This is without doubt one of the reasons a black actress in 1955 found herself cast in the lead on a network series. Even so, someone as high up the network food chain as CBS Chairman William S. Paley would not simply allow her to play the part as it was written, given the potential problem her portrayal posed with racist viewers:

> During dress rehearsal, Mr. Paley came into the studio and saw this soliloquy where Salome says to the soldier, "Get me the head of John the Baptist," and she rams him down the stairs in anger because he refuses. When Mr. Paley saw this, there was a conference, and the result was the whole soliloquy was cut out because Mr. Paley said, "A white person can hit a black person, but a black person cannot hit a white person."[8]

In a 1968 issue of *TV Guide*, writer-producer Gene Roddenberry cited a "sin of omission" that demonstrated how difficult it was for black actors in the early '60s to get roles on network TV shows: "When the Writers Guild struck in 1960 on the issue of money, the strike should have been on the issue of *River Boat*, a series supposedly set on the Mississippi. The producers warned us, 'No negroes.'"[9]

There were a couple of places in the network television firmament where African-Americans were allowed to carve out relative "safe spaces" for themselves in the early days of the medium. Black athletes were granted tacit waivers for the purpose of batting balls and taking gloved punches at opponents' faces on the various sports programs during this period. Likewise, black entertainers were allowed to perform (as themselves) on the decade's many white-run and white-hosted music and variety shows— singing, dancing and then removing themselves from the stage. Producer Max Liebman hired a few black singers for *Your Show of Shows*. Both Kate Smith, who had an afternoon variety show on NBC, and the great video impresario Ed Sullivan frequently included African-Americans on their broadcasts.[10] There were consequences, though, for the racial integration of TV variety programming, as Eddie Cantor learned in 1952. On the February 17 *Colgate Comedy Hour*, host Cantor whipped out his own handkerchief to wipe the perspiration from Sammy Davis Jr.'s face. NBC was subsequently flooded with letters from angry and appalled white viewers. One wrote, "How dare you mop that coon's face with your handkerchief on national TV?"[11]

A black performer named Amanda Randolph got lucky. She also holds title to a television first for black female performers. When the coaxial cable finally linked up the East Coast and the Midwest in January 1949, the DuMont network began to send four and a half hours of daytime programming from its New York City flagship station WABD to its East and Midwest affiliates. As a result, the owners of television receivers in several American cities got the chance to see a live broadcast of Ms. Randolph singing and playing the piano on her own program. *Billboard* was complimentary in its brief mention of the show and so far as anyone knows, there was no white backlash (either because the viewing audience was so small, or because the South wasn't watching):

> Amanda, a Negro lass, comes on at 9:40 for about 15 minutes of well-sung tunes ranging from spirituals to boogie woogie, accompanying herself on the piano. The gal is by far the most entertaining part of the early stretch.[12]

Network television viewers had to wait another eight years to find a black male entertainer hosting his own music program—in this case *The Nat King Cole Show*. Unfortunately for the popular singer, the show was doomed to cancellation because no national sponsor cared to connect its product with him (there *were* a few regional sponsors). Cole's memorable remark "Madison Avenue is afraid of the dark" was expanded upon in a piece he wrote for *Ebony* magazine. In it, the singer asserted, "Madison Avenue, the center of the advertising industry, and their big clients didn't want their products associated with Negroes." Addressing the elephant in the advertising agency boardroom, he added, "Madison said I couldn't be sold, that no national advertiser would take a chance on offending Southerners."[13]

Otherwise, there weren't too many other places on the tube for African-Americans to appear, given the lack of interest the industry's overlords had in them.

With a couple of exceptions.

One was Edward R. Murrow's interview show *Person to Person* (1953–1961). Although most of Murrow's African-American interview subjects were singers, musicians and sports figures (Harry Belafonte, Mahalia Jackson, Sugar Ray Robinson, Jesse Owens, W.C. Handy *et al.*), Murrow also video-visited the home of NAACP executive secretary Walter White and U.S. diplomat Ralph Bunche. And one assumes that Murrow's conversation with famed American contralto Marian Anderson wasn't limited to her pipes. (Murrow's documentary series *See It Now* covered Anderson's successful goodwill tour through Asia in 1957.)

The other area of television programming in which some modicum of respect and visibility were afforded members of Ralph Ellison's race was quiz shows. If black actors and entertainers were denied TV exposure even minimally reflective of their race's increasing stake in America's expanding middle class, the television game shows of the 1950s and early 1960s gave black Americans some measure of on-camera dignity as contestants. Here audiences came to discover that the lives of black men and women in America were, paradoxically, both the same and different when compared with white Americans. White viewers were left to make that comparison and to ponder the reasons for the discrepancy. Several of the panel shows demonstrated that African-Americans held many of the same kinds of jobs as did white Americans. Their race made them interesting to those white viewers who had never been allowed to contextualize them in any way different from how network television seemed to always want them seen: through the gritty lens of stereotype and bigotry. Otherwise, more innocuously, black Americans were shown on TV game shows to be very much like their fellow white citizens.

These shows didn't remove blacks entirely from the shadows, but they did allow a little light to penetrate the darkness.

One of the first winners of *The $64,000 Question* was a 12-year-old African-American girl named Gloria Lockerman. An expert speller, she won $16,000 and was invited back for the show's first anniversary broadcast in 1956, where she was asked to do the honors of blowing out the candle on the celebratory cake. Later that summer, Gloria's TV fame won her a speaking slot at the Democratic National Convention. She added another $32,000 to her winnings when she competed on *The $64,000 Challenge*.

Also coming out big winners on *The $64,000 Question* were dancer Geoffrey Holder ($16,000) and Frances DeBerry, a 74-year-old Shakespeare expert ($16,000). Singer-actress Ethel Waters won $10,000 on *Break the $250,000 Bank*. Ex-boxer Beau Jack left with $1900 from his stint on *Strike It Rich*, singer Leslie Uggams—at age 15—won $25,000 on *Name That Tune*, and Steve and Dorothy Rowland earned an eye-popping $75,000 on *Do You Trust Your Wife?*

Ebony magazine tallied the winnings of over 25 African-American quiz show contestants during this period and came up with over half a million dollars. The magazine also estimated that their triumphs were viewed by a video audience of over 120 million. This figure may or may not include several black Americans who competed in talent competitions of this era, including Johnny Nash, Gladys Knight and Diahann Carroll. And though not a contestant, singer-pianist Bob Howard was a regular performer on the musical quiz show *Sing It Again* during its 1950–51 season.[14]

Not that African-Americans were ever invited to appear on any of the celebrity panels in that decade. It wasn't until the 1960s that blacks finally got the chance to serve as panelists on the socially progressive (comparatively speaking) *What's My Line?* By the series' final prime time broadcast, three had been given that opportunity: Harry Belafonte in 1961 and 1962, Sammy Davis Jr. in 1964 and broadcast journalist Joan Murray in 1967 (two weeks before the program went off the air). The unfortunate consequences of Belafonte's groundbreaking appearance are related below.

On November 4, 1963, *To Tell the Truth* invited actor Ossie Davis to sit on its panel. This occurred by either consequence or design only a few weeks after Martin Luther King delivered his historic "I Have a Dream" speech at the Lincoln Memorial (and a mere 18 days before the assassination of John F. Kennedy).

No black man (or black woman) was ever hired to emcee a network television game show in the 1950s. African-American bandleader Cab Calloway did have the distinction of serving in 1941 as quizmaster for a *radio* game show, a rollicking music-based program called *Quizzical*. NBC's Blue Network kept *Quizzical* on the air for nearly a year as a sustainer, but the program's eventual cancellation was attributed, in a fate identical to that of Nat King Cole and his television variety show, to a failure to secure a national sponsor for it.[15] Nor was a black woman in the 1950s ever given the chance to model a fur or gown on a TV game show, or to demonstrate any of the other prizes awarded on these shows.

For every two steps forward in the advancement of civil rights in America via the video medium, there was inevitably one, sometimes even two steps back. For as remarkable as it was that African-Americans were being let through the gates to participate in game shows, what if a black contestant won a trip instead of a cash prize? And the trip package included a free stay in a hotel with a color bar? The NAACP's Odelle Clark raised this issue of "false salesmanship" in 1955: "The main prize is sometimes a free trip to a nice hotel in Miami, Florida. If I won that prize, I'm sure they would ask me what I came down there for."[16] (One wonders if there was a disclaimer in the appearance contracts which quiz show contestants were required to sign, related to such race-related exclusions.)

Even the panel shows were most comfortable hauling in "safe Negroes": athletes, singers, dancers, the occasional actor. *What's My Line?* presented as mystery guests the aforementioned Mr. Calloway and fellow bandleader Duke Ellington; boxers Joe Louis, Floyd Patterson, Sugar Ray Robinson and Archie Moore; entertainers Pearl Bailey, Johnny Mathis, Louis Armstrong, Eartha Kitt and Lena Horne; baseball players Roy Campanella and Willie Mays; the Harlem Globetrotters and actor Eddie "Rochester" Anderson. (Anderson was always required to include the name Rochester as if it were his middle name—to remind viewers of the role with which he was best identified: Jack Benny's loyal assistant and factotum.)

Famous and semi-famous African-Americans also made *To Tell the Truth* and *I've Got a Secret* appearances. The Globetrotters' captain Clarence Wilson and two black imposters challenged the *To Tell the Truth* panel on May 5, 1958. Jackie Robinson's *I've Got a Secret* appearance coincided with a *Look* magazine article that announced Robinson's retirement from baseball and his joining the Chock Full o' Nuts restaurant chain as vice-president of personnel—the first black man to hold such an office in a major American corporation. Instead of playing the game, Robinson fielded questions from the studio audience about his decision, touching as well on aspects of his groundbreaking career.

You Bet Your Life, to its credit, made it a mission of sorts to give its contestant slots to people of a variety of races and religions. Contestants competing on the show were both well-known people of color as well as those who would otherwise never be known. On its May 12, 1960, broadcast, actress Louise Beavers shared with the audience the fact that she had been a board member of the Screen Actors Guild for 12 years. Her fellow competitor was a young black man named Thomas Yangha, who hailed from the Belgian Congo.

The April 16, 1959, broadcast included Earlene Brown, a black champion female shot putter, and Kenny Washington, the first African-American NFL player. Washington joined the Los Angeles Rams on March 21, 1946 (over a year before Jackie Robinson broke the color barrier in baseball), his hiring representing significant forward momentum in the civil rights movement. When it was decided that this Cleveland-based team would become a Los Angeles–based team, it was also decided that they would play their home games in the publicly owned Los Angeles Memorial Coliseum. Since the taxes of both white *and* black Los Angelinos had financed the facility's construction, it stood to reason that Jim Crow would not be welcome there—a civil rights victory based on simple fairness and common sense.[17]

The December 16, 1954, *You Bet Your Life* featured a white Methodist minister and his wife, the Reverend Karl and Helen Doss, who had adopted 12 mixed-race children—kids who'd been classified as unadoptable. An exchange between Groucho and the reverend illustrates the efforts made by this particular game show not only to entertain its audience but to enlighten them—something that probably made the high-principled NBC president Pat Weaver quite happy.

> GROUCHO: Reverend Doss, you have a wonderful family and I want to ask you one question: the experience you've had so far—would you do the same thing all over again?
> DOSS: Sure would, Groucho. It's been an enriching experience for us. We've discovered for one thing, that all races are basically alike. These differences that we call racial differences that divide us are cultural differences. It's something acquired after birth. That all people are born alike.

The industry rarely put into writing its reticence about populating the airwaves with too many black folk. But it was hard for producers, ad men and network execs to hide their collective discomfort. Their squeamishness was clearly evident both in their actions and in their frequent *in*action. In spite of gains won by African-Americans throughout the decade (Truman's Executive Order 9981 desegregating the Armed Forces, the Supreme Court's landmark Brown v. the Board of Education of Topeka ruling, and the end to segregation of the races on public transportation following the Montgomery, Alabama bus boycott), there was a feeling among both provocatively unrepentant white racists as well as those whose racist feelings didn't go *quite* so far as endorsing lunging German Shepherds and industrial-strength fire hoses, that black Americans should be grateful for what they were getting and "shouldn't make waves."

Advertisers shared that discomfort (as the Sidney Poitier example above demonstrates). Because sponsors feared boycotts of their wares by racist viewers, the advertising account executives who represented them had to walk a fine line between trying not to vex white Dixieland consumers (who could become a little annoyed by too much black skin on their TV screens) and respecting the indisputable fact that a not insignificant number of black Americans were also consumers of the products manufactured by their clients.

On certain occasions, a program might become so popular that it could defy its sponsor and the advertising agency that ran interference for it, and get its way. Such was the case in 1955 when the producers of *You Bet Your Life*, demonstrating the show's preference for partnering mixed-gender couples as game contestants, brought out a white woman and a black man as side-by-side players. Director Robert Dwan remembered that the ad agency representing the interests of its client, the DeSoto division of Chrysler, "raised a major fuss. They predicted dire consequences springing from the predictable reaction of the Southern DeSoto-Plymouth dealers." In the face of agency objections, the show refused to back down. And, according to Dwan, in spite of "vociferous response from some of the Southern dealers ... no reprisals were taken."[18] A possible reason for this: *You Bet Your Life* was doing well. There existed the distinct possibility that any Southern-based DeSoto dealer who put pressure on an NBC affiliate to pre-empt the show just might catch hell of a different sort from those loyal fans who also happened to live in the South and who would rather have Groucho quizzing two racially controversial contestants than not have Groucho at all.

You Bet Your Life also succeeded in racially integrating its orchestra. When he was hired as the show's orchestra leader, Jerry Fielding realized that *You Bet Your Life* had something in common with nearly every game and music-based program on network television: It employed only white musicians. This went for motion picture studio orchestras as well. Fielding couldn't go along with that. When it turned out that the best man for the wind section of the show's ensemble was a young musician who could not only double on sax and clarinet, but was also an accomplished flute player,

Fielding immediately snatched him up. The musician's name was Buddy Collette. He told Dwan in 2000 that he was more than willing to break the color barrier among TV musicians. Collette said he "felt like Jackie Robinson in the band." Fielding had discovered Collette when he attended a concert by an interracial symphony orchestra formed by Collette, famed double bass player Charlie Mingus and others. Collette and his fellow trailblazing musicians were also successful in ending the longtime separation, by race, of unionized musicians in Los Angeles. No longer would there be a Local 47 for white musicians and Local 767 for blacks (who got only a fraction of the work their white counterparts did). Now everyone, regardless of color, would come under Local 47.[19]

Procter and Gamble, the medium's #1 advertiser (by 1960, the company's TV advertising budget had risen to just over $100 million, or 92 percent of their total advertising outlay[20]), is a good example of how to have your cake and eat it too. (Duncan Hines was bought by Procter and Gamble in 1957.) Among the most scrupulous enforcer of taboos on TV game shows, Procter and Gamble went so far as to put into writing a lengthy list of dos and don'ts (mostly don'ts) which the makers of the TV shows the company sponsored were required to follow *if* the shows wanted to keep getting Procter and Gamble's ad bucks.

However, found nowhere on that list was anything approaching the statement, "Negroes should neither be adversely characterized nor disrespectfully marginalized in the programs you produce for us."

Instead, the Procter and Gamble-authorized protocol proscribed all "material dealing with miscegenation." This meant that mixed-race couples were banned from all P&G-sponsored programming, including game shows, through which the company did a significant amount of its advertising. Harold Mehling commented: "From Mount Cincinnati, it has decreed that love and marriage between whites and Asians, or Bantus and Arabs, is to be lumped with carnal lust in the minds of television viewers."[21]

And though the company included a long paragraph in its editorial policy guide disallowing "material that may give offense, either directly or by inference, to any organized minority group, lodge or other organizations, institutions, residents of any state or section of the country, or a commercial organization of any sort," one might interpret the statement to apply to both the NAACP *and* to the White Citizen's Council. In addition, nowhere in any of the other paragraphs of proscription were TV producers asked not to give offense to black viewers through disrespect shown to a black person individually. Furthermore, "residents of any state or section of the country" was a clear expression of Procter and Gamble's pledge to Southern white racists that the shows *it* sponsored would be kept free of the creative involvement of integration-minded northern liberals. Even more revelatory is this directive: "We will treat mention of the Civil War carefully, mindful of the sensitiveness of the South on this subject." This guideline was especially important coming as it did on the eve of the war's centennial.[22]

In other words, don't touch slavery with a ten-foot pole. One supposes this also applied to any new dramatizations of *Uncle Tom's Cabin*.

When black guitarist and civil rights activist Josh White was blocked by Sara Lee from singing a song about integration on a Chicago-based television special, its director William Friedkin withdrew from the broadcast and had his name removed from its credits. Later, in explaining his actions to *Variety*, he said, "They gave all kinds of reasons for wanting the number removed, but it is obvious why they wanted it cut. I've got to live with myself, and to put up with this kind of thing is to me an ugly way to make money."[23]

And yet this incident points up another way blacks were kept off television shows: a contention by those assembling the 1950s blacklists that the decade's civil rights movement was in actuality a communist plot. If one was fighting for the right of black Americans to secure the same status and opportunities afforded white Americans, then one had to be—according to the McCarthy crowd—either a communist or a "fellow traveler," and therefore the person shouldn't be permitted to work in television, where their mere presence might be perceived as an endorsement of Soviet Marxism.

This is probably the very good reason why black actor-singer Paul Robeson, a prominent civil rights activist, who also espoused support for positions and policies advocated by the Soviet Union, never made a celebrity guest appearance on a 1950s (*or* 1960s) network television game show.

Sometimes when black celebrities did go on quiz shows, their behavior was restricted to only those forms of interaction deemed least offensive to segregation-minded white audiences. When that line was crossed, there were consequences. Mark Goodson remembered negative audience reaction when *What's My Line?* panelist Arlene Francis kissed guest Ella Fitzgerald on camera as she was leaving the set after her appearance as mystery guest.[24] Even more consequential was Harry Belafonte's 1962

9. Guess Who's Probably Not Coming to Dinner 103

appearance as guest panelist on the show, when in accordance with the usual "girl-boy-girl-boy" seating arrangement, the singer was planted right between Arlene and fellow female panelist Dorothy Kilgallen. In retaliation for this perceived insult to white womanhood, a dozen CBS affiliates in the South removed the show from their schedules for several months.[25] (One presumes that neither black Southern viewers nor those occupants of pockets of Southern liberalism who also enjoyed *What's My Line?* had any say-so in the matter.)

Game shows offered radio and TV audiences the chance to hear about the accomplishments of black men and women in fields besides sports and entertainment. Diplomat and political scientist Ralph Bunche appeared on *Information Please* when the United Nations began meeting in New York. Bunche was a U.N. mediator, and he later became the first African-American to win the Nobel Peace Prize, for brokering the 1949 Armistice Agreements between Israeli and the neighboring states of Egypt, Lebanon, Jordan and Syria, which officially ended hostilities in the 1948 Arab-Israeli war.

On August 15, 1954, one of the challengers on *What's My Line?* was a man who would go on to become in 1975 the first African-American to attain the rank of four-star general, and one of only three men of Sub-Saharan origin up to that time to reach high military rank in the Western world. (The other two were Thomas-Alexandre Dumas, a general in Revolutionary France, and Toussaint Louverture, leader of the Haitian Revolution.) At the time of his *What's My Line?* appearance, Daniel "Chappie" James Jr. was a U.S. Air Force jet fighter pilot and commander of the 437th fighter interceptor squadron base at Otis Field. In Korea, he'd flown 101 combat missions.

On December 21, 1958, *What's My Line?* featured the African-American commander of the Nike missile base in Washington, D.C., Captain DeReef A. Greene. He had served in the U.S. Army for seven years, and had been a paratrooper in the Korean War, his combat service winning him a Bronze Star. There wasn't a single reference from either host or panel to his race.

Nor was the race of a contestant named Laoma Byrd acknowledged in her March 29, 1953, appearance on the show. Ms. Byrd ran a training camp for prizefighters. *What's My Line?* viewers got a good sense from both Captain Greene and Ms. Byrd's appearances as to what a colorblind American future might look like.

The same prospect of eventual racial assimilation came in the form of a now all-but-forgotten children's stunt game show similar to *Beat the Clock*, which aired on Saturday mornings on NBC in early 1956. Hosted by a very young Gene Rayburn, *Choose Up Sides* pitted two teams of four kids each, who competed in various stunts, cheered on by kids in two sets of onstage bleachers (each team's respective adolescent supporters). The cheers came from both white kids and black kids.

As for the gains made by black Americans in television over the coming decade, not all of them can be attributed to the programs of the Great Society, or to a general expansion in civil rights activism after so long a relative absence of black Americans from the airwaves. Movement in that direction should also be credited to simple pragmatism on the part of advertisers. When growing black purchasing power in the '60s was weighed against the possible loss in revenue from anti-black boycotts, the calculus came ultimately to favor racial integration in American broadcasting, as well as increased visibility for people of other races (as well as adherents to non–Christian religious faiths). As a result, the African-American actor Ossie Davis was cast as a prosecutor in the courtroom series *The Defenders*, a black dancer joined June Taylor's troop on *The Jackie Gleason Show*...

And *I Spy* was just around the corner.

But it was the television game shows of the 1950s that helped to show the way to that corner.

◆ 10 ◆

A Beautiful Mosaic (Still Under Construction)

> We become not a melting pot but a beautiful mosaic. Different people, different beliefs, different yearnings, different hopes, different dreams.
> —Jimmy Carter[1]

Inroads made by black Americans into the relatively closed shop of 1950s television were matched by those of Americans of other ethnic identities, who also had their own arguments to make and battles to wage in their overall struggle for traction and respect. People of color and/or non–Judeo-Christian religious affiliation found themselves either unrepresented or significantly under-represented in most forms of non-news television programming, with the exception of variety, audience participation and game shows. Here, though, these minority-group Americans faced the same hurdles to which African-Americans were being subjected, with limited opportunities for a full and authentic expression of their identity, uncontaminated by caricaturized distortion and ridicule.

People of color, when given the chance to participate in quiz shows, all too often found themselves having to shake off stereotypical characterization, racial prejudice and insensitive lampooning. The June 4, 1957, *To Tell the Truth* is characteristic. It included among its contestants a Native American named Cornelius Vanderbilt Seneca, who was described as chief of the Seneca Tribe. As the round began and Chief Seneca and the two pretenders stood waiting in silhouette for their introduction, the audience was already laughing at the outlines of the elaborate Indian headdresses which the trio of challengers were required to wear. When the lights came up on each individually, the expressions of audience merriment did not subside. Such a reaction might even have been intended by the show's producers, since the war bonnets seemed purposefully exaggerative, and it is doubtful any member of the trio (all three men were Native Americans) would have been in a position to refuse to wear the get-up.

When it was time for panelist Jack Paar to ask his questions, he mischievously sought the meaning of "Kee-mo Sah-bee," and again the presumably majority-white audience vocalized their delight, this time at his perceived cleverness. Kitty Carlisle, in explaining her vote for one of the two imposters, said she did so because "he seemed like a proud descendant of Hiawatha." The Indian of Ms. Carlisle's reference was thought to have been leader of either the Onondago tribe or the Mohawk, or both. But Ms. Carlisle gets a half-point for effort, since it was Hiawatha who was influential in banding together the Five Nations of the Iroquois Confederacy, which also included the Senecas. Panelist Hy Gardner eliminated the real Chief Seneca from consideration by claiming facetiously that "he looked like he posed for the radiator cap of a Pontiac." Host Bud Collyer was quick to add, "More like the nickel to me." After the real Seneca leader authenticated himself by standing up, the imposters were asked who they really were and what they did. One of the fakers, a member of the Cherokee tribe, said he was an engineer for St. Joseph's College for Women, which led Collyer to quip, "What better job for an 'Injun' than engineer."

To the show's credit, as the trio was leaving, Collyer mentioned that Chief Seneca was involved in efforts to "convince the authorities in Washington not to appropriate part of his reservation for a reservoir." He claimed that such appropriation "would be in violation of a treaty signed with George Washington," and then wished the chief good luck with his fight. Luck, unfortunately, wasn't on the side of the Senecas. They lost their lawsuit, President Kennedy denying their appeal on the basis of the need for flood control, and the Kinzua Dam on the Allegheny River was erected between 1961 to 1965. As a result, approximately 600 Seneca Indians were forced to leave the 10,000 acres they had occupied since the 1794 Treaty of Canandaigua, and relocate to Salamanca, New York (within the Allegany Reservation of the Seneca Nation of New York).

The *To Tell the Truth* panelists weren't any more ethnically sensitive later that summer when trying to guess which of three competitors was Delores Shorty, "Miss Indian America of 1957," winner of the pageant portion of the annual All-American Indian Days Festival in Sheridan, Wyoming:

10. A Beautiful Mosaic (Still Under Construction)

HY GARDNER: Are there any blond Indian girls?
POLLY BERGEN (after the real Ms. Shorty stood up, and Ms. Bergen realized she'd guessed incorrectly): It's not fair because they're all Indian.
BUD COLLYER: Nobody tried "Ke-Mo Sah-bee" on any of them.

American Indians were treated slightly better on an episode of *It Could Be You*. A contestant, who was Cherokee, was singled out for her missionary work and given a church organ so worshippers on her reservation could have music. But even still, the woman first had to be subjected to a lame joke about not being able "to get the flap of her wigwam open."[2]

It wasn't necessary for a Native American to even appear on a game show in the '50s for his or her ethnicity to receive comical disparagement, and such on-camera insensitivity continued well into the '60s. On a November 13, 1961, *I've Got a Secret*, host Garry Moore did a live commercial for the dessert topping Dream Whip, with the help of a young white woman dressed in parodic Indian garb (complete with single head feather). As she and Moore salivated over a piece of pie smothered in Dream Whip dessert topping, the woman hoked, "Dream Whip: white man's magic. Little box will stay fresh for many moons on pantry shelf.... For next big family powwow, serve-um pumpkin pie...." "And Dream Whip," Moore closed.

One of the contestants in a March 1956 *Queen for a Day* was a "full blooded Pima Indian." One winner the previous month was a Mexican-American widow with three children. On June 18, 1957, *To Tell the Truth* featured Chinese-American Olympic high diving champion Dr. Sammy Lee (who had appeared on *You Bet Your Life* a year earlier); and five weeks later, the show featured early Bollywood Indian actress Mohana.

A big winner on the June 9, 1956, telecast of *The Big Surprise* was a woman named Maisie Chen, who had immigrated from China in 1950. Her knowledge of the Brooklyn Dodgers won her $100,000. The producers of the large-payout quizzers of the mid–1950s had a special interest in contestants whose ethnicities and life stories seemed at odds with the players' own areas of interest and expertise. The opera-loving Italian-American cobbler Gino Prato, who won $32,000 in the second month of *The $64,000 Question*, would soon become the exception rather than the rule when it came to contestants and their fields of knowledge. This is one of the reasons that psychologist Dr. Joyce Brothers' professed interest in boxing made her a far more intriguing contestant than, say, an art dealer who knew a lot about art. (Art appreciation, as viewers of *The $64,000 Challenge* came to learn, was more fun when it was being taught by art collectors with names like Edward G. Robinson and Vincent Price.)

Although appearances by contestants like Dr. Lee and Ms. Chen tended to reflect a best-intentions form of ethnic tokenism, *You Bet Your Life* actually did play a big role in promoting the career of performer Pedro Gonzalez Gonzalez. The Mexican-American actor, singer and dancer was discovered at the San Antonio television station where he worked as a handyman when he had the chance to perform in a local telethon. Gonzalez Gonzalez (the double-name a combination of his father's surname and his mother's identical maiden name) was an instant hit with both Groucho and the audience during his January 7, 1953, *You Bet Your Life* appearance, in no small part due to exchanges like the following (probably completely scripted, but still funny):

> GROUCHO: Pedro, we could do a great act together. We could make a tour of Vaudeville, you and I. What should we call our act? Two Hot Tamales?
> PEDRO: No, we would call it Gonzalez Gonzalez and Marx.
> GROUCHO: That's great. Two people in the act and I get third billing.

John Wayne caught the broadcast that night and within six weeks, a William Morris representative was at Gonzalez Gonzalez's door with a contract. The Mexican-American actor ended up working with Wayne for almost 20 years.[3]

A Mexican-American with a similar name also appeared on *You Bet Your Life*—tennis player Pancho Gonzales. He was the world's #1 tennis player for eight years, from 1952 to 1960, winning 17 major singles titles, including two Grand Slams and 15 Pro Slams.

The beautiful mosaic that has always been America was finally starting to come into focus as TV camera lenses were more frequently trained on people of color from diverse ethnic backgrounds on the medium's game shows. As seen above, white America didn't always regard them with respect, but strides were still being made in the direction of inclusion and humanization.

And this is the best that can be said about a country involved in the very long and laborious process of cultural assimilation and social evolution.

❖ 11 ❖

And Now a Mandate from Our Sponsor …

> Advertising may not be the best method, but no one has evolved a better one, or indeed any alternative which does not entail either government control or indirect but effective government influence on what goes on the air.
> —William Paley[1]

The prosperity that characterized the United States in the 1950s had as one of its biggest engines, the advertising industry. Never in any previous decade had the country's economic vibrancy been more dependent on its advertising sector. The amount of money spent by advertisers more than doubled during the decade, going from $6 billion in 1950 to $9 billion in just the first five years. By 1963, that figure had jumped to $13 billion.[2]

That's $13 billion *1963* dollars expended for reasons of vital importance to the future of the nation—for example, convincing American consumers to switch from Gleem toothpaste to Colgate (with decay-fighting Gardol!).

In television's infancy, the cost of assembling and broadcasting a television program that wasn't sustained (that is, with all costs borne by network and/or producer) was shouldered by corporate America in the form of program sponsorship. This tidy arrangement, a holdover from radio, was facilitated by advertising agencies, which wielded great power in network radio. In fact, the sponsorship model had worked so well in radio—and mostly to the benefit of advertisers, who exercised significant control over the shows they sponsored—that there was little doubt the same system could be applied with equal success to commercial television. This somewhat arrogant assumption by agents and sponsors ticked off the *New York Herald Tribune*'s radio and television critic John Crosby, who boldly pronounced in a 1946 column that "the greatest problem in broadcasting [is] the control exercised by the advertiser."[3] Either Crosby was coming late to the radio complaint window, or he was exercising amazing prescience when it came to the imposition of the monocratic sponsorship model on the new medium, and, ultimately, how it would fail.

No doubt, in the early days of television, the agencies and the sponsors held the field, the advertising agencies in many cases becoming the actual show creators, producers and packagers. In other cases, an agency might devote its time and resources to looking for just the right advertising vehicle for its client from among independent producers clamoring to get their shows plugged into a limited number of network television slots.

Agencies felt they had the right to call the shots on behalf of the sponsors who were writing the checks. For this reason, there were TV shows in the early days that, in keeping with radio tradition, incorporated the names of their sponsors in their show titles. There were sometimes "alternate" sponsors, but control of a large number of programs still rested not in the hands of the network or even independent packaging firms like Goodson-Todman Productions, but with the ad agencies which, with unwavering loyalty to their clients, did the sponsors' bidding, regardless of what was asked. For this reason, there were in the days of television's infancy, programs that bore such billboard monikers as *Paul Whiteman's Goodyear Review*, *Chesterfield Sound-Off Time*, *The Philco Television Playhouse*, *The Voice of Firestone*, *The Speidel Show*, *Texaco Star Theater*, *Armstrong Circle Theater*, *Kraft Television Theater* and *The Gillette Cavalcade of Sports*. Even NBC's nightly news broadcast, because it was sponsored by Camel cigarettes, carried its benefactor's name in its title: *The Camel News Caravan*.

Curiously, there were few network television game shows from the late '40s and early '50s that took this route. The exceptions were *General Electric Guest House* and *Messing Prize Party* (sponsored by the Messing Bread Company). However, one presumes that *local* quiz shows were more likely to accommodate sponsor ego in this manner.

The model held fast for a while. But then along came Pat Weaver, who became head of NBC-TV in 1949 and then served as president of the network from 1953 to 1955. Weaver arrived at NBC's doorstep fresh from the advertising world (he'd supervised radio programming for the Young and Rubicam advertising agency), but this fact didn't deter him from efforts to put his network in control of its own programming, which meant dismissing the long-held belief that a television show's advertiser should have autocratic control of program content. Weaver struck at just the right time. Networks were growing tired of not being able to program the shows they offered their affiliates, with the freedom to move them around on the broadcast schedule in ways that made sense in terms of viewer needs and interests. Also, because television was far more expensive to produce than radio, and only the giants of American industry (at least those that advertised) could afford the higher price tags, it made sense that the long relationship between commercial television and its commercials should undergo some serious reevaluation and revision.

And a lot of advertisers were just fine with that. Smaller companies, which had long sought a national sales presence, had pockets that weren't deep enough to pay the production costs for an entire show, or even, in many cases, *half* of one, and therefore these businesses had no way to get their own brands on the air and before the eyeballs of new customers. Weaver had a solution, which he maintained would be good for everyone.

Weaver was famous for his ideas; his frequent brainstorming over ways to improve the medium while offering culture and class to viewers (a goal which even earned itself a nickname: "Operation Frontal Lobes") gave NBC fresh-concept programming like *The Today* Show, *The Home Show* (a generously budgeted magazine show for homemakers) and *The Tonight Show*. It also brought network television stand-alone "spectaculars" like *Peter Pan* (in living color!). Here was an idea that was visionary *and* practical: spot advertising based on the magazine format, administered not by Madison Avenue, but by NBC itself. The magazine ad-like concept would allow for a more diverse mix of television advertisers, more advertising opportunities for smaller businesses, *and* more control by networks over the shows in their stables. Although there was balking from some of the major players, even they couldn't help seeing a certain logic behind the change, for by the mid–50s, after the FCC freeze on new TV stations had been lifted, and the number of homes with TV receivers began to mushroom, the costs related to a sponsor affixing itself to a specific show also skyrocketed.

And yet, because TV quiz shows were far cheaper to produce than filmed sitcoms and live teleplays, it was the quiz show that had the honor of being the last hold-out from the days of single, sometimes double, sponsor control. As late as August 31, 1964, *To Tell the Truth* was still seating its host Bud Collyer and celebrity panelists behind placards for "our sponsor this week," in this case, Dristan nasal mist. This was, however, the exception to the rule, as even reasonably budgeted game shows were destined to switch to magazine-style pay-as-you-go advertising after the quiz show scandals of the late '50s put the networks securely in the driver's seat.

The history of early television is rife with examples of sponsor intrusion in the production of programs. Theirs was a form of extra-creative interference that gave raging migraines to writers, directors and actors, who just wanted to do their work with as few problems as possible. Content creators were opposed all along the way by sponsors and their ad agency mouthpieces, who sought to monkey with that content for the purpose of

(A) Not giving offense to certain viewing constituencies and thereby avoid provoking product boycotts or inciting affiliates not to clear (or air) those national network programs into which the sponsor had sunk so much of its advertising budget.
(B) Obviating any negative feelings about the sponsor's product, which might come from a word, phrase or image that might be misconstrued.
(C) Avoiding the possibility of accidentally or even tangentially endorsing a competitor's product.

Weaver, in a long memo written to NBC president Joseph McConnell, expanded the argument against advertiser power when he stated that major clients "want shows of their own. [But] they want to be able to cancel every 13 weeks. They want to take the summer off.... They have no real interest in public service. They have no real interest, in most cases, in giving the public anything but escape, and selling them their products."[4]

CBS broadcast journalist Edward R. Murrow was one of the few TV producers in the years that preceded the full switch to magazine-style advertising, who could brag on air that *his* sponsor, Alcoa (the Aluminum Company of America), kept its hands off his show, the documentary series *See It Now*. Alcoa confirmed the truth of this statement, and continued to grant Murrow and his partner Fred Friendly total creative independence in spite of some of the very controversial topics explored on the show.[5] One wonders, though, if Murrow would have had it so easy had his sponsor been a cigarette company, since the legendary journalist devoted two entire broadcasts (May 31 and June 7, 1955) to the connection between smoking and lung cancer (shows that inveterate smoker Murrow, who died of lung cancer in 1965, obviously did not heed).

Big tobacco was big on TV quiz shows. From the tap-dancing packs of Old Gold on *Two for the Money* and *Stop the Music* to Winston cigarettes' grammatically incorrect brag on *I've Got a Secret* that "Winston tastes good like [*sic*] a cigarette should," game shows of the 1950s functioned under a perpetual smoke-filled cloud of burning brightleaf and burley. (Winston's maker, R.J. Reynolds, caught flack for its problematic slogan, which was repeated by everyone from the Beverly Hillbillies to the Flintstones. The widely discussed controversy possibly played a role in boosting sales of the brand to #1 cigarette in the nation by 1966.[6])

As sponsors go, Winston wasn't always an easy one to deal with. *I've Got a Secret*'s problem with its sponsor was one that was typical of the kind of wrinkles—and sometimes full rumples—that turned up in the program-sponsor relationship: Winston cigarettes got word from a viewer of a television show hosted by one of *I've Got a Secret*'s regular panelists, Henry Morgan, that Morgan had made an unpardonable crack about cigarettes. Famous for his crusty, shoot-from-the-hip bluntness, the veteran broadcaster had offhandedly remarked, while lighting a cigarette on his show, that he was "creating his own cancer." As evidenced by *See It Now* taking up the issue long before the seismic release of the 1964 U.S. Surgeon General's report confirming that smoking was indeed injurious to human health, there had been a number of studies that had come to the same conclusion, and millions of Americans, including Morgan, had become aware of the simple fact that tobacco companies didn't want people to know: cigarettes just weren't very good for you. According to Morgan, such a thing wasn't said without consequence. The powers-that-be at R.J. Reynolds in Winston-Salem, North Carolina, took swift action against him for his apostasy. Morgan said he was "fired at dawn."[7]

But Morgan had an ace in the hole: his friendship with Garry Moore. Popular with viewers (and perhaps acting at the behest of Messrs. Goodson and Todman) the *I've Got a Secret* host flew straight down to the tobacco company's North Carolina headquarters and talked the company out of dumping loose-lipped Morgan. And by the way—Moore may very well have argued—weren't those loose lips of Henry's frequently seen dutifully sucking the sponsor's cigarette?[8]

By way of sadly relevant sidebar, Morgan and Moore died about six months apart, both in their late seventies, Morgan from lung cancer and Moore from emphysema. Cigarette smoking was implicated in the deaths of quite a number of TV game show hosts and panelists active in the 1950s, just as it took the lives of thousands of others who made a living in the high-stress, tobacco-tranquilizing early years of television. Hal March

(*The $64,000 Question*), Bert Parks (*Break the Bank, Stop the Music*), and Dennis James (multiple shows) all died of lung cancer. Bud Collyer (*Beat the Clock, To Tell the Truth*) succumbed to circulatory problems. Johnny Carson and Robert Q. Lewis (*The Name's the Same*), like Moore, died of emphysema. John Charles Daly had a heart attack. Jack Barry (*Twenty-One*) also suffered a heart attack, his at just 66; Sam Levenson (*Two for the Money*) was 68 when he suffered the same fate. On the flip side, two iconic game show emcees who pursued healthy lifestyles, Ralph Edwards and his *Truth or Consequences* protégé Bob Barker lived very long lives. Edwards died at the ripe old age of 92 and Barker, as of the year of this book's publication, is still spry at 93.

Old Gold cigarettes was a heavily advertised brand on both radio and TV; they not only sponsored Paul Whiteman's radio show in 1929 but paid the bills for Artie Shaw's *Melody and Madness* show on CBS radio in 1938 and '39. But Old Gold wasn't always the pack of preference for the staff of the television shows it sponsored. In spite of Old Gold's endearingly kitschy dancing cigarette boxes (sometimes it was a cigarette pack and a lighter), Norm Blumenthal, producer of the 1950s game show *Concentration*, had a difficult time following his sponsor's rule that everyone connected with the show had to smoke Old Golds, *whether they were smokers or not*. "The only way I could calm [my people] down," Blumenthal remembered, "was to ban smoking on the set. The biggest problem I had was unloading all those cartons of their product; nobody wanted that brand."[9]

Cigarette company decrees weren't limited to TV quiz shows. Creators of the highly rated live detective drama *Man Against Crime* (1949–1954) were leaned upon quite heavily by the aforementioned R.J. Reynolds, maker of Camels. The mimeographed instructions to the writers and directors of the show from the William Esty agency—acting on behalf of its client, Reynolds—dictated that the series "have no heavy or any disreputable person smoking a cigarette." Furthermore: "Do not associate the smoking of cigarettes with undesirable scenes or situations plot-wise." Whatever that meant.

A viewer should never see a cigarette offered to a character to "calm his nerves," to avoid the implication that cigarettes possessed narcotic properties. Arson was never mentioned as a possible crime-as-plot-element because it might remind the audience of the thousands of fires caused each year by ill-placed cigarettes.[10]

Camel cigarettes created challenges for other broadcasters through dromedary-related dictates, such as those made to the makers of *The*

Camel News Caravan. Producers of this forerunner to *The Huntley-Brinkley Report* prohibited the filming of any NO SMOKING signs. Writer for the show (and, later, an NBC news producer) Reuven Frank remembered that the news broadcast couldn't include an image of a camel. "To them a camel is not a stinking animal, it's a cigarette. You could not use anybody smoking a cigar. I got the rule changed for Churchill. He was probably the most famous living human being, and every time you took a picture of him he had a cigar.... But that was it. I couldn't use Groucho Marx."[11]

Despite Big Tobacco's denials that cigarette smoking caused cancer, Reynolds took no chances. *The Camel News Caravan*'s senior editor Arthur Holch recalled that there couldn't be any news story about cancer, "*any cancer*" (presumably, even a story about a breakthrough in cancer research). If it became necessary to include an obituary for someone famous who had died of the disease, the writers were instructed to use the euphemism "long illness."[12]

Likewise, according to behind-the-camera game show lore, a *Do You Trust Your Wife?* contestant lost title to her astrological sign when a representative of the cigarette brand that was sponsoring the show, L & M, asked that a segment be re-shot (like *You Bet Your Life, Do You Trust Your Wife?* was filmed and edited) so the husband-contestant, who was asked his wife's sign, could answer "Aries." The man's wife wasn't born under the astrological sign of Aries, but no matter: It was far less offensive to the tobacco company than her real sign: "Cancer."[13]

Fast-forward several decades to the 1990s, when the CBS news magazine *60 Minutes* found itself in a standoff with Brown and Williamson over Jeffrey Wigand's scheduled-for-broadcast on-camera claims that the company for which he'd served as vice-president of research and development intentionally manipulated its tobacco blend with additives meant to increase the effectiveness of nicotine in cigarette smoke. The network initially put the kibosh on the interview, fearing a gigantic lawsuit by Brown and Williamson for facilitating the breach of Wigand's confidentiality agreement with his former employer.[14] This corporate showdown was dramatized by Michael Mann in his 1999 film *The Insider*, and was presented to audiences as a fight for journalistic freedom and integrity.

The *60 Minutes* correspondent in the hot seat was Mike Wallace, who had begun his long broadcasting career as a game show host and panelist. Wallace was actually one of several newscasters who straddled the news and entertainment divisions of their respective networks in the

'50s by both delivering the news and serving as a quiz show emcee. Douglas Edwards, Walter Cronkite, John Cameron Swayze and John Charles Daly all did double duty at one time or another. For several years, while Daly was serving as moderator of CBS's *What's My Line?*, he was also employed as vice-president in charge of news at an entirely different network, ABC.

Wallace's pre–*60 Minutes* game show credits included *The Big Surprise*, *Who's the Boss?* and *Who Pays*? He was also a guest on the radio quiz show *Information Please*, served as the voice of Elgin-American in the commercials that aired during *You Bet Your Life*, and from time to time sat in on the *To Tell the Truth* panel. Wallace's association with cigarettes went back to the early 1960s, when his primary income was derived from pitching Parliaments in commercials; Parliament was the original sponsor of *The Mike Wallace Interview* (ABC, 1957–58).

Parliament cigarettes turn up in a funny anecdote by Goodson-Todman director Franklin Heller, who was interviewed by Jeff Kisseloff for his oral history of early television, *The Box*:

> *To Tell the Truth* was sponsored [at one point] by Marlboro. We had on two people pretending to be Israeli aviators. Before the show aired, we had a panel of actors, who would play a game with the liars to give them a chance to practice. In the course of the rehearsal, the agency man heard one of the actors ask, "What's the name of the Israeli parliament?"
> Afterward, the agency man came up to me and said, "You're going to have to change that question."
> I asked him why. He said, "This is a Marlboro show. Parliament is a competing cigarette."[15]

Of course the joke was on the agency representative. It wasn't these actors who'd be asking the questions when the show was broadcast (live); it would be that week's celebrity panelists (Polly Bergen, Jackie Cooper, Kitty Carlisle and Hy Gardner), and it would have been impossible to pre-censor the on-camera interlocutors and still preserve their right to independent and undirected examination of the three aviatrix-looking females, one of whom really had been the first woman pilot of the Israeli air force, Yael Finkelstein.

As it turned out, by the end of the round, none of the panel members had thought to ask about the Knesset. The closest anyone came was Jackie Cooper's oddball question about potato kugel.

Sometimes it was the sponsors who won the tussles to protect and promote their brands irrespective of how inconvenient or just plain absurd their requests might seem to the people who put the nuts and bolts of their shows together. On other occasions, it was the creators and packagers of the shows who prevailed. And even when the creative types lost the bout, they didn't lose the overarching argument. One comedy writer even had the chutzpah to go after General Motors: "We can't offend teenagers on the Chevrolet show because, after all, they steal a lot of Chevys."[16]

Problems arising from the often strained relationships between quiz shows and their sponsors go back to the days of radio. The creator of *Information Please*, for example, strongly resented its sponsor American Tobacco's heavy-handed Lucky Strike commercials and he refused to kowtow to the company that footed his bills. As it turned out, Dan Golenpaul was a longtime cigar smoker, and as such, he declined to take up the cigarette habit. Clearly biting the hand that fed him, he was more than once heard to say on air, "*Every* brand of cigarette is as bad as every other brand."[17]

And got away with it.

"Today, the sponsors pull the strings and we are the puppets," Groucho Marx grumbled to *Printers Ink* magazine in 1953. "Radio and television announcers have to be liars."[18] Producers of Marx's own quiz show *You Bet Your Life* were at one point required to defend a contestant's right to keep his own name. The surname was Ford and the sponsor was DeSoto ("Tell them Groucho sent you"), and the DeSoto Plymouth folks were afraid that the name would remind viewers of their competition.[19]

William Clotworthy, DeSoto's representative on the show, remembered things somewhat differently: "If there was someone named Ford, they just didn't get on. These were all handpicked people."[20]

Norm Blumenthal recalled an incident involving the host of *Concentration*, Hugh Downs, refusing to stand before a camera, eat from a bowl of rice and then lick his chops with delight:

> Hugh refused because he felt it could send a message of personal endorsement. Pretending to savor any product was not something he would ever do. The irate sponsor, who wielded lots of power, insisted, and threatened to pull out of the show. Hugh stood his ground, won out, and a compromise was reached. He held the bowl up, looked at it, and gave it a sort of friendly smile.[21]

According to *I've Got a Secret* producer Allan Sherman, there were even advertisers who had a thing or two to say about how the women on their shows did their hair. He wrote in his memoir, "The president of Prom Home Permanent was violently opposed to Laura Hobson, and later to Nina Foch and Faye Emerson because they had straight hair. In this man's mind," Sherman opined, "there was something basically disgusting about any woman with straight hair. He would rather have Harpo Marx than Faye Emerson, because Harpo's wig would have showed the advantages of a Prom Home Permanent."[22]

And what if a game show *didn't* balk at advertiser demands? What if it went along with every change requested by the sponsor—especially those that rose from alleged viewer complaints? It didn't take very much to induce sponsors to tighten the screws on the shows they superintended (even if viewer unhappiness stemmed from extreme parochialism, prudery, race prejudice or other forms of bigotry). There was, after all, a prevailing theory in the TV industry that for every viewer letter of complaint received, there were 50,000 viewers who *didn't* write but were nonetheless in full agreement with the letter writer.[23]

But whereas there was often a price to be paid for the crime of fighting a sponsor's demands, no matter how unreasonable or even ludicrous, there were consequences as well for those game show producers who capitulated too willingly to sponsor wishes, especially if the impetus for the changes constituted reckless overreaction to nothing so much as the usual assortment of viewer kvetches and nitpickings.

In the case of *Masquerade Party*, the price was direct targeting in 1960 by the pioneering underground magazine *The Realist*, largely regarded as a grown-up version of the sophomorically satirical *Mad* magazine. (*The Realist*, in fact, was first published in the spring of 1958 out of the New York offices of *Mad*.) *The Realist* chose to reward *Masquerade Party* for overly accommodating the whims of its sponsors with a hoax perpetrated by readers of the magazine itself.

In its March 1960 issue, editor Paul Krassner wrote that a TV network executive once told the magazine that the relationship between advertiser and broadcaster had reached the point where "if a sponsor wanted to show a couple fornicating, the network wouldn't prevent it—and if the sponsor thought it would increase sales, he'd go right ahead and *do* it."

That is, if there were no viewer complaints.

Krassner proceeded to his proposal:

> Let's take what, to us, is just about the worst program on television—a thing called *Masquerade Party*—on which a panel ... has to guess what celebrity is dressed in an idiotic costume and mask. We'll pick a specific date—Friday night, April 1st—NBC, 9:30 EST—but you don't have to watch. Your job then: the next day, write a letter complaining about the offensive thing that was said on the program. Use your own wording. *But don't mention anything specific.*

11. And Now a Mandate from Our Sponsor ...

Krassner provided the addresses of the show's sponsors, the Block Drug Company and the Hazel Bishop cosmetics company (whose profitable sponsorship of *This Is Your Life* had convinced Revlon to ante up for *The $64,000 Question*).

> But—hoaxwise—doesn't it give you a nice warm feeling inside just to picture all these TV officials, sponsor representatives and advertising men sitting around the screening room in their gray flannel ulcers watching a kinescope of *Masquerade Party* and trying to find something offensive....[24]

The Realist reported on its success in its June 1960 issue, quoting from readers' own reports of their twitting of the show's sponsors. One subscriber wrote to "The Green Mint, Nytol People":

> I am a teenager and my parents have tried to raise me as a decent god-fearing person and have tried to keep me and my mind pure. We often *used* to watch *Maskkeraid Party* and we thought it was a dandy show. But once in a while those people got on their big-city high horse and said some pretty bad things. Of course my parents were upset and turned the sound off so I wouldn't be perverted.
>
> I always used to wash [my] mouth out with Green Mint because I think Dick Clark is a pretty swell fellow and a really cool guy and he said he liked Green Mint and wanted me to use it too.... I just poured all the Green Mint in the toilet and flushed it away. NEVER AGAIN!!! I am going to tell everyone I know never to use your products again. Just who do you think you are?[25]

Krassner defended his hoax by noting that it "was precisely because *Masquerade Party* is the epitome of *in*offensiveness that we chose it for our hoax" and stated that there was "more than one way of smiling into a TV camera." He related a confession by *I've Got a Secret* panelist Henry Morgan that the show got letters asking them to fire him because he doesn't smile *enough*.[26]

It isn't clear how much sponsors and producers of *Masquerade Party* were smiling after the stunt had run its course. But the point had been made, capped by an impish Alfred E. Neuman–like grin.

There are other examples of sponsors and the packagers of the shows they sponsored getting along quite well with one another, neither making too strong a demand on the other. Such was the case with *What's My Line?* Its producers were quite fond of the program's hands-off benefactor. Jules Montenier, a chemist and inventor, is best known for giving the world Stopette antiperspirant, effectively turning his skills in the laboratory into a lucrative cosmetics company. Montenier—mystery guest for the show's February 12, 1956, broadcast—was praised on-air by moderator John Charles Daly for having been with *What's My Line?* for six years, but more importantly: for being a sponsor who "did not interfere with the production of the series."

When Remington Rand (maker of electric shavers, office machines and the UNIVAC line of mainframe computers) stepped in as co-sponsor for the show six months later, an effort was made by *What's My Line?*'s staff to schedule a mystery guest appearance by former President Harry S. Truman, since its August 12, 1956, telecast would be coming out of Chicago, and it was assumed that Truman would attend the Democratic National Convention there that week. But as it turned out, the hands-off approach to television program sponsorship exhibited by Mr. Montenier wasn't one shared by the new chairman of the board of Remington Rand. He vetoed the very suggestion of an invitation to Truman, and thus prevented the former president from appearing. One suspects he did this without compunction. The name of the new chairman was Douglas MacArthur.[27]

As a side note, Dr. Montenier, though he never meddled with the running of the show he was paying for, did have some say in where *What's My Line?* was broadcast, since there were costs to his company in every market where the series aired. And because there were parts of the country where Stopette, Poof! deodorant power and Finesse ("the flowing cream shampoo") weren't sold, it wasn't until 1956, when Jules Montenier, Inc. was sold to Helene Curtis (a nationally marketed cosmetics company), that television viewers in Columbus, Georgia; Jackson, Mississippi; Lancaster, Pennsylvania; Lexington, Kentucky; Memphis, Tennessee; Spartanburg, South Carolina; and Tallahassee, Florida, got the chance to see the show, which by that point had already been on the air for six years.

Some of the most egregious examples of sponsor control of 1950s television programming took place in the world of live television drama, which had earned an early reputation for examining serious issues related to human relationships, human rights and America's place in the world. And though these incidents didn't have a direct impact on game shows, they did send disturbing reverberations throughout the television industry in terms of the kinds of restraints that could be placed on those who created original material for the medium.

Perhaps the most execrable example of sponsor infringement upon the right of television show creators to put their shows together without interference had to do with an episode of CBS's *Playhouse 90* series, broadcast on April 16, 1959. The televised play that week was the serious and

11. And Now a Mandate from Our Sponsor ...

substantive courtroom drama "Judgment at Nuremberg." Inspired by the U.S. military tribunals that took place after World War II in the Palace of Justice in Nuremberg, Germany, the teleplay later became a 1961 award-winning movie (as happened with quite a few live television dramas of the 1950s).

The incident in question involved a character railing against those who had sent "innocent men and women into gas ovens." But the television audience never heard the words "gas ovens," because the show's sponsor, the American Gas Association, had requested that the sound be turned off at the moment of the phrase's utterance, which the sound engineer unquestioningly did. To add insult to injury, Nicholas E. Keesely, senior vice-president of the advertising agency that handled the episode, Lennen and Newelly, defended the decision:

> In going through the scripts, we noticed gas referred to in a half dozen places that had to do with the death chambers. This is just an oversight on somebody's part. We deal with a lot of artistic people in the creative end, and sometimes they do not have the commercial judgment, or see things as we are paid to see [them], and we raised the point with CBS and they said they would remove the word "gas," and we thought they would, and they did in some cases, and at the last minute we found that there were some still left in.[28]

In other words: "This wouldn't have happened if CBS had done its job and made the writer strike out all references to gas chambers so as not to give viewers the idea that gas is *always* a bad thing."

Sponsors of the big money quiz shows that crashed and burned once proof of game-rigging was brought to light, also faced accusations that they too played a role in all that nasty business. They were charged with encouraging the makers of the shows to find ways to remove certain less appetizing contestants, while keeping around those contestants whom audiences seemed to approve.

In October 1959, when the House Subcommittee on Legislative Oversight, chaired by Congressman Oren Harris, met to investigate the scandal, both Charles Revson, head of Revlon, the sponsor of *The $64,000 Question*, and his adjutant, his brother Martin, were questioned about their involvement in the "fix." Nothing definitive was admitted to, but both brothers found it hard to deny that certain suggestions had been made as to which individuals the cosmetics company wanted on the show and which they did not. This fact was corroborated by Steve Carlin, executive producer of Entertainment Productions, Inc., which produced *The $64,000 Question* and its spin-off *The $64,000 Challenge*. Carlin testified,

"There is a tradition in television ... of trying to please the client. We were willing to please the client."

From Andrew Tobias's biography of Charles Revson, *Fire and Ice*:

> Martin [Revson] admitted that he would voice opinions at these meetings as to which contestants had audience appeal and which he hoped would lose. He admitted that his opinions could be forcefully stated. But he claimed to have no idea that his wishes would be taken as orders, or that the producers had some way of carrying them out. Neither was he apparently surprised to notice, as the weeks and months went on, the remarkable consistency with which his idle wishes, expressed innocently at these meetings, seemed to be fulfilled.[29]

Charles Revson was the recipient of some particularly pointed grilling by Congressman Walter Rogers of Texas, and ended up saying without a full admission what had been observed about sponsor control of television game shows for years: that it was the sponsor who had the final say, and so when things went wrong, the sponsor had to shoulder some of the blame, whether the culpability was explicit or implicit:

> ROGERS: You have branded this, you and your brother both branded this as a deceitful practice and a reprehensible practice. Yet you are willing to accept the profits from it and let the contestants take all of the blame. Both of you said you had nothing to do with the running of it. The most you did was to make suggestions, isn't that correct?
> REVSON: Yes, sir.
> ROGERS: Were those suggestions subtle suggestions, Mr. Revson?
> REVSON: The suggestions made as far as I am concerned had no relativity to that.
> ROGERS: You mean they were about as subtle as a blow by a baseball bat?
> REVSON: I certainly do not.
> ROGERS: That is what the evidence would indicate, as you know. You heard the testimony.... It would indicate [that] when ... Mr. Martin Revson made a suggestion, there was not any question in his mind or anyone else's mind as to what he meant and what he intended to have.
> REVSON: That is correct.
> ROGERS: That is actually what happened. A suggestion was made and you expected it to be carried out?
> REVSON: Pardon me?
> ROGERS: A suggestion that was made in one of these meetings you expected to be carried out, didn't you?
> REVSON: I didn't get the first part, then. I thought I got it.
> ROGERS: I say, that in these meetings you had, when you made a suggestion, which you claim you had the right to do under your contract, you expected that suggestion to be carried out, didn't you?
> REVSON: The few infrequent times that I was there, I don't remember discussing anything about a contestant or anything like that. The times that I would be in there would have relation to the format of the show, or possibly a change

in the plateau aspects of the money part, or the show could be more interesting, or something such as that.³⁰

In other words: "Pin it on my brother, not me. I just run the company."

Having cast the advertising industry in a fairly harsh light throughout this chapter, and with an apology-in-apostrophe to the author's late father, who worked as a commercial artist for a small Memphis advertising agency, I give the last word in this chapter to two prominent ad men who, by the early 1960s, had had their fill of disparaging comments about an area of enterprising American commerce without which, they contended, the country could not survive. The first from the president of the D'Arcy advertising agency, Harry W. Chesley: "Let's recognize that the fuzzy thinking of some of our critics both inside and outside government has already placed us at a disadvantage—that it already represents an even more serious threat than anything Russia can do abroad or that inflation or recession can do at home."³¹

Max Banzhaf, advertising director for the Armstrong Cork Company, unfurled—metaphorically speaking—an even larger American flag when he said, "Advertising is under attack because it represents a skirmish which must be fought in the battle of big government versus private enterprise—the battle between the advocates of state socialism and the advocates of free enterprise, the free market economy and individual liberty."³²

Or rather: Ignore the First Amendment and keep your criticism of Aunt Jemima; Speedy, the Alka-Seltzer boy; and the Jolly Green Giant to yourselves. You *do* want to keep the Giant jolly don't you?

◈ 12 ◈

Walpurgisnacht

> It went to ridiculous extremes. We had a lipstick shade called Red Caviar, and people said we were pro-communist. I remember our TV executive was on the phone with this woman. He was holding the phone about a foot away from his ear. Finally, he said, "Madame, do you shop at Macy's? What about their red star?"
>
> —Tom Quinlan, marketing director at Revlon[1]

One of the biggest quiz show-related casualties of the McCarthy-communist witch hunt era was *What's My Line?* panelist Louis Untermeyer. The well-known poet, editor and anthologist, who was with the show from its first broadcast on February 2, 1950, was ignominiously terminated on March 11 of the following year. Untermeyer had the same pun-loving sense of humor as his replacement, Bennett Cerf. Cerf remembered that once Untermeyer had become implicated in the 1950s anti-communist hysteria, right-wing organizations demanded his removal from the panel. War veterans picketed the show's live broadcasts and the pressure became, according to Cerf, too great for sponsor Jules Montenier to withstand. "After all," the antiperspirant king is reputed to have said, "I can't afford to have my product picketed."[2]

Franklin Heller, CBS director who worked on *What's My Line?*, put it succinctly and somewhat callously: "Then Untermeyer got mixed up with McCarthy, and he was dropped."[3] An interpretation of callousness on the part of everyone affiliated with the show was confirmed by Untermeyer in 1977:

> Besides murmurs of personal regret, no one connected with *What's My Line?* attempted to do anything on my behalf. Intimidated as they all were by McCarthyism (or sympathetic to it), the feeling must have been: the less said the better. I can't say Dorothy Kilgallen behaved worse than anyone else. There was little behavior.[4]

12. *Walpurgisnacht*

The truth of Untermeyer's firing from the show to please the pitchfork-brandishers (no hammers and sickles allowed) and the sponsor of the show that employed him doesn't permit such a facile dismissal as Heller's. In his memoir *Timebends: A Life*, playwright Arthur Miller, a friend and colleague of Untermeyer's, wrote that the editor's misfortune had largely to do with his having attended the 1949 Cultural and Scientific Conference for World Peace, held at the Waldorf Astoria Hotel. The gathering was a quixotic attempt to rescue the United States' wartime alliance with the Soviet Union as the increasingly gelid Cold War pushed the two nations farther apart. Miller wrote that "there [was] no denying the probability of retribution against the conference participants"—participants that included, in addition to Miller, Albert Einstein; Harvard astronomer Harlow Shapley; composer Aaron Copland; Congressmen Adam Clayton Powell Jr. and Vito Marcantonio; playwrights Clifford Odets and Lillian Hellman; novelist Norman Mailer; and poets Langston Hughes and Mark Van Doren (father of the 1950s' most famous game show contestant, Charles Van Doren), all of whom had their photographs published in *Life* magazine as "supporters and participants" of the conference, or in *Life*'s decidedly non-objective take on the gathering, "dupes and fellow travelers [who] dress up Communist fronts."[5]

Or, in Miller's words, "a veritable gallery of rogues."

Yet none of these socialists and other left-leaning men and women of national prominence suffered the kind of career assassination faced by Louis Untermeyer, who, to his grave misfortune, happened to be working less than a year later in the industry which, because of its strong commercial underpinnings, was most susceptible to backlash. At the nadir of those dark times, many TV and film actors, writers and directors did something that Untermeyer was unable to do: They fled back to the sanctuary of the theater, where even brazenly left-wing dramatists like Odets and Hellman could continue to work relatively unmolested. Miller himself enjoyed the political immunity of the legitimate stage. It was only five weeks after *Life* magazine pronounced Miller's *Death of a Saleman* "one of the finest tragedies written by an American" that the magazine lumped him, with journalistic contempt, into the "dupe" and "fellow traveler" category for having participated in the Waldorf Astoria conference. And yet Miller's own literary career remained untarnished by this supposed misstep.[6]

Miller wrote of his friend Louis that he had "instant recall of every joke and pun he had ever heard," and that he loved poetry and young women, but "not necessarily in that order." On his eighty-fifth birthday, as Miller told it, "Louis would say, 'I'm still chasing them. The only difference is that now I can't remember why'":

> I suppose his innocence was what left him so unprepared when one day he arrived as usual at the television studio an hour before the program began and was told by the producer that he was no longer on the show.... [He] went back to his apartment.... Louis didn't leave his apartment for almost a year and a half. An overwhelming and paralyzing fear had risen in him. More than a political fear, it was really that he had witnessed the tenuousness of the human connection and it had left him in terror. He had always loved a lot and been loved, especially on this TV program where his quips were vastly appreciated, and suddenly he had been thrown into the street, abolished.[7]

And yet as Americans in the entertainment industry were being hounded and harassed and losing their livelihoods as a result of tenuous accusations of disloyalty toward the United States, there was solid work being done by the Eisenhower administration to find and prosecute traffickers in actual Soviet espionage. Ike's assistant attorney general charged with going after Russian spies, William F. Tompkins, appeared on *To Tell the Truth* on June 24, 1958, after stepping down as the Department of Justice's Chief of Internal Security. Tompkins had, by that point, supervised the conviction of over 100 Communist Party leaders for illegal and subversive activities. One of his better-known courtroom victories involved Soviet spymaster Rudolf Abel (born Willie Fisher), who, finding himself luckier than Julius and Ethel Rosenberg in being spared the death penalty, was ready and available when, on February 10, 1962, he was exchanged for the Soviet-captured American spy-plane pilot Francis Gary Powers. (The exchange took place on the Glienicke Bridge, which became known during the Cold War as the "Bridge of Spies," the incident being dramatized a few decades later by Steven Spielberg in his film of the same name. Tom Hanks played James Donovan, Abel's lawyer and negotiator of the exchange. Mark Rylance won numerous awards for his portrayal of Abel, including an Oscar. Stephen Kunken played Tompkins.)

Although Edward R. Murrow's documentary series *See It Now* had been on the air for over a year when the legendary broadcaster made a December 7, 1952, appearance as a *What's My Line?* mystery guest, it would be another 15 months before Murrow's special broadcast "A Report on Senator Joseph McCarthy" would do so much damage to the Senator's reputation that he was never able to recover. The country, which had finally had its fill of the crippling lies and innuendo emanating from McCarthy and his forces, expressed their agreement with the broadcast via tens of thousands of letters, telegrams and phone calls, running, all told, 15 to 1 in favor of Murrow's show's decision to confront McCarthy.[8]

To some in the broadcast industry, the "Red Scare" appeared to have come out of nowhere. Those with high-profile jobs—actors, entertainers, writers and directors—felt in some ways that they had woken one morning to find that the ground beneath them had shifted in a profound and frightening way. But in truth, the anti-communist crusade had started several years before it succeeded in getting its tentacles into American television. The House Un-American Activities Committee was created in 1938 for the purpose of investigating citizens and organizations suspected of having communist ties, even as Lady Liberty was headed down the aisle for her World War II marriage of convenience to Papa Joe Stalin. The campaign hit its stride after the war when it went after Hollywood, giving fresh currency to the word *blacklist*.

In a period in which commercial television was taking its first baby steps, industry leaders were already glancing nervously over their shoulders. General David Sarnoff, chairman of the board of RCA—which begot NBC—made certain that everyone knew exactly what side he and the National Broadcasting Company were on: He publicly declared in 1950, "The communists smother the truth with their falsehoods. Through radio and television, the motion picture and the printed word, we have a great opportunity to reveal the truth to the rest of the world. We must expose [their] lies and spike [their] false propaganda."[9]

In 1949, FBI director J. Edgar Hoover opened the door to the abuse of human rights that was sure to follow any ramping-up of anti-communist activism when he stated that the advent of television "offers a new adjunct to law and order, and I see in this new medium an instrumentality of great aid and assistance in the future protection of society."[10]

So by all means, gentlemen, *let the witch hunts begin*!

One of those who appeared to have done his part for the good of the hunt was TV critic Jack O'Brian, mystery guest on the November 4, 1956, *What's My Line?* As documented in the George Clooney-directed 2005 film *Good Night, and Good Luck*, O'Brian, who worked for the same paper as panelist Dorothy Kilgallen, the *New York Journal American*, was among the most tenacious of those newspapermen making charges of communist ties against members of the TV industry, and against CBS in particular. *Good Night, and Good Luck* alleges that it was a series of published attacks by O'Brian against WCBS correspondent Don Hollenbeck that either led to or contributed to his suicide. Luckily for O'Brian, *I've Got a Secret* panelist Henry Morgan wasn't subbing on *What's My Line?* for that 1956 broadcast (something he did eight different times), since the columnist, whom Morgan described as "a popeyed little golliwog [who] had the intriguing habit of saving the country from Godless Red Communists," had also gone after Morgan, and the cantankerous humorist wouldn't have pretended otherwise.[11]

O'Brian, by the way, was also known for helping to bring the rigging of NBC's *Twenty-One* and other quiz shows to light in 1958. It was O'Brian who first published Herb Stempel's claim of fixing by the show's producers. Following the death of Ms. Kilgallen on November 8, 1964, the journalist took over her "Voice of Broadway" column.

McCarthy was invoked slyly and repeatedly throughout the broadcasts of *What's My Line?* which coincided with the Army-McCarthy hearings in 1954. Though the hearings of the Senate's Subcommittee on Investigations convened on March 16, it was their live gavel-to-gavel coverage on ABC and DuMont from April 22 to June 17 which became "appointment television" for those Americans who owned a TV receiver or at least had access to one.[12] When emcee John Charles Daly went into a private *tête à tête* with a "lady trolley driver" on the show's May 30 broadcast, Steve Allen joked, "Just like Cohn and McCarthy." One of the purposes of the hearings was to investigate charges that chief committee counsel Roy Cohn had pressured the Army into giving preferential treatment to his friend (and possible crush) David Schine, a former McCarthy aide. During the hearings, Cohn was frequently picked up by TV cameras whispering into the Senator's ear.

Two weeks earlier, Dorothy Kilgallen at one point appropriated the most overused phrase of the hearings when she called out, "Point of order!" Steve Allen had some fun with, "Can we have that read back, please?" and the producers of the show got into the spirit by bringing on the manager of a "pizza pie" factory (in the parlance of the '50s, a whole pizza was always a *pie*). The gentleman was the spittin' image of Senator Joseph McCarthy. (*What's My Line?* did something identical later in the decade, when they produced a gentleman who was a dead ringer for Soviet leader Khrushchev.)

On the show's May 23 telecast, Lt. Lewis Disney stumped the panel with his "line": "head of the uniformed guards at the Army-McCarthy hearings." Chairman of the hearings Karl E. Mundt had his turn on the show on June 27. Regular panelist and resident punster Bennett Cerf, after correctly identifying the mystery challenger, wisecracked that in the publishing business, "we've even named something after him: the 'Book of the Mundt Club.'"

What's My Line? executive producer Gil Fates wrote with unbridled resentment about what shows like his were up against, trying to keep sponsor and network happy, while reining in the indignation of having to submit their casting decisions to what seemed like cruel and arbitrary outside scrutiny:

> There was a vice-president at CBS (I'm sure he had a counterpart at each of the other networks) with whom I had to check the name of every prospective guest on our shows. We would call him and he would call back in an hour or so with a "no problem" or a "could be trouble." Sometimes names previously unchallenged would become "not recommended" and names still prominent on the printed blacklist would be okayed. It was very mystifying until we found out that some people had found methods of buying their way off the list.[13]

Fates doesn't even mention the overall climate of paranoia that propelled CBS to establish a loyalty oath in 1950, and then in 1951 to appoint an executive in charge of "security." Some of Fates' colleagues called him, with wry contempt, "vice-president in charge of treason."[14]

Henry Morgan's entanglements with the blacklist—especially after finding his name inside the dreaded publication *Red Channels*—was both typical and atypical of what entertainment professionals, a good many of them employed in the radio and TV industry, were put through.[15] *Red Channels* purportedly only listed "Red Fascists and their sympathizers" but, like the other blacklists then being compiled, the net was cast wide and benefit of the doubt seldom applied. As a result, a lot of the individuals who wound up on the list were guilty only of the crime of having been in the wrong place at the wrong time, having been friends with the wrong person, having been married or otherwise related to someone with communist ties or, as Nancy Davis discovered when she accidentally turned up on a Hollywood *liste noir*, due to confusion between two people with the same name. (SAG president Ronald Reagan fixed the problem and then asked Nancy to marry him.)

There were several groups gunning for people in the film-TV-radio business. The conservative American Legion's "Americanism Division" had issued its own blacklist in 1949. *Red Channels*, which focused exclusively on broadcasting, was put out by a group called American Business Consultants, Inc. Formed in 1947, the organization, run by a "group of former FBI men," published a weekly newsletter called *Counterattack: The Newsletter of Facts to Combat Communism*. Within two years of its publication and the investigative service it also offered, the group appeared to be making $200,000 annually for its "assistance."[16] Stepping things up a notch, they brought out *Red Channels* on June 22, 1950.

When Morgan learned that his name was on the list of 151 "dangerous" individuals named in the publication, he came to understand why over the last several months he'd stopped getting calls for television jobs. In February 1952, he received a letter from a gentleman named Vincent Hartnett, who was heavily involved with the publication of *Red Channels* and would later found the anti-communist organization AWARE, Inc., which offered a "clearance" service to networks and advertisers for a fee.[17] The letter was accompanied by a "confidential memo," which itemized "reported affiliations on your part with communist fronts and causes," most of which had been left out of *Red Channels*. In other words: "We've got you over a barrel, so play ball with us, and let's see what we can do for you." The stick was obvious; the carrot was unique to Morgan. The letter went on:

> I wish to make it crystal clear that I am tendering you this opportunity to comment not because I have any obligation or desire of personal gain of any sort. I am acting out of a wish to protect you from undue hardship, in view of your position taken on January 24, 1952, a position which was productive of patriotic gains in the entertainment industry, no matter how belated.[18]

The "position" the magnanimous Mr. Hartnett was referring to was a speech Morgan gave at a meeting of AFTRA (the American Federation of Television and Radio Artists) which, according to Morgan, "made a nice impression on the blacklist folks."[19] Morgan had been asked to take the floor at the meeting to condemn efforts by a blacklisted actor named Philip Loeb, late of the soapy sitcom *The Goldbergs*, to rally the union behind his efforts to get back on the show. Morgan decided not to deliver the speech that had been prepared for him by the head of the American Legion's "Americanism Committee," which began, "This rotten swine..." and instead pen his own. But the speech Morgan came up with on his own did just as much damage to Loeb. Morgan's reward was the offer of a course of rehabilitation by which he could get himself back in the broadcasting saddle.[20]

This involved mandatory attendance at a Park Avenue cocktail party at which "shoulder-to-shoulder, cigarette-to-cigarette and drink-to-drink stood every professional anti-communist in the Western World. There were the people who made a living from it." (Both from the sale of their publications and the fees required to "clear" actors, writers, directors and

12. *Walpurgisnacht*

musicians whose talents were needed by the various producers, packagers and networks.) "There were perhaps a hundred and fifty of them," Morgan wrote in the chapter of his autobiography aptly entitled "Kindergarten Kafka," "smug and creepy, and happy to be in one another's company. I had trapped myself." He continued:

> I said to the man on my right, "Well, I'll tell you one person I really can't stand. Whittaker Chambers."
>
> The man smiled and reached across me to tap another guy on the shoulder. A short, rumpled man turned toward us. The guy on my right said, "Mr. Morgan ... I'd like you to meet Whittaker Chambers."[21]

In other words, Henry Morgan had done what he needed to do to protect his career. A lot of other broadcast professionals did the same. However, for some, like Philip Loeb and Louis Untermeyer, the chance for redemption and rehabilitation was never offered. As a result, Loeb went into a depression spiral that ended in suicide.

Broadcasting history scholar J. Fred MacDonald uses the jargon of the day to classify the "political deviants" who were targeted by the putative anti-communist campaign:

> ... card carrying members (actually dues-paying members of the CPUSA), "dupes" (those fooled into supporting Red goals without realizing the error of their ways), "Pinkos" (those who were leftist but not red enough) [and] "Comsymps" or "fellow travelers" (those who sympathized with Communist ends without joining the party).[22]

The blacklist made no apologies about going after the "Pinkos"—the public figures in the entertainment industry who supported or espoused progressive causes. While those who were singled out argued the very real possibility that the storm of anti-communism fervor in the country was largely a tool used by American conservatives to dismantle the New Deal, stymie the growing civil rights movement, and obstruct the advance of other left-wing causes, those who were behind the witch hunts turned those arguments in on themselves. In Hartnett's introduction to *Red Channels*, he volleyed the countercharge that it was those very left-wing causes that *attracted* Communist Party organizers; liberal gatherings (like the Waldorf Astoria conference of 1949) were but facilitating venues for the spread of anti–Americanism among liberal chumps.

> No cause which seems calculated to arouse support among people in show business is ignored: the overthrow of the Franco dictatorship, the fight against anti–Semitism and Jim Crow, civil rights, world peace, the outlawing of the H-bomb are all used. Around such pretended objectives, the hard core of Party organizers gather a

swarm of "reliable" and well-intended "liberals," to exploit their names and their energies.²³

Which, perhaps, is the reason several high-profile black entertainers and writers, each working to advance civil rights for members of their race, found themselves blacklisted, Canada Lee, Paul Robeson, Richard Wright, Langston Hughes, Harry Belafonte, Ossie Davis and Ruby Dee among them.²⁴

Also, because of a long history of liberal activism in the American Jewish community, a large number of Jewish-Americans working in TV and radio in the 1950s also found their professional reputations besmirched (or far worse). Playwright and game show panelist Abe Burrows and stage actor Martin Gabel (husband of Arlene Francis and a frequent substitute panelist on *What's My Line?*) were placed on the *Red Channels* list in the company of a number of other prominent Jews in the entertainment industry—everyone from Pulitzer Prize and Academy Award–winning composer Aaron Copland to writer Dorothy Parker to beloved stage and screen actress Judy Holliday.²⁵

When in 1953 the House Un-American Activities Committee set up shop in Hollywood, a subpoena went out for the Jewish orchestra leader of *You Bet Your Life*, Jerry Fielding, who confessed to Hector Arce, co-author with Groucho Marx of the 1976 book *The Secret Word Is Groucho*, that of the 240 communist, "communist front," "fellow traveling" or otherwise allegedly un–American organizations, "I belonged to at least 60 of them."²⁶ Rather than wait to see how the show would react to his appearance before the committee—an appearance in which he intended to be an unfriendly witness and cloak himself in the Fifth Amendment—Fielding quit the show.

And no one tried to stop him.

Years later, when Fielding and *You Bet Your Life* director Robert Dwan looked back on the orchestra leader's departure, it came to light that NBC had been nervous about the possibility that Groucho Marx might be dragged before the committee. After all, Marx had been a member of at least one organization on the subversive list: the Independent Citizens Committee of the Arts, Sciences & Professions.²⁷ Fielding didn't want to put either Groucho or any of his other friends in hot water with the committee. Even so, taking the Fifth ended all chances of Jerry Fielding ever returning to the show. According to Dwan, producer John Guedel said the order to remove its orchestra leader came down from the show's long-time sponsor, the DeSoto Division of the Chrysler Corporation.²⁸

12. Walpurgisnacht

Fielding had just beat everyone to the punch.

Dwan remembered how vulnerable they had all felt at the time: network personnel, the account executives at the advertising agency, Groucho, producer Guedel and, not least of all, Dwan himself. "We were all vulnerable because everyone was vulnerable. The foe was faceless, something called public reaction. The weapon of the zealots was the threat of a boycott." Dwan wondered: "Would people stop buying DeSotos because Jerry Fielding took the Fifth Amendment? Would people stop watching *You Bet Your Life*?"[29]

No, and no.

Fielding went on to a long career in music. He conducted in Las Vegas, and later wrote film scores, three of which were Oscar-nominated. With the end of the blacklist, he wound up back in television composing music for *Mission: Impossible* and *Star Trek*.

He was also hired to conduct an orchestra that toured military bases and other government installations for the purpose of selling U.S. Government Bonds for the Treasury Department. This was something that Dwan said Fielding found bitterly amusing: "It was okay for me to work for the United States Government, but not the Chrysler Corporation on a quiz show."[30]

Gentiles weren't spared either. Leon Janney (born Leon Ramon), panelist on ABC's *Think Fast* and host of NBC's *Stop Me If You've Heard This One* (both broadcast in the late 1940s), landed on the blacklist in all likelihood because of his fluency in Russian. A voice actor who learned the language to help him play Russian characters, Janney's language skills had been considered an asset to the U.S. government during World War II; but later, in the anti–Soviet maelstrom of the 1950s, it might very well have been turned against him.[31]

There might have been something in the water at ABC in 1949 and 1950, because the host of *Think Fast* also found herself listed among the 151 television and radio folk cited by *Red Channels* for possible communist ties: Gypsy Rose Lee, actress and famed former ecdysiast. One cannot help wondering if, as the list was being prepared, one of the former FBI agents putting it together (three gentlemen by the names of Kenneth M. Biery, John G. Keenan and Theodore C. Kirkpatrick) simply shrugged at his cohorts and said, "What the heck. Let's just toss in the stripper for kicks."[32]

Orson Bean, panelist and celebrity player on numerous game shows from the '50s through the '80s, including 110 appearances on *To Tell the*

Truth, was probably doomed to the dreaded list from birth; his father, George Burrows, was a founding member of the ACLU and a fundraiser for the Scottsboro Boys. (Bean's father appeared on the July 5, 1965, *To Tell the Truth*, with Bean obviously disqualifying himself from the guessing panel.) What incensed Orson Bean the most about the modus operandi of those involved in the blacklist was its shakedown component:

> [It] was a protection racket. The networks had to pay 50 bucks a head to clear people and they would have to do it week after week. If someone was a series regular, they had to pay to clear them *again* the next week. So they didn't want the blacklist, but it was Campbell's Soup and people like that who did the blacklist. The reason the blacklist never took hold on Broadway was because there were not sponsors.[33]

But there were a few whose fame and popularity protected them. Even though proof existed of former communist ties or close affiliation with known communists, nothing was taken from members of this small privileged group, and nothing asked of them.

Henry Morgan writes about a red tinge to Lucille Ball that had nothing to do with her hair:

> There was a flurry in 1952 when it was revealed to the House Committee on Un-American Activities that Lucille Ball's father had been a declared Socialist and an admitted contributor to the Socialist Party. What happened was that when these facts were revealed, the members of the Committee just shrugged, looked at one another and then laughed. I mean, after all, *Lucille Ball*, for chrissake. And that was the end of that.[34]

What Morgan neglected to mention is that Ball had in fact registered as a Communist Party member herself in 1936. But Morgan's point still held. "The lesson learned," Thomas Doherty observed in his book *Cool War, Cool Medium: Television, McCarthyism, and American Culture*, "was that while the small fry were hooked and gutted, the big fish would be tossed back."[35]

Morgan also wrote about Ruth Cosgrove, secretary of a post of the American Legion that had been, in Morgan's words, "dominated by communists." When Morgan (also a member of this post) recognized the political leanings of this particular group of legionnaires (odd, for a veterans' group that had long been virulently anti-communist—but Morgan doesn't elaborate on this paradox), he left. Ms. Cosgrove left. And Milton Berle, who married Ms. Cosgrove, was never called on the carpet for having married a fellow traveler.[36]

He *was* Mr. Television, after all.

Some historians peg the end of the blacklist to Kirk Douglas's decision

12. Walpurgisnacht

to give public credit to Dalton Trumbo for writing the screenplay to 1960's *Spartacus*. Since 1947, Trumbo, blacklisted as one of the Hollywood Ten, had written as many as 30 screenplays, all without credit. Now he was being allowed to come out into the light, and Douglas dared anyone to give him trouble.[37]

Others attribute the end of the blacklist to the lawsuit won by radio personality John Henry Faulk in 1962. Faulk also appeared as a celebrity panelist on the news-related game show *It's News to Me* in the early '50s. The Texas-born broadcast raconteur was fired by CBS Radio after he was targeted by AWARE and lost the sponsor for his radio show, *Johnny's Front Porch*. The charge: that he had once attended a dinner at the United Nations for Soviet foreign minister Andrei A. Gromyko. The *actual* crime: that Faulk, CBS news correspondent Charles Collingwood and others who opposed the blacklist gained control of the leadership of AFTRA from officers backed by AWARE in 1955. It was an anti-blacklist coup that took place in the union. And Faulk was branded a communist in retaliation, AWARE listing him in their February 1956 pamphlet. But unlike almost everyone else in the industry who faced accusation, innuendo and efforts to extort money for their "clearing" and/or turn in others of a suspiciously red or pink tint, Faulk decided to retaliate. He got himself a good lawyer and sued AWARE in 1957. The attorney was Louis Nizer, who for a number of years was listed by *Guinness Book of World Records* as the "highest-paid lawyer in the world."

The lawsuit, which was stalled for several years by attorneys for AWARE (including McCarthy's own Roy Cohn), resulted in the largest libel judgment in history up to that point, $3.5 million. According to Faulk, his willingness to take on the culture of destruction and intimidation that characterized the 1950s TV industry was galling to the powers-that-were, not only because of the audacity of what he was doing, but because of who he was. "It was one thing to be a radical Jew from the Bronx, but a down-home, church-going boy (like me)?" he waxed later. "They hated me worse than anyone. They had to get me."[38]

Though an appeals court lowered the amount of the judgment, and legal fees and related debts left him with only $75,000, Faulk had succeeded. His struggle was supported by quiz show pioneer Parks Johnson (*Vox Pop*) and Walter Cronkite, who in the 1950s had acted as emcee for *It's News to Me* and served as a judge for *Two for the Money*, in addition to making celebrity guest appearances on *What's My Line?* and *I've Got a Secret*.

The courtroom win represented a public victory for Faulk. But there was a private one as well. One of the men who had lost his seat on the 35-member AFTRA board when Faulk and company took over was also one of the staunchest supporters of the blacklist and its efforts to cleanse the broadcast industry of purported communist subversion: Bud Collyer. The longtime host of two of the most popular shows from the Goodson-Todman stable, *Beat the Clock* and *To Tell the Truth*, must have assumed that John Henry Faulk would receive his comeuppance for sidelining the "patriotic" wing of the industry. And Faulk did struggle financially for several years as he awaited his day in court. But in the end he triumphed, and even got an Emmy-winning TV movie made about his experience, *Fear on Trial*, taken from the same-name book he wrote. Faulk never returned to game shows, but he did get a recurring storytelling gig on the cornpone, down-home variety show *Hee Haw* from 1975 to 1982.[39]

For Collyer's part, he continued to host *To Tell the Truth* until a year before his death in 1969, his career unaffected by his anti-communism fervor.

The result of Faulk's courtroom victory was that the blacklisters and all those who abided by their wishes were put on notice that they could be legally liable for the damage caused by their recklessness. Still, there was long-lasting fallout in the industry. Those who refused to cooperate with the House Un-American Activities Committee or jump through all the hoops placed before them by groups like the American Legion, AWARE and the publishers of *Counterattack* and *Red Channels* severed their friendships and professional relationships with those who sold out. As late as 1999, director Elia Kazan, called to the stage of that year's Academy Awards broadcast, was given a standing ovation by some of the Academy members in recognition of his powerful body of work, while other audience members remained in their seats, some with arms folded and faces set in unforgiving scowls.[40] Folk singer and actor Burl Ives, whose name turned up in *Red Channels*, saved his career by naming names. As a result, he was able to continue acting in films (and winning awards for his performances), as well as appearing as guest on the TV game shows *What's My Line?* and *High Low*. But there was a price to be paid. Fellow folk singer Pete Seeger accused Ives of betraying his colleagues and selfishly turning his back on the cause of cultural and political freedom. The two weren't reconciled for 41 years, when they finally made up to sing together at a benefit in New York.[41]

There were those who found it in their hearts to forgive. But never to forget.

12. Walpurgisnacht

One unsettling coda to this dark period in our nation's history comes courtesy of a survey conducted in 1954 by the Gallup Poll and the National Opinion Research Center, located at the University of Chicago. Its results, published in 1955 as *Communism, Conformity, and Civil Liberties: A Cross Section of the Nation Speaks Its Mind*, reveal that support for Edward R. Murrow in his joust with Senator McCarthy notwithstanding, America still had strong feelings about communism, born of a largely irrational fear of its influence and potential for government and societal infiltration.[42]

There had never been strong support for communism in the U.S. No communist had ever been elected to Congress. Even in the grimmest moments of the Great Depression, when struggling Americans might have been rethinking the effectiveness of their long-standing form of republican government, no Communist Party candidate for president ever received more than one quarter of one percent of the vote.[43] According to J. Ronald Oakley's detailed history of the decade, *God's Country*, Americans were "still worried about the communist menace and were still distorting its nature and influence," given the fact that over half of those who had been canvassed in the Gallup/NORC poll felt that communists should be thrown in jail, and rooted out, even if the result caused innocent people harm. An astounding 89 percent of respondents thought communists should be fired from college teaching positions. Over 60 percent were comfortable with removing books from library shelves if it was discovered that their authors were self-avowed communists; and 73 percent of those polled were okay with reporting possible communists among their friends and neighbors to the FBI.[44]

Yet, only three percent said they had ever known a communist.[45]

Although they'd heard that sometimes you can find them on the television...

◆ 13 ◆

Jackpot!

> What might be the final word on give-aways comes from TV comedy Writer-Director Nat (*Phil Silvers Show*) Hiken, who whimsically suggests a show called *A Million or Your Life*. "The contestant will stand in front of the TV camera and face two gun barrels. He will have a string leading to the triggers on the two barrels. One will be loaded with a dud containing a check for $1,000,000—the other with a live 37mm shell guaranteed to tear his head off. If he pulls the wrong string—kaputt!"
> —*Time*, September 3, 1956[1]

After years of economic depression and idled industrial plants, followed by a world war that required the conversion of factories from the manufacture of home goods to the building of bombs and tanks, all of America was ready for that long-promised postwar consumer spending spree. Which did come.

Just not as quickly as everyone would have liked.

It took time to retool the factories and then ramp up production so that shelves could again be fully stocked and new car lots once again filled to capacity. And inflationary pressures (too much money but too few goods) also put that spending spree off for a while. Americans with fat wallets, thanks to an industrious postwar economy, yearned for the nicer things they hadn't been able to buy for years. But when those things came on the market, they were initially too expensive—even for people with fat wallets. Things did get better, but for the remainder of the 1940s and the early part of the 1950s, there was only one place where you could get everything your heart desired: the radio and TV game show.

Game shows had the *best stuff*.

And with each passing year in the war recovery era, the prizes got bigger and more impressive. Though consumer envy grew, no one even thought of not tuning in. There was always a vicarious thrill attached to watching a game show contestant take home the store.

Quiz shows crowded the airwaves. By late 1957—their peak year on television—there were 37.5 hours of game programming airing each week. This translates to 75 different half-hour game show episodes broadcast weekly in that bumper year—both once-a-week prime time series and daytime series that aired each morning or afternoon.[2]

The winners of *The Big Payoff* were especially well-treated (although treating women especially well was the show's *raison d'être*). Lucky contestants received "stunning dresses," "chic hats by the world's greatest designers," matched luggage, hosiery, jewelry and lingerie. The "big payoff" was a trip to Paris, and "the breathtaking gift of a woman's dream: a beautiful mink coat."[3]

Bid 'n' Buy rewarded some of its winners Mercedes-Benz sports convertibles, an $11,000 Bergdorf-Goodman wardrobe and a trip to London to see *My Fair Lady*, its West End production having opened just a few weeks before *Bid 'n' Buy* went on the air in 1958.

The original *The Price is Right* had an even more impressive reputation for doling out outlandish loot. Winning contestants received for their shopping smarts such odd and arguably wonderful prizes as a part in the TV show *Jefferson Drum*,[4] a mile of hot dogs and a six-foot jar of mustard, a home soda fountain, a 16-foot Ferris wheel, a 1928 Rolls-Royce (with chauffeur), 12 jars of caviar and a case of champagne, a live Angus steer, a live peacock to go with a new color television set (this was, without doubt, when the show was being broadcast by NBC), a sable coat valued at $23,000, 50 pairs of shoes and 250 pairs of stockings to go with them, 100 shares of Union Pacific railroad stock, and an elephant, valued at $4000 and flown in from Kenya (which the contestant—a Texan, with apparently a few acres to his name—decided to keep).[5]

Even before television game shows had gotten a good foothold, radio quizzes were increasing the number of prizes lavished on winning contestants, and upgrading their valuation. Only three months after VJ Day, ABC brought out a program that was less game show and more early reality show: *Bride and Groom*. Couples got hitched in a chapel next to the studio and then within minutes were trotted in to answer questions about how they met and all the particulars of their engagement, in exchange for appliances and furnishings, many of which were still being rationed to less fortunate postwar newlyweds.[6]

When the show moved to television, first to CBS and then to NBC, the gifts kept coming.

A similar radio program, *Second Honeymoon*, was also all about the merchandise. And, one assumes, for the sake of convenience, it was broadcast from Bamberger's department store in downtown Newark, New Jersey.[7]

The creators of a different radio show, an ambitious couple of game show promoters with the familiar names Goodson and Todman, sought to add a little cachet to their new quizzer *Hit the Jackpot* by awarding their big winners $1000 worth of books, courtesy of the publishing house Rinehart & Co. This decision may have been in reaction to charges made in the press (and referenced by Todman in a 1949 article he wrote for *Variety*) that give-aways were "a form of lunacy for which give-away producers will be held accountable on the day of judgment."[8]

Perhaps the biggest prize-giver in the history of television game shows was *Queen for a Day*. With the exception of the interview portion of the show between master of ceremonies Jack Bailey and each of his four contestants, and then the time required for the studio audience to pick its winner by their applause, *Queen for a Day* was one long succession of commercials, both those of the "and now a word from our sponsor" variety, as well as those product plugs blatantly woven into the body of the show itself.

In spite of its long run, very few episodes of the Southern California–based *Queen for a Day* are available for viewing. However, a 1960 broadcast, which has been preserved, should be illustrative of the extremes to which video hucksterism could go. In a broadcast that lasted around 29 minutes, only ten and a half (roughly one-third of the show) were devoted to actual conversations between Bailey and the contestants. And it took only two and a half minutes for Bailey to recap each woman's qualifying tribulations and then allow the studio audience to cast their collective vote. No sooner had the winner been royally draped than the procession of prizes—presented as a series of micro-commercials—began. The following list of winner-boodle doesn't include the *real* commercials that nominally sponsored the show (the Pan American Coffee Bureau, Ex-Lax chocolate-flavored laxatives, Hartz Mountain Cat Yummies, Arrestin cough medicine, Sta-Puf laundry rinse and Borden Starlac non-fat dry milk):

- A private screening of the film *Spartacus* (members of its illustrious cast noted)
- An assortment of Merle Norman cosmetics
- A ladies' watch (the maker's name indiscernible)

13. Jackpot!

- Five off-the-rack dresses and accessories presented in a mini-fashion show
- An indeterminate number of pairs of Mojud nylons
- A pair of Sarah Coventry "starburst" ear rings
- A West Bend electric griddle
- A Hamilton Beach food converter
- A Hoover floor polisher
- A bottle of Fame perfume by Corday
- Four dozen roses from Carl's of Hollywood florist
- An Everson Jennings wheelchair (for the winner's son, who had cerebral palsy)
- Lunch at the Brown Derby restaurant
- A personalized tour of Universal-International studios
- Dinner at the Sportsmen's Lounge
- Attendance at the late show at the Crescendo nightclub starring Bob Newhart
- A Revere still camera and 777 Revere slide projector
- A weekend at the Jamaica Inn in Corona del Mar
- A Spiegel catalogue gift certificate
- Four Westinghouse small appliances
- A set of Club Aluminum cookware
- An Adler sewing machine and cabinet
- An Imperial dishwasher-dryer
- An Amana freezer
- $100 worth of records at House of Sight and Sound
- $100 worth of books at a local bookstore of the queen's son's choosing
- $100 worth of clothing at a men's clothing store (the name indiscernible)

Shows like *Queen for a Day* did their part to contribute to the rise in consumer spending after 1945, especially in the category of lower-priced household goods. Coincident to broadcasts of *Queen for a Day*'s wildly popular radio incarnation, consumer spending in this category increased 60 percent in the five years that followed the end of the war. Though this growth was attributable to a large degree to the end of wartime rationing and Americans being freed up to buy things again, spending on household goods in particular—the kind of small-ticket goods advertised on game shows—rose an impressive 240 percent.[9]

It was CBS's *The $64,000 Question*, which ushered in the era of the really big *money* TV quizzes. Although this show and its several imitators tried to emphasize the personalities of its contestants, and while many tuned in to root for their favorites and to vicariously match wits with the smart people on the screen, it was the unprecedented amount of money being given away that piqued viewer interest just as the proletariat down through the ages has always fascinated itself with the lives of the rich and famous ... famous quite often only because they are rich.[10]

An instant sensation, this summer replacement for the so-so sitcom *Life with Father* took only three weeks to fly past *I Love Lucy* and *The Ed Sullivan Show* to reach the #1 spot in the rankings, grabbing an incredible 84.8 share in the Trendex ratings. Sponsor Revlon experienced a 54 percent increase in sales. Its Living Lipstick flew off the shelves, literally leaving them empty.[11] In 1956, the company's net earnings after taxes were over $8,000,000, compared to $1,300,000 before it began sponsoring *The $64,000 Question*.[12] Richard A.R. Pinkham, one of the senior assistants to NBC's Pat Weaver, was as surprised as anyone else over the incredible early success of CBS's new quiz show, telling nervous NBC affiliates, "[It] falls into the category of the lucky break that hits broadcasting every couple of years and is almost wholly unpredictable."[13]

As evidence of the show's popularity, emcee Hal March's six-week leave of absence in the summer of 1957 to appear in the film *Hear Me Good* left the door open to clamoring requests by half of Hollywood to fill in for him. As a result, Charlton Heston, Gene Kelly, Celeste Holm, Ginger Rogers and Fred MacMurray all got to add the title "quizmaster" to their lengthy résumés.[14]

Quiz show winners were elevated to the status of national folk heroes. Their photographs graced magazine covers, while feature articles about them appeared in newspapers and magazines across America. Running counts of their weekly winnings were published in the papers as if they were baseball box scores.

In the May 25, 1985, *New York Times*, Maureen Dowd wrote a poignant elegy about one such hero, whose life came to a tragic end a few days earlier. At the age of ten, Lenny Ross won $100,000 on *The Big Surprise*. A year later he racked up another $64,000 on *The $64,000 Challenge*. A child prodigy with a special gift for understanding the workings of the stock market, he was honored for his stock-smarts by being the first outsider to ring the opening bell of the New York Stock Exchange.[15] His brilliant intellect and interest in politics and economics landed him jobs in the administrations of California Governor Jerry Brown and President Jimmy Carter. But the same "Whiz Kid" brain that made Ross a juvenile household name in the '50s later sent him into depression and despair over his inability to turn off its racing synaptic engine. The result was suicide at the age of 39.[16]

In a televised 1957 interview, 12-year-old Ross was asked by Mike Wallace if he minded not having a "normal" childhood, both because of his game show success and because of his above-average intellect. Ross refused to accept the premise of the question. Whether he'd succeeded on TV or not, he was, in his own mind, as normal a kid as he cared to be.[17] The culture of American game shows, and especially its lionization of the big jackpot winners, called into question preconceptions about big game show winners, including the idea of luck (shouldn't TV game show winners be considered the luckiest folks on the planet?), success (is doing well on a quiz show a measure of personal success?) and celebrity (should fame be aspired to or avoided for all the inconvenience, headache and heartbreak that might attend it?).

In the pre-broadcasting era, abstractions such as "phenomenal overnight success" and "instantaneous celebrity" were foreign to most Americans, whose lives were localized and parochial. The idea of having a national conversation along these lines was unfathomable. But this was a new America, its people having gathered themselves around the "box," in a formation of national community and cultural unification. In his *One Nation Under Television*, J. Fred MacDonald wrote of the promise television held for those who anticipated and welcomed its arrival—forging "a more perfect national consensus, spreading over regional, ethnic, religious, linguistic and cultural differences, creating a common 'language,' rooted in shared tastes and a popular desire to understand the world."[18] But there were weaknesses and fractures to this coalescence, and those elevated by the medium and lavished with all of its goodies found within it no cure for simple, human frailty.

And besides, the jackpots won by the Lenny Rosses and the Charles Van Dorens and the Teddy Nadlers (Nadler won the top prize of the era: $262,000 on *The $64,000 Challenge*) weren't even all they were cracked up to be. One of the dirty little secrets of the big money games (among several that came to light), and one that was a fairly open secret should anyone have been familiar with U.S. tax law in the 1950s: Game show jackpot winners took only a portion of that money home with them, thanks to a very stingy Uncle Sam. For example, an $8000 winner on *The $64,000*

Question had to give up $2000 in federal taxes. At the next level, $16,000, the IRS grabbed $4,640. Win $32,000 and a contestant gave up $11,910—over a third of his winnings. This was also one of the reasons some of those who were eligible to answer the final, eponymous question, declined. The show's first $64,000 winner, Marine Captain Richard S. McCutchen, was required by the strongly progressive tax code of the day to give nearly half of his winnings, $31,150, to the federal government. One didn't have to be a Quiz Kid to calculate that risking $20,090 (after-tax winnings at the $32,000 question level) to win only an additional $12,760 (the difference in after-tax winnings between the $32,000 level and the $64,000 level) just wasn't worth it. Of course, these calculations would have been made in the absence of game manipulation on the part of the show's operatives. In truth, a good many of *The $64,000 Question*'s contestants didn't have to make any calculations at all, because they were given clear guidance as to just how far they would be helped to advance and when it just might be wise for them to bow out.

Hollywood had its fun with the travails of a quiz show jackpot winner and his subsequent indebtedness to the U.S. government in the 1950 film *The Jackpot*. Just by answering his phone, Bill Lawrence (played by James Stewart) wins $24,000 worth of merchandise from a radio quiz show, which includes 7500 cans of soup, 1000 fruit trees, a diamond ring and the services of a French maid, an interior decorator and a portrait painter. Good luck for Bill turns to bad when he realizes he has to pay $7000 in income tax. He gets fired from his department store job for trying to raise money by selling some of his loot, he's arrested when he tries to fence the diamond ring, and to make matters worse, his wife suspects him of having an affair with the portrait painter.

Be careful what you never wished for.[19]

The television game show had, by 1958, hit the jackpot in the American consciousness. American capitalists couldn't have dreamed up a better example of the possible perquisites awaiting champions of the free enterprise system. But the riotous success of network game shows in mid-century America was more than just a propaganda tool. It became a cultural phenomenon, which, like all the other fads and trends of the decade, unified the country in a shared avocation: Baseball, Mom, apple pie and *The $64,000 Question*.

And there was even room for the kids.

◈ 14 ◈

What's the Matter with Kids Today?

> The children now love luxury. They have bad manners, contempt for authority; they show disrespect for elders and love chatter in place of exercise.
> —Socrates[1]

The word *teenage* has been with us since the early '20s, *teenager* since roughly the '40s, though it didn't come into wide usage until the mid–50s, around the same time America started paying heed to rock'n'roll, youthful angst and an uptick in juvenile delinquency. With the phenomenal profits raked in by the record companies and clothing manufacturers which targeted teenage consumers, those aged 13 to 19 had become an economic force to be reckoned with. Much of the concern, as well as the respect shown to young Americans for taking their destiny into their own hands, found its way into game shows, sometimes in ways that were supportive and affirming but just as often with all the animus of the proverbial geriatric fist-shaker guarding his front lawn.

It was customary for game show panelists, hosts and their predominantly post-teenage audiences to make known their displeasure with the corrupting influences of youth. But it went both ways. According to *You Bet Your Life* director Robert Dwan, on a February 1958 broadcast of the show, Groucho's voiced affection for a song written back in the 1930s (coincidentally called "The Object of My Affection") received a nice, concurring round of applause from the audience. But mixed in with the general approbation were some noticeable boos. They came from a few brazenly opinionated younger members of the audience. The boos were there because of Groucho's contention that the song was "as good today as it was 25 years ago, and a vast improvement over many of the songs that you hear now."[2]

Fightin' words, Groucho. Fightin' words.

Allen Freed, the disc jockey who coined the phrase "rock'n'roll," was featured on a March 1957 *To Tell the Truth*. Panelist Polly Bergen, only 26 at the time, decided to take the side of the panel's resident fogies, who were protesting and decrying all of that Elvis-engineered music of rebellion. She asked one of the two imposters:

> POLLY: Don't you feel guilty some time?
> IMPOSTER: About what?
> POLLY: Bringing about this whole terrible thing.

On March 9, 1958, partners Jerry Leiber and Mike Stoller took their turn at having their profession guessed on *What's My Line?*. Two of the decade's most successful rock'n'roll songwriters, they penned some of Elvis Presley and the Coasters' biggest hits. When Dorothy Kilgallen correctly guessed that the two young men made their living writing pop songs, she clutched her breast and cried out, "That inflicts pain!" Citizens of the 21st century can get only a small sense of how insurrectionary this music phenomenon was viewed by people of Ms. Kilgallen's generation, even though its television ambassadors—gentlemen like Messrs. Leiber and Stoller—couldn't have been by appearance and demeanor, any more cleancut and disarming.

The conversation between the two partners and show moderator John Charles Daly and the panel concluded:

> DALY: Actually the effect or the popularity [of rock'n'roll] is fascinating. "Hound Dog" has sold something like five million records, hasn't it?
> STOLLER: That's right.
> LEIBER: That's right.
> KILGALLEN: That's no excuse.
> [Later:]
> DALY: Congratulations to you. I hope you have the chance to enjoy it and go on and perhaps do more serious things in music.

Because, after all, who could ever believe Danny and the Juniors' songful contention the very next year that rock'n'roll "is here to stay"?

That inflicts pain!

Resistance to rock'n'roll by older generations of Americans became a running gag on *You Bet Your Life*. Groucho often found himself in the role of mediator. On some days, he could take the same potshots at the music as most everyone else past the age of 25, as demonstrated in his exchange with Roberta Rene, the 30-something president of the San Diego Elvis Presley Fan Club and defender of rock'n'roll musicians from coast to coast:

14. What's the Matter with Kids Today?

GROUCHO: Do you have any other interests?
RENE: You haven't mentioned Elvis Presley.
GROUCHO: I seldom do unless I stub my toe.

And after Ms. Rene explained that she was also honorary president of over 100 Southern California chapters of Elvis Presley fan clubs, Groucho came back with: "Well, I'd love to join the Elvis Presley Fan Club, Rene, but I'm too busy with my other groups. You see, I happen to be Sergeant of Arms of the Rudy Vallee Raccoon and Adenoid Club."

Most *You Bet Your Life* fans came to realize that Groucho's adolescent daughter Melinda (born when Groucho was 55) enjoyed rock'n'roll just like every other kid her age, and this fact gave her father a perspective on the music that most television personalities—even several decades his junior—did not have.

Ms. Rene was brought on the show to rebut strong comments against rock'n'roll made the week before by concert baritone John Charles Thomas. During the discussion, the singer doubled down, contending that rock'n'roll music was "just too frothy. It's like it has no truth in it. It has no expressive beauty." His comments the previous week had been even more dismissive:

> I know teenagers like it, but they also like watermelon and if you eat too much of that you'll get a tummy ache. The present-day jitterbug music seems to me to not have been written even in Tin Pan Alley. From the odor of it, I think most of it comes from the Chicago stock yards.

Rene was loaded for bear:

GROUCHO: Your name is...?
RENE: Roberta Rene and I'm mad.
GROUCHO: What is your reason for sticking up for rock'n'roll?
RENE: That doesn't make any difference whether I'm a teenager or not, Groucho. I think the world is changing. It *has* changed. It's going at a pretty fast pace. We've got to have the kind of music to go along with the trend we're living in. And all this malarkey and jazz, "unspeakable rock'n'roll," lewd, vulgar—what's it gonna do, "wreck the teenagers"—that's absolute malarkey. It is not so because you have *got* to love it.
GROUCHO: Whose records do you buy?
RENE: Elvis Presley. [*Gasps from the audience.*]
GROUCHO: Why do you pick Mr. Presley's records as opposed to Tommy Sands or Perry Como or Eddie Fisher or some of the other singers?
RENE: Because Elvis has the know-how and the gimmick to put this stuff over in the way that it ought to be done. He is a great outlet and release for every growing teenager today. I see nothing wrong with his music. I think it's great.

Perhaps in an effort to offset growing reports of juvenile delinquency, *I've Got a Secret* decided to devote its whole March 26, 1958, episode to "teenage appreciation." Garry Moore introduced the program by telling his audience, "We're meeting some of our country's most important natural resources." He rattled off stats that cast American youth in the most positive light possible:

> There are more than 16 million of them in the United States. Almost ten million of them work at either full or part-time jobs. Each year they save or spend more than nine billion dollars. Sixty-one percent of them go to church regularly and that figure is increasing every year. Seventy-eight percent of them read books in addition to their regular schoolwork.

The show was largely devoted to showcasing the talents of nine special teens. Among them were several young Americans who would go on to great fame and accomplishment in their lives, and a couple who were already famous in the there-and-then. Teenage actress Carol Lynley was appearing at the time on Broadway in *Blue Denim,* an unflinching look at teen pregnancy and abortion. It was later made into a film, which also starred Lynley. In keeping with the times, the word "abortion" was excised from the screenplay, and whereas the character portrayed by Lynley in the play ultimately had an abortion, her film counterpart did not. (Censorship in movies and television was still firmly in place in the late '50s.)

The ennead of gifted teens included 19-year-old basketball player Oscar Robertson, then playing for the University of Cincinnati. He later played point guard for the Cincinnati Royals and Milwaukee Bucks. He was a 12-time All-Star, an 11-time member of the All–NBA team, and is the only player in NBA history to average a triple-double for a season.

Sixteen-year-old songwriter prodigy Paul Anka already had two one-million sellers with "Diana" and "You Are My Destiny," and sang (or, rather, lip-synced) his latest, "Let the Bells Keep Ringing." (By either design or coincidence, teenage America's favorite adult authority figure, Dick Clark, was present that night as a member of the celebrity panel.)

A chess whiz from Brooklyn, who at 15 was both the United States chess champion and the youngest grandmaster up to that time, had the chance to tell Garry Moore about the invitation he'd received to attend the World Youth and Student Festival in Moscow. His name was Bobby Fischer, and Moore surprised him with the announcement that the show would pay for his sister and him to fly to the USSR so he could participate.

In the spirit of giving American kids—both teens and those of the

14. What's the Matter with Kids Today?

pre-pubescent variety—their own voice and constituency in the game show arena, there were several shows, besides *Quiz Kids,* geared to young Americans (as well as to anyone, for that matter, interested in watching kids playing games on the small screen). One of TV's earliest quizzers, *Americana*—premiering in December 1947 on NBC—switched three months later from an adult celebrity panel to one which included five bright high school students, called the "board of experts." The teens answered questions on American history and folklore as skillfully as did their adult predecessors.

Other game shows that targeted a young viewing market were *Funny Boners* (a junior version of *Truth or Consequences*), *Giant Step* (contestants from seven to 17 playing for college tuition and an all-expense-paid trip anywhere in the world after high school graduation) and *It's a Hit* (a quizzer with a baseball-playing format).

In truth, teenagers, and adolescents for that matter, were anything but radical during the 1950s and posed little threat as a demographic to the country at large. J. Ronald Oakley argued that if there was anything wrong with the kids of the '50s, it was the fact that they were fairly humdrum. Fifties teens were big consumers (spending around $75 million a year just on records), politically conservative (or simply politically unengaged), conventionally religious, and somewhat prudish when it came to views on sex. Not only weren't they rebels, but they actually *had* a cause: keeping their noses clean, getting good grades, landing a good job, making a good marital match, having several kids and living happily ever after in a comfortable house in the 'burbs. In short, teenagers in the 1950s, unlike their radical younger siblings in the 1960s, just wanted a sliver of the American dream, even if that dream was somewhat unimaginative and uninspiring.[3]

And as the first generation of Americans to grow up with television, they watched a lot of it. And they were certainly *on* lots of TV shows. Especially game shows.

And what of the larger context—the families from which these teenagers came? Game shows of the 1950s give us a very good look at mid-century American family dynamics, and with far more accuracy and trenchancy than family photo albums, home movies and "Wish You Were Here" postcards and letters could offer. On television, parents and children faced cameras and studio lights in imposed settings that sometimes created the opposite of a realistic family paradigm, but just as often cut to the meat of relationships that were never perfect, were frequently quite funny, and always very American. *Beat the Clock* generally involved contestant partnerships between husbands and wives, but it had plenty of room for the couple's kids to come on stage and watch Mom and Dad make temporary fools out of themselves before millions of American viewers. *There's One in Every Family* highlighted family members with special attributes, talents or accomplishments to their credit.

Keep It in the Family (1957–58), a forerunner of *Family Feud*, pitted two families against each other, each bidding for control of the questions. The show appears to have been completely scripted, with the youngest members of the two families receiving helpful prodding from emcee Bill Nimmo, and the older members expressing themselves with dubitable cleverness. When one of the "moms" was asked about her line of work, she replied, without skipping a beat, "I'm superintendent in charge of dishwashing, ironing, cooking, cleaning, sewing, painting and plastering." *Keep It in the Family* was one of a large number of game shows that served largely as advertising vehicles for a litany of sponsors, with every successfully played five-part question resulting in a lengthy prize-package-presentation interlude.

With the exception of the agony shows, the heartbreak of infidelity wasn't the usual sort of thing to find expression in the context of a TV game show (in which contestants—even those related to one another—were obliged to pretend that all was wine and roses between them). But it did turn up on occasion among the 4000 letters that came each week to *I've Got a Secret*. The confessional nature of the letters, each suggesting that his or her "secret" might be worth sharing with the show's millions of viewers, sometimes crossed the line into the creepy and tragic. Producer Allan Sherman remembered one letter in particular:

> At first I felt guilty and couldn't eat or sleep and lost weight but now I am feeling better and like to think of our times together as I feel I deserved them. I hope my god will understand because my wife never will. I even told my wife I hate her looks now. I don't even want her to have new clothes. My new love has had four beautiful coats this year and I smile as I see her wear them. This is my secret.[4]

Thanks for sharing. Bath anyone?

◆ 15 ◆

The Love That Dare Not Speak Its Name

Don't you like girls?—Groucho Marx

LGBTQ people didn't exist in the United States in the 1950s. At least that's what anyone watching television in the mid–20th century might take away from their viewing experience. Granted, the country had a long way to go in acknowledging the civil rights of those Americans who didn't happen to be born straight. Formed in 1950, the Mattachine Society, one of the gay rights movement's earliest advocacy organizations, wasn't that widely known through the decade, and struggled to disseminate its message in a climate of societal antipathy toward gay people.

There was, however, one place where the existence of homosexual Americans *was* acknowledged.

Just not to their benefit.

There was a concerted effort in the 1950s to remove homosexuals from all federal government employment. This campaign—known as the "Lavender Scare"—comported with the routing of communists (far more likely: *alleged* communists) from all the nooks and crannies of the federal bureaucracy. Throughout the decade, the result was mass firings of presumed gay federal workers, the justification being that homosexuals were thought to be security risks, susceptible to blackmail and, even more troubling, that gay people, because of their reputed "perversion," were likely to be communist sympathizers (a familiar trope in Marxistphobic 1950s America). In 1953, newly installed President Eisenhower made everything official by signing Executive Order 10450, which barred gay Americans from employment with the federal government.

If one hid his or her lavender light under a bushel, while ostensibly walking the straight and narrow, a person needn't fear anti-gay persecution.

The pianist Liberace, who just "hadn't found the right girl," was the spangled darling of millions of American women. If there were whispers about his sexuality, they were loudly drowned out by the vocal raptures of Liberace's legion of middle-aged female fans. (This author's own grandmother assembled several scrapbooks of Liberace-related magazine and newspapers clippings when she was well into her forties, this interesting family discovery made after her death.) Liberace was the *What's My Line?* mystery guest on three occasions, and once served on the show's panel of interrogators. (Another well-known gay pianist, Van Cliburn, was also three times a mystery guest and also once a guest panelist.)

At least two game show hosts (and panelists) of the era were generally known to be gay. But given the times, and given his apparent desire to stay employed, one of them, Robert Q. Lewis, never came out. (Hardly any well-known person, with the exception of Beat poet Allen Ginsberg, were "out" in the 1950s.) Wildly successful game show producer (and game and talk show host) Merv Griffin kept himself largely in his closet, except for those times when in the absence of a television camera he dared to sneak a toe or two outside the door. Griffin's life as a gay man is documented in Darwin Porter's unambiguously titled unauthorized biography *Merv Griffin: A Life in the Closet*.[1]

On occasion, TV game shows would give an indirect wink at homosexuality, or at least at gender fluidity. The March 11, 1958, *To Tell the Truth* featured a University of Pennsylvania undergrad who, in addition to being head cheerleader *and* company commander of the Naval Reserve Officers Training Corps (the latter being of no inconsequential mention), was set to appear in the university's upcoming Mask and Wig Club spring show ... in drag. (All parts in Mask and Wig Show productions were played by men.) Which is why this particular young man, as well as his two assigned imposters, appeared on the broadcast clad and coiffed as females. For their trouble, the three men were rewarded with guffaws from the audience and tickled expressions on the faces of the panelists. "Now, panelists," laughed Collyer, "if I can tear your gazes away long enough to follow along with this affidavit as I read it, I'd appreciate it."

This particular segment, incidentally, plays a small role in highlighting the negative reaction to Christian Dior's beltless sack dresses. In telling why he voted for the collegian he did, Hy Gardner remarked, "I was going to vote for number one, but I switched to three because he's the first person I've ever seen to make one of those chemise gowns look flattering." While there were many who praised the style because of its comfort, there were

15. The Love That Dare Not Speak Its Name

others, including a great many heterosexual men like Gardner, who complained that they did too good a job of concealing the feminine figure.

On the March 8, 1959, *What's My Line?*, John Charles Daly took pains to defend the masculinity (read that: heterosexuality) of one of his contestants, even though he was brought on the show for the explicit purpose of fooling the panel and leaving them clueless as to his decidedly *un*-he-man profession. The gentleman managed a chain of charm schools called "The Loretta Young Way." The program, as it was explained when all the guessing was done, "teaches young women about wardrobe, poise, makeup, modeling and more." Daly also felt it important to mention that the schools' manager, a Robert Reinhart, had played for the Toronto Argonauts and that in 1956 he'd been the third-ranking passer in all of college football.

They were simpler times; sociologically speaking, much more rigidly prescribed times; and for gay people in particular, much more dangerous times. For this reason, a *You Bet Your Life* conversation between Groucho Marx and an unapologetically homosexual contestant—a young man who resembled actor Michael J. Pollard—stands out. This part of the interview never made it into the show:

> CONTESTANT: I don't have a girl, Groucho.
> GROUCHO: You don't have any girl?
> CONTESTANT: No, sir.
> GROUCHO: How old did you say you were?
> CONTESTANT: Thirty-one.
> GROUCHO: You *had* a girl, I'd imagine.
> CONTESTANT: How do you mean that?
> GROUCHO: I mean it in the nicest way you possibly could. Some time in these 31 years there must have been some girl you liked, wasn't there?
> CONTESTANT: I like traveling better, I'm afraid.
> GROUCHO: Well, I don't see the comparison, I suppose. I know you need a bag when you travel.

This exchange, which can be found among the *You Bet Your Life* blooper and outtake videos on YouTube, was also remembered by director Robert Dwan in his book *As Long As They're Laughing*. Dwan contended that the reason this portion of the conversation didn't make the cut had to do with Groucho's "vulgar" use of the word "bag."[2] One wonders, though, if that was merely a pretext, and the real reason was the far more obvious—and in the 1950s, uncomfortable—one.

Groucho may have feigned ignorance of non-binary sexual identification, but he was also known to toss in a Christine Jorgensen reference now and then for a guaranteed laugh. In the early 1950s, Jorgensen was the recipient of a series of well-publicized sexual reassignment surgeries, this making her the decade's best-known transgender woman. For example, another casualty of the censor's scissors:

> CONTESTANT (in the middle of a story): A gentleman from Laguna Beach ...
> GROUCHO (interrupting): There *are* no gentlemen in Laguna Beach.
> CONTESTANT: No, the gentleman is now abroad.
> GROUCHO: This couldn't be Christine, is it?

One interview segment that did make it on the air was no less to-the-point than the excised chat between Groucho and the young man who preferred travel to girls. The contestant's name was Air Force pilot Charlie Jones, who was partnered with a very beautiful young woman name Lily Badalian from Iran. Groucho, as usual, was up to his matchmaking tricks:

> GROUCHO: Are you married, lieutenant?
> JONES: No, I'm not.
> GROUCHO: Well, neither is Lily, you know. What do you think of marrying her?
> JONES: I haven't given it much thought.
> GROUCHO: Why not? Don't you like girls?
> JONES: Well, maybe that's why I haven't given marriage too much thought, Groucho.
> GROUCHO (after a contemplative pause): Oh. I see.

❖ 16 ❖

All Fall Down

> The *New York Daily News*' Inquiring Photographer asked six New Yorkers a question: "Would you have any qualms about appearing on a [rigged] quiz show?" Answered five of the six: "No, I'd take the money."
> —*Time*, October 16, 1959[1]

Despite the overall popularity of game shows as a programming format in the mid–1950s, there is a false narrative that has long circulated among media historians that big-money-prize shows, when the scandals broke, fell much harder and much farther because of the heights to which viewers had sent them soaring. The truth is that while *Twenty-One* had some success, especially when Charles Van Doren was in the booth, it was only *The $64,000 Question* which received high-enough ratings to land in the Nielsen top 20. Television scholars tend to interpret the attention given these shows in East Coast newspapers and magazines as evidence of a popularity that, in truth, was largely limited to the Northeast, and, even more locally, to the New York metropolitan area. Writes James L. Baughman in his examination of the first decade and a half of American television, *Same Time, Same Station*, "Reporters and editors, notably at the nation's two leading news magazines, *Newsweek* and *Time*, confused local attention with national interest. Simply put, much of the national journalistic community was guilty of overplaying what in many ways was a New York story."[2]

Based on the NBC radio show *Take It or Leave It*, which later became *The $64 Question* when it moved to CBS (thereby giving us the popular catchphrase, "That's the $64 Question"), the big-bucks television version, *The $64,000 Question*, had only been on the air for seven weeks when its creator Louis G. Cowan was rewarded for delivering such a tasty TV plum to CBS by being made a network vice-president. In Harold Mehling's indictment of the TV industry, *The Great Time-Killer* (1962), he points out the irony of Cowan having landed his cush job at Columbia thanks to the success of a quiz show, and then having lost it in disgrace four years later because of that very same show, which stood at the sullied center of the 1958–59 quiz show scandals.[3]

The game show train, which had begun to wobble several months earlier with uncorroborated accusations of game-tampering, officially jumped the rails when a stand-by contestant on the game show *Dotto*, aspiring actor Edward Hilgemeier Jr., took a surreptitious peek at a notebook that had been carried around by fellow contestant Marie Winn.[4] The notebook revealed to Hilgemeier that Winn was being fed the answers to the questions she'd be asked on the show. He sent an affidavit to the FCC in May 1958, stating what he'd seen.

Several months later, disgruntled quiz show contestant Herb Stempel was interviewed by New York prosecutor Joseph Stone before a grand jury about the allegations of game-rigging Stempel had been making against NBC's *Twenty-One* (the network's answer to CBS's *The $64,000 Question*). (See Robert Redford's film *Quiz Show* for an entertaining and largely faithful dramatization of this particular chapter in the saga.)[5]

Other ex-contestants were interviewed as well, and not just contestants on Cowan's *The $64,000 Question* and Dan Enright and Jack Barry's *Twenty-One*. Also placed in the hot seat were sponsor representatives, program producers and staff supervisors. As a result of the inquiry, several shows were implicated, and charges that had previously gotten little or no traction (because of a shortage of Hilgemeier-like smoking guns) were now being given appropriate prosecutorial scrutiny. *The Big Surprise, The $64,000 Challenge* (a spin-off of *The $64,000 Question*), *Dotto* and *Tic Tac Dough* also came under investigation. In fact, virtually every big-money quiz on TV had now fallen under suspicion.

After nine months of collecting testimony from 150 witnesses, Judge Mitchell D. Schweitzer reported that the hearings had done a good job of showing that there were corrupt practices in the television industry, but that no laws had been broken (there being nothing on state statutes at the time which criminalized "faking" a game show). Since the grand jury report would not lead to a trial, and the accused individuals would therefore be provided no legal avenue to explain or defend themselves in the light of these revelations, the judge decided it would be best to simply seal and impound the findings.[6]

Case closed.

For about two minutes.

Responsibility for picking up where the New York grand jury left off fell to Congressman Oren D. Harris, chairman of the House Committee on Interstate and Foreign Commerce. He announced that his Subcommittee on Legislative Oversight would hold public hearings in October 1959. Although there had been a decided difference of opinion among those witnesses who testified before the grand jury as to whether or not contestants had been coached, and whether or not the quiz shows had been "overly controlled," everyone was ready to come clean under the bright beam of a Congressional spotlight. (New York District Attorney Frank S. Hogan estimated that only 50 of the witnesses who had testified told the truth.[7]) Many of those who testified confessed that, yes, they'd perjured themselves, but there was justification: Admitting culpability in the fraud would have demolished their reputations and subjected them to public backlash. So many of the contestants, having achieved a comfortable level of celebrity, weren't willing to give it all up, or even worse: to be so roundly discredited and disgraced. And no one had more to lose than Columbia University professor and Herb Stempel's nemesis Charles Van Doren. Van Doren was one of the last to deliver his mea culpa to Harris' committee—after having protested his innocence to NBC, protested his innocence to his own lawyer, protested his innocence to viewers of *The Today Show* (his big gig after *Twenty-One*), and after having finally protested his innocence to the grand jury—a protest that constituted a clear act of perjury.[8]

The upshot was that no one went to jail for their involvement in the rigging or paid even a single cent in fines. Those who pled guilty to charges of second degree perjury in Special Sessions Court in New York drew suspended sentences. Judge Edward A. Breslin felt so sorry for all of the actors in this sad tragedy, that he even spared them probation.[9]

In the end, humiliating lessons had been learned, reputations tarnished, once bright, promising TV careers crippled or even destroyed. A cloud of notoriety settled over all the participants and would remain there in perpetuity.

It had all been done for ratings, for money, to please the sponsors, to please the networks. Contestants were coached. Contestants who found favor with audiences were kept on the show by whatever means possible, those who weren't liked all that much were kicked to the curb.

Most of those who have assessed both the short- and long-term effects of the quiz show scandals tend to use a very broad brush, painting every participant in dark hues, and raising the industry's misdeeds to the level of national tragedy. Even quiz show fan President Eisenhower likened the whole thing to the 1919 "Black Sox" World Series baseball fix and Van Doren to Shoeless Joe Jackson,[10] although, curiously, Ike's successor in the White House was more sanguine in his assessment. Addressing the Association of Radio and Television Directors in January 1960, John F. Kennedy reminded the gathering that "the mistakes or misjudgments of a comparatively few" were merely "a misstep in a long climb to usefulness in the public interest."[11]

Columnist (and founding editor of *The New Republic*) Walter Lippman was far less equanimous with his opinion:

> Television has been caught perpetrating a fraud which is so gigantic that it calls into question the foundations of the industry.... There has been, in fact, an enormous conspiracy to deceive the public in order to sell profitable advertising to the sponsors.[12]

Even FCC commissioner Robert E. Lee wailed that the scandals were a reflection of "the Godless materialism which is the cancer of American life."[13]

"So gigantic that it calls into question the foundations of the industry"? "Cancer of American life"? Granted, there was plenty of blame to go around: from the on-staff fraudsters themselves to the contestants who played along for the financial gain that would redound to them, to the sponsors and advertising agencies which, if they hadn't been overtly complicit, still encouraged a culture of manipulation and control of the quizzes for the purpose of heightening the drama and intensifying audience investment—this leading to a generous patronizing of the sponsors' products at supermarkets, department store perfume counters and drug stores across the land.[14] Even the networks (excepting ABC, which didn't have a horse in this rodeo—all of its horses being rounded up for the cattle drive of its many TV westerns) weren't completely absolved. Had they not *allowed* this system to thrive?—one in which the sponsors ran the shows with an independent hand, and if anything went wrong, CBS and NBC could simply claim plausible deniability? Called before the House subcommittee, NBC President Robert E. Kintner proclaimed with a straight face, "We were just as much a victim of the quiz show frauds as the public." Not to be outdone, CBS president Frank Stanton told the committee that he'd known absolutely nothing about "program irregularities" until he started hearing "gossip" around the network in late 1958.[15]

16. All Fall Down

The bandwagon from which the opprobrious heavy brickbats were hurled at the big-money quiz shows was capacious. It had room for every American who felt manipulated, disappointed, disillusioned and appalled. Some of television's longtime critics took this opportunity to remind the country of what they'd be saying in different terms for the last several years: that television was falling short of its potential, that it was missing the mark in demonstrable ways. Media critic John Crosby spoke for most of his colleagues when he wrote, "The moral squalor of the quiz mess reaches through the whole industry. [Almost] nothing is what it seems in television.... The feeling of high purpose, of manifest destiny that lit the industry when it was young ... is long gone."[16]

But how did America itself feel about having been "played"?

Quite ambivalent, actually.

In a *Miami Herald* straw poll conducted during the Congressional hearings, outrage among the suntanned populi was in short supply. Most of the respondents said they wanted the cancelled shows back. One Miamian was cynical but forgiving: "Everything on TV is somewhat of a lie. But it's still entertainment."[17] Very few Americans were motivated by the hearings to dash off an angry letter to their Congressman. Years later, journalist Russell Baker asked, "Was America really deceived? Of course not, except for the usual saps (there's one born every minute, Barnum noted) who always want to be deceived."[18] A December 1959 issue of *Broadcasting* referred to a public opinion survey which showed that the quiz show scandals had hardly put a dent in the popularity of the medium. One respondent spoke for many when he said, "My only regret is that I didn't have a chance to get on one of the shows before they were discovered rigged."[19]

Twenty-One producer Albert Freedman dared to take off the sackcloth and shake off the ashes when he remarked that his show and the others should have been judged as mere entertainment from the very beginning (not everyone being as insightful as that Miami observer). The real crime, he said, was trying to convince audiences that the shows weren't approximations of reality, but actually reality itself. "Our only error was that we were too successful. The stakes were too high, and the quiz winners fused themselves into the home life and the hopes and aspirations of the viewers."[20]

In an October 26, 1959, *Life* magazine cover piece written just after an "ashen-faced" Charles Van Doren appeared at a "stormy" press conference to explain why, by all appearances, he'd ducked the subpoena that would place him before the Harris committee, attendees at a broadcast of the NBC game show *Treasure Hunt* shared their feelings about all the recent revelations of fixing and contestant collusion, in anticipation of the even more damaging revelations that were certain to come.

There was no consensus.

Opinions ranged from hard denunciations ("There isn't any honesty left in the world"; "Television has lost my confidence") to the more tepid ("It was foolish"; "It wasn't right, but I'll keep watching the shows") to '50s-era versions of shrugging mehs ("So what? I still love quiz shows"; "It rocks confidence. [But] I'm not mad or anything.")[21]

After all, they're just *games*, right?

With all the hard times now supposedly in the country's rear-view mirror, promises had been made to the American people, which the 1950s were tasked to deliver. By the end of the decade, it had become clear that while some of these promises had been kept, a good many remained unfilled. Americans, while continuing to believe that their country—for the most part—was still that bright, shining democratic light of the world, had swallowed a big dose of castor oil realism.

In retrospect, Americans concluded that "of course a bunch of those quizzes were manipulated. How else could it have been possible for so many of those *Twenty-One* contestant face-offs to end in ties—ties that forced viewers to have to tune back in the following week?" But on the other hand, "I see the corner butcher put his thumb on the scale every now and then. And why is Benny at the service station always saying I need a new oil filter? And I can't believe there isn't a single colored family that can afford to move to my neighborhood; something's fishy there too."

And less than a year later, the American people (along with the rest of the world) would be lied to by the Eisenhower administration over events surrounding the downing of Air Force captain Francis Gary Powers' Lockheed U-2 plane over the Soviet Union. What was actually a failed spy mission was purposefully presented as a NASA flight that happened to have "gone missing" north of Turkey.

There were far greater lies told to the American people than Van Doren's self-absolving opinion of opponent Herb Stempel's charges against the producers of *Twenty-One*: "Reports of fixing are greatly exaggerated. I was completely fooled. I thought he was sweating as hard as I was."[22] In other words, Van Doren was "shocked, SHOCKED to learn that rigging was going on there," and purposefully neglected to mention that sweating had nothing to do with a contestant's laborious efforts to answer a difficult multiple-part question: *Twenty-One* contestants perspired because the air conditioning was intentionally turned off in their "soundproof" booths for brow-trickling dramatic effect.

In fact, America's TV viewers saw very little on their home tubes that wasn't or hadn't always been in some way manipulated, if not wholly manufactured, for a particular purpose or effect. Even the supposed spontaneity of Groucho Marx's *You Bet Your Life* was a fabrication; guests weren't plucked right out of the audience and placed on the stage as viewers were led to believe. They had actually been selected beforehand and were subjected to interviews, the contents of which were used by the show's writers to construct script outlines that guided Groucho's interchanges with them.[23]

"Control" had been a part of game show culture from its infancy. Many years after the scandals, Albert Freedman was still sticking to his guns when it came to his earlier assertion that any and all means should be used to serve the single end of entertainment:

> Traditionally, all panel and quiz shows, from the time of radio, had a form of control. Entertainment was the key. Without entertainment you had no show. Everybody knew what was going on—the agencies, the sponsors, the networks. A producer knew what he had to do to make a show successful, or he would no longer be producing. It doesn't make it right but that's the way it was.[24]

According to veteran TV producer and director Joseph Cates, going back as far as the 1930s, radio shows like *Quiz Kids* and *Information Please*, while not actually feeding answers to their panelists, used a system which tailored questions to panelists based on their personal interests and knowledge specialties. "It wasn't an accident that they asked [*Information Please*'s] John Kieran questions on nature and Oscar Levant questions on baseball."[25] There was also the precedent of radio quizzers hiring so-called professional contestants. These were regulars who appeared on multiple shows using a variety of aliases and different home towns. It wasn't a problem, writes Stan Opotowsky in his 1962 examination of the good and bad of television, *TV—The Big Picture*, "because radio had a $64 question. It took television to produce a $64,000 question."[26]

In his 1958 novel *The Hot Half Hour*, Robert Foreman, account executive for the BBD&O (Batten, Barton, Durstine and Osborn) ad agency, had an advertising man explain the extent to which controls were used on an ostensibly "spontaneous" game show: "You've control over the questions, the contestants, the timing, the spacing of the contestants, and therefore as complete control over the results as does the director of a dramatic show."²⁷

Producer and CBS network executive Perry Lafferty noted that sometimes the control was to the contestant's benefit:

> On *Name That Tune* we had a thing where, if you kept a contestant on five weeks, he would get up to $25,000. Well, the audience would go nuts because [show creator Harry Salter] had a hot couple going, and Harry didn't want them to lose, so the band is playing and he's going (in a loud whisper), "Blue Skies. Blue Skies," three feet from the mike boom.²⁸

And if the above were true, there may be less cause to contest Albert Freedman's contention that "a friend of mine [who] produced *Name That Tune* gave the answers to John Glenn, who won a lot of money."²⁹ That large amount of money added up to $25,000, which Glenn split with his partner, child actor Eddie Hodges.³⁰ (On the other hand, since the late astronaut and U.S. Senator was believed by most to be an American hero beyond reproach, the reader has the author's permission to view that supposed revelation with whatever degree of skepticism makes one comfortable.)

Oscar Katz, the head of CBS's daytime programming, said there were times when the *Name That Tune* staff were called upon to depose a contestant who wasn't getting sufficient love from his audience:

> One time they had this obnoxious kid on the show, and they couldn't knock him off. They put the other kid's chair closer to the bell. That didn't work. You know what they finally did? The idea was if you knew the song you would run down the stage and ring the bell. Now, this is in front of the audience, they weren't hiding anything. They raised the bell! He couldn't reach it. That's how they knocked the little son of a bitch off.³¹

Game controlling took a variety of different forms. In the course of an internal investigation undertaken by CBS, it was discovered that the "dancing decimal machine" on Walt Framer's *For Love or Money* had been jiggered with to give players no chance whatsoever of winning its much ballyhooed top monetary prize.³²

Even Barry and Enright's production company's infamous manipulation of *Twenty-One* and *Tic Tac Dough* might have had intra-company precedent as far back as 1953. On one of its early programs, *Juvenile Jury* (a show in the "Kids Say the Darndest Things" category of advice-panel offerings), one of the youngest of the advice-givers, a preschooler named Michelle Fogel, let it slip that her "Mommy" had told her what problem would be put before her on that day's broadcast and instructed her in how

16. All Fall Down

to respond. Host Jack Barry protested that such couldn't possibly be, because the child panelists were *never* given the questions ahead of time. He made this on-air claim more than once, each time with awkwardly expressed adamancy. Years later, Albert Freedman, who also worked on *Juvenile Jury*, admitted to interviewer Jeff Kisseloff quite matter-of-factly, "Sometimes we fed them answers. Sometimes, we didn't have to. They were very bright."[33]

But just how many pitchforks *did* the country raise over sworn revelations that the producers and staff of several of television's big-money game shows had committed fraud? As it turns out, not nearly so many as TV historians want us to believe. It's a narrative that conveniently services the trope of lost American innocence. Yet at the end of the day, the facts don't necessarily support it.

And it was the network overlords who, when all the dust had settled, benefitted the most from the scandal. Because of it, they could make a convincing case for rescuing television game shows from their advertisers. And since full or shared sponsorship of a whole television show ("and now a word from our *alternate* sponsor") was by the late 1950s largely limited to game shows, it would be the nail in the coffin for a form of programming control that harkened all the way back to the earliest days of radio.

But any network that thought its newly minted reputation for probity and high-mindedness put it in the video catbird seat, ignored the growing dislike for other areas of programming for which the networks had long been responsible: programming that subjected television viewers to hourly orgies of gratuitous violence dealt by cops and robbers, itchy-trigger-finger private eyes and shoot-'em-up cowboys. While the country was focused on the crimes and misdemeanors of the makers of *The $64,000 Question* and *Dotto*, there was far more insidious villainy afoot elsewhere on the dial: a least-common-denominator species of television storytelling that sacrificed artistic nuance and all of the medium's better angels upon the altar of video guts and gore, and on an unprecedented scale. Groucho Marx wrote cynically in February 1959 that "the air is now completely filled with cowboys, fertilizer and inanity. The country is full of jerks and they're now getting exactly what they deserve."[34]

Several of television's game shows might have been corrupted for the purpose of expanding viewership and raking in profit for their sponsors, but the industry's love affair with violence (with a pinch of titillating T&A thrown in) was, at the same time, raising hackles of a different sort. And viewers who were turned off by all the mayhem knew just who to blame: the networks themselves.

Plausible deniability didn't work here.

Among those attendees of that earlier referenced *Treasure Hunt* broadcast who had been interviewed by *Life* reporters prior to Charles Van Doren's spilling of every single bean related to his *Twenty-One* participation, was a woman who, without explanation or elaboration, was given to remark, "I feel sorry for all the people involved in this mess ... except for the executives at NBC."[35]

Take *that,* Peacock.

We'll give the garrulous Mr. Freedman the last word on the quiz show scandals and how they defined the frightening potential of television to shape American society:

> Believe me, the decadence in America started long before the quiz scandals. What the scandals showed me was the extraordinary power of this visual medium.... It creates celebrities and even elects presidents. The power of television started branching into everything in the '50s.[36]

For good *or* bad.

◆ 17 ◆

They Were the Best of Times; They Were the Most Stupid of Times

> Having Groucho as emcee of a quiz show is like using a Cadillac to haul coal.
> —John Guedel[1]

Considering that so many radio and TV quiz shows were broadcast live, it is astonishing, given the record we have, how seldom the programs actually went off the rails, both in terms of descents into havoc and mayhem, stunts and demonstrations that went disastrously wrong, notoriety-hungry studio crashers trespassing before cameras, and moments when the shows went blue—sometimes *very* blue. Of course, with so many of the game shows unrecorded or having had their videotapes erased or their kinescopes destroyed, what exists today is but a remnant of what was actually aired. Most of what we have to go on are the memories of the shows' participants, not all of which are trustworthy or fully extractable. Viewings of videotaped oral history interviews on the Archive of American Television website (www.emmytvlegends.org) of several celebrities who guested on the various panel shows reveal a recurring theme of faulty recollection. Some of these individuals, perhaps given the difficulty of remembering details from long careers on numerous television shows, could not even recall the names of the panelists or even sometimes the names of the hosts of the shows on which they appeared.)

But when game shows did wade into bawdy waters, they did so with quite a bit of splish and splash. On the radio version of the quiz show *Double or Nothing*, quizmaster Walter O'Keefe found himself blindsided by a contestant who seemed to have no idea she was saying anything untoward. The contestant was a waitress, and during her chat with O'Keefe on a show broadcast in October 1948, he happened to ask if she'd ever had any unusual customers. "Well, Mr. O'Keefe," the waitress responded, "yesterday a man asked me a question. He had a sick friend needing advice. This friend can't go out nights, can't eat, can't do nothing. Even had to send his wife away on a vacation. This guy asked, 'What do you think we should do with him?' I said I didn't really know. 'Well,' he replied, 'I think he should get a good-looking girl like you and take her home and just have a big screwing party.' I said, 'What! Why don't you go down to the hardware store and get some ... a screw ... and go home.'"[2]

O'Keefe wasted no time in getting to the quiz part of the show and then having the poor woman removed from the microphone. In the meantime, the NBC switchboard lit up like the proverbial Christmas tree, callers expressing predictable outrage over hearing about screwing parties "on such a fine family show."[3]

Bill Cullen had trouble keeping a straight face twice on the October 14, 1954, *Name That Tune.* In an attempt to help young female contestant Rose find her way to the song title "Christopher Columbus," he encouraged her to "think of an Italian man who did something very, very important. In fact, if he hadn't done what he did, you wouldn't be here tonight. Who is this Italian man?"

Rose's face brightened. "My father!"

When the audience's laughter and applause finally died down, Cullen confessed that it was "pretty hard to call an answer like that wrong."

Later in the broadcast, a contestant had trouble identifying a song played by the show's orchestra, "Under a Blanket of Blue." Another hint from the ever-helpful Mr. Cullen: "If it was a girl baby, you could tell because she would be under a blanket of pink. Therefore, if it was a boy baby, how could you tell?"

The contestant responded, "By looking under its diaper."[4]

Because *You Bet Your Life* was filmed and edited, and because many of the show's outtakes were kept around for posterity (largely to be compiled into stag reels for annual DeSoto Plymouth dealer conventions[5]), we have a good idea of the kinds of things that were considered too risqué to make the final cut for broadcast. Much of the rejected material had to do with overly suggestive Grouchoian ad libs. Though tame by today's standards, Marx's offhanded remarks were lewd enough for the times to be cut out without objection from the star. In fact, quite often, after making a statement he knew wouldn't make it past network censors, Groucho

17. The Best of Times; The Most Stupid of Times   167

would chirrup, "Clip, clip!"—the sound of an editor's scissors snipping out the offending section of the show, that moment then either winding up on the cutting room floor or finding its way to that particular season's blooper reel.

Everyone knew the drill, even the contestants and the audience members who attended the filming. Many, in fact, came to the show just to see Groucho, prince of the double entendre, raising his brows and twirling his ubiquitous cigar, as he milked a line for the naughty laugh he hoped it would elicit. Inevitably, everyone knew there would be conversations that wouldn't pass muster with NBC's morality gatekeepers, but everyone was having too much fun to care. On one occasion, a woman, originally from France, tried to explain to Groucho what a certain brand of electric kitchen mixer did: "They call it a 'Mixed Master.' You put your business in there." Groucho seemed to know at that moment that this conversation had reached the point of no return. Turning to his off-screen producer, he asided: "Clip, clip, clip. Here we go again."

The contestants themselves weren't always total innocents in the proceedings. On a different outtake, a female player was delighted to serve as accessory to Groucho's rascality.

> GROUCHO: Pete, are you married?
> PETE: Yes, I am.
> GROUCHO (indicating the female contestant standing next to Pete): You don't subscribe to her philosophy at all?
> PETE: Well, I've been at it for 33 years.
> GROUCHO: You've been *at* it?
> FEMALE CONTESTANT: He must be worn out by now.
> GROUCHO: I have a line which we can't use. The line is: A man is as young as the woman he feels.
> FEMALE CONTESTANT: You're gonna be censored! Groucho, you're gonna be censored as of right now!

That was the advantage of the fact that *You Bet Your Life* wasn't live. Marx and his guests could say virtually anything they pleased and know that when all the mischief was clip-clipped away, the network and the sponsor would be left with a show that would score respectfully low on the raunch meter.

In the meantime, TV's beloved mustached dirty old man had nothing to fear about exchanges like the following:

> GROUCHO: John, are potatoes really fattening?
> JOHN: No, sir. It's what you put on them that's fattening.
> GROUCHO: What do you mean?

JOHN: Oh, butter, gravy, cheese, but if you put that on a mattress, it would fatten you too.
GROUCHO: That's one of the few things I've never had on a mattress.

And ...

GROUCHO: Do you like to cook? Let me put it this way: Do you like to fool around in the kitchen? Because, if you like to fool around in the kitchen, you don't have to be able to cook.

and ...

GROUCHO: When a fellow takes you home at night, does he say, "Good night, Irene?" ("Goodnight, Irene" was a popular song from the '30s.)
IRENE: It depends on the particular case.
GROUCHO: If he's real lucky, he doesn't say good night at all. [Groucho turns to the show's producer.] Clip. Clip.

When Groucho Marx was scheduled to make appearances on other game shows—most of them live—one can imagine producers breaking out in cold sweats. On the September 20, 1959, *What's My Line?*, considered by many aficionados to be the funniest in the show's 17-year history, Groucho, onboard to promote his just-published autobiography *Groucho and Me*, seemed to have an additional reason for coming on the show: to blow the whole thing up. Amazingly, no one paid a price for Groucho's pushing the envelope of decorum on this particular broadcast to the point of full rupture. Marx interrupted panelists, asked nonsensical and comically unconstructive questions, wore his mask upside down so he could clearly see that the mystery guest for the evening was Claudette Colbert (and was thus disqualified from participating in that round) and at one point followed a long-winded clarification by host John Charles Daly with the observation, "You realize that no one's listening to you."

So flustered had Groucho gotten his fellow panelists, that Dorothy Kilgallen, the epitome of white-gloved primness and propriety, temporarily lost title to her on-air reputation:

GROUCHO: It's up to you, Mrs. Kilgallen, errr, *Miss* Kilgallen.
DOROTHY (addressing a beautiful blonde named Judy Grable, whom the panel would later learn was a professional wrestler): Miss Grable, are the men and women you come in contact with ... are they grown up human beings?
MS. GRABLE: Yes.
DOROTHY: Now, would you say that you deal with more sex—
GROUCHO: You think I'm the only one that's obsessed with that subject, huh? Oh boy, what a Freudian panel this is! If people would only talk!
JOHN CHARLES DALY (after allowing everyone to regain composure): Uh, Dorothy, before we pursue this subject any further ...
DOROTHY (through mortified laughter): I don't *want* to pursue it any further!

17. The Best of Times; The Most Stupid of Times

Of course, when game shows were good, there was nothing more entertaining in all of television.

And when they were dirty.

Usually unintentionally. But it can't be mere coincidence that over the course of *What's My Line?*'s history in prime time, the show booked several managers and owners of nudist camps, more than one lingerie and/or foundation garment model, a bubble dancer, a can-can dancer, a fan dancer, a store-window vibrating mattress demonstrator, a sweater model and more than one operator of an amusement park skirt-blowing machine.

The show also hosted Kathleen Winsor, author of the racy 1944 novel *Forever Amber*, which was banned as pornography in 14 states. Despite all the criticism she received for its frank sexual references—or perhaps because of them—Ms. Winsor's nearly 1000-page tale of an orphan who either sleeps or marries her way to the top of English society, sold over 100,000 copies within a week of publication and had reached over three million by the time of her October 1, 1950, *What's My Line?* appearance to promote her latest bodice-ripper *Star Money*.

On the flip side, *What's My Line?* had, for one of its occupation-related challengers, Frances Vaughn, who served on the Kansas State Board for Movie Censorship. She ended up stumping the panel and after pocketing her $50, no doubt returned to making sure married couples in movies didn't share the same bed, never had extra-marital affairs, and never used the toilet.

When *I've Got a Secret* producer Allan Sherman was brainstorming with his partner Howard Merrill over a possible panel show idea with which to win over Mark Goodson and Bill Todman, *What's My Line?*'s border-line roguery did not go unmentioned. The conversation, as Sherman remembered it, went roughly as follows:

> ALLAN: Let's think up the most successful type show there is.
> HOWARD: Good idea.
> ALLAN: Like *What's My Line?*, for example.
> HOWARD: Precisely. Now, what is the basic reason for the success of *What's My Line?*
> ALLAN: Well, it's dirty.
> HOWARD: Right. And the panelists wear tuxedos.
> ALLAN: All the better. That makes it a typical American family show.[6]

Sometimes the mistakes made on TV game shows had nothing to do with an errant dirty word or off-color observation getting a live airing.

Though it happened slightly outside the time frame addressed in this book, a remark by Merv Griffin on his 1963–64 game show *Word for Word* demonstrates that things can go wrong even when a show has been videotaped. Following the assassination of John F. Kennedy, all non-news broadcasting was suspended. When normal programming resumed four days later, the networks asked producers to check all their pre-recorded material to make sure that anything said about the slain leader, which could be conceived as dishonoring his memory, be excised. Unfortunately, whoever was in charge of doing this for *Word for Word* dropped the ball. On a cringe-worthy pre-recorded episode, the first contestant, who mentioned that she was from Dallas, Texas, received in return—delivered in a comical Lone Star State accent—an inquiry from host Griffin as to whether she'd "checked her guns at the door."

Griffin had to go on the next day and ask audience forgiveness for the offensive oversight.[7]

Game shows were the best places to go in the 1950s to check in with the fads and fancies, crazes and manias swirling about the pop culture ethos. *To Tell the Truth* gave us in 1957 the Bubblegum Blowing Champion of Chicago. Enrico Caruso appeared on the show—not the famed opera singer, who would have had to show up as a 36-year-dead ghost, but a hairstylist by that name, whose claim to fame was the Italian and poodle cuts. Without Caruso, it leaves one to ponder just how Lucy Ricardo would otherwise have done her hair. The April 8, 1958, *To Tell the Truth* brought together *Vogue* fashion model Joan Pederson and two equally beautiful pretenders wearing the seminal fashions of that year, which they modeled to commentary by host Bud Collyer: an example of Christian Dior's "trapeze look," Roberto Capucci's "cocoon silhouette" and Ceil Chapman's organza "balloon."

I've Got a Secret panelist Henry Morgan, became for a time a beatnik. He was booked into the Village Vanguard cellar night club in Greenwich Village to recite his hip poetry. His gig was such a hit that he was invited to return there nightly. (Unlike Maynard G. Krebs, Morgan chose not to grow a goatee.) On the May 28, 1959, *You Bet Your Life*, rookie stand-up comic Ronnie Schell (who later worked in sitcoms) schooled Groucho on San Francisco beatnik culture. Groucho asked Schell if there was truth to the stereotype: "Aren't they supposed to sort of be a long-haired, egghead crowd? Poets, students, philosophers." Schell, apparently no fan of beatniks, agreed that they were beard- and sandal-wearing non-conformists, the girls favoring black leotards. (Groucho required an explanation of

17. The Best of Times; The Most Stupid of Times 171

what leotards were.) But Schell's general assessment was basically a rebuke: "A beatnik is a fellow on the bottom looking down."

By all appearances, Schell had never met Kerouac, Ginsberg or Burroughs.

On November 18, 1958, young Connie Hagedorn twirled 20 hoops on *To Tell the Truth*, demonstrating conclusively why she had just been named National Hula Hoop Champion. In the competition, Connie had gone for the endurance record, spinning a hoop for an impressive ten hours, one minute, nine seconds (quite a feat for this not-very-big-girl from Royal, Iowa). In the course of questioning, Polly Bergen happened to ask the "real" Connie Hagedorn why she decided to take up hula hoop spinning "as a profession." Connie answered ingenuously, "Well, everyone else had one!" (Polly got a chance to hoop it herself at the end of the round.)

Eleven weeks earlier, the *I've Got a Secret* panel received hula hoop lessons from a spinner from Pasadena named Susan Molin. At the height of the craze, which took off only a few months before this broadcast, Carlon Products Corporation, one of the first manufacturers of the hoop, was producing more than 50,000 of the rings a day. Within the first four months, 25 million plastic hoops had been sold, more than 100 million after only two years.[8]

A novelty line dance, the "Madison," created in Columbus, Ohio, in 1957 and first popularized in Baltimore, Maryland (as fans of John Waters' movie *Hairspray* already know), reached national popularity at the tail end of the 1950s. On April 7, 1960, George Foster (host Garry Moore's stand-in) and a gentleman named Don Creighton were contestants on *I've Got a Secret*. They were there to teach Betsy Palmer and Bess Myerson the dance.

In that same vein, *What's My Line?* featured both a Rumba teacher (December 30, 1951) and a Mambo instructor (June 26, 1955). Both dances were popular in the '40s and '50s.

One of the crazes most identified with the 1950s hit *What's My Line?* on June 5, 1955, with an appearance by Alex Tansman, whose line was making Davy Crockett hats for pint-size fans of Walt Disney's "Davy Crockett" mini-series. Before exiting the stage, Tansman passed out coonskin caps to host John Charles Daly and each of the panelists, including "Daisy Crockett" (otherwise known as Arlene Francis). Bennett Cerf casually remarked to Francis that she should "send that back to Kefauver." Senator Estes Kefauver, a Tennessean like ol' Davy, wore a coonskin cap for many of his public appearances. He was even photographed for the cover of the March 24, 1952, issue of *Time* sporting both his trademark toothy grin and the now familiar raccoon hat on his head.

To Tell the Truth featured Chuck Weiss, inventor of AromaRama, used in the theatrical presentation of the film travelogue *Behind the Great Wall of China*. The movie was released in specially equipped theaters three weeks ahead of *Scent of Mystery,* which was presented in competing Smell-o-Vision. *Scent of Mystery* was produced by Mike Todd Jr. and promoted on the February 17, 1960, *I've Got a Secret* by one of its stars, Peter Lorre. (Of this film, the comedian Henny Youngman joked, "I didn't understand the picture. I had a cold."[9]) *Variety* called the competition between the two films the "Battle of the Smellies." Although *The World Telegram* gushed, "You've got to breathe it to believe it—scented movies are here to stay!," a 2000 survey of *Time* readers counted movies that smell among the "Top Worst 100 Ideas of All Time."[10]

I've Got a Secret, fairly obsessed with national obsessions and the Elvis phenomenon in particular, featured Freddy Renucci ("I gave Elvis Presley a haircut"); draft board member Jane Patrick ("I am going to draft Elvis Presley"); and Ira Jones ("I was Elvis Presley's platoon sergeant"). And on July 9, 1958, the show introduced the country to Elvis' grandfather Jesse, for whom Elvis's stillborn twin had presumably been named.

Likewise, the Marilyn Monroe obsession was personified through an appearance of Marilyn's drama coach Natasha Lytess (aka Tala Forman) and a man who sold Marilyn Monroe calendars, both on *What's My Line?*

◆ 18 ◆

Future Dark, Future Bright

> Let us make our future now, and let us make our dreams tomorrow's reality.
> —Malala Yousafzai[1]

At decade's end, the American television game show, though rattled by scandal, wasn't ready for Boot Hill. Some of the genre's most successful shows were born in the first half of the 1960s. *Password*, debuting in 1961, *(The) Match Game* (1962) and *Jeopardy!* (1964) had large, devoted followings, and all three became game show mainstays over the years that followed.

But there were also dramatic failures—an indication that the new decade was going to be even more disorderly and unpredictable than the decade that preceded it. In fact, most contemporary historians agree that on a domestic level, the 1960s were the most turbulent ten years of the century. That tumult created uncertainty in network TV programming. That uncertainty made for chaos, disappointment, bumbles and miscalculations.

When game shows flopped—as many did in the 1950s and '60s—they did so without drawing much attention to themselves (drawing insufficient attention being a big reason for their demise). One show in the annals of game show failure deserves mention here not only because of its unusual flame-out but because its miscarriage became a news story in itself. *You're in the Picture* was hosted by Jackie Gleason who, at the time, was attempting to demonstrate a performing versatility, which, it was hoped, would revive his slipping brand. Gleason wasn't alone in trying to "find himself." A number of TV personalities who had staked a place for themselves in the national consciousness during the '50s, were now seeking relevance and reinvention in a hip new, youth-obsessed entertainment terrain, ushered in by America's youngest elected president. Similarly, Milton Berle, once so popular with TV audiences that he was given the soubriquet "Mr. Television," found himself on September 19, 1960, the new host of—with unavoidable abasement—*Jackpot Bowling*.

The concept of *You're in the Picture*, which premiered on Friday, January 20, 1961, was a simple one. It was dreamed up by three gentlemen, each of whom spent his game show career thinking big: Steve Carlin, who, having had a hand in the infamous *The $64,000 Question*, decided two decades later to create for syndication (what else?) *The $128,000 Question*; Bob Synes, who later produced a dozen episodes of the big pinball machine game show *The Magnificent Marble Machine*; and Don Lipp, best known for *The Moneymaze*, a show that actually had contestants running through a maze like rats while George Clooney's father Nick cheered them on.

You're in the Picture featured four celebrities—each an actor, and each playing for the chance to have 100 CARE packages sent to needy folk in their name. To play the game, they put their heads through holes cut into life-size illustrations of famous historical scenes or come-to-life song lyrics, in much the same way county fair-goers used to make sillies of themselves in the "funny-foto" tent. Clueless as to how ridiculous they looked, the four good sports—Pat Carroll, Pat Harrington Jr., Jan Sterling and Arthur Treacher—duteously peppered Gleason with questions they hoped would produce clues helpful to them in determining the nature of the cartoon murals for which they'd been asked to donate their heads.

The show bombed. Infamously.

Gleason readily admitted this the very next week when he made an on-air apology on behalf of himself and all the "300 years worth of show business experience" involved in putting the program together. Seated on a bare stage, totemic coffee cup and cigarette in hand, he rambled on for the entire 30 minutes allotted to the show's second episode.

Such an apology was unprecedented. By their nature, game shows don't lend themselves well to extensive deconstruction, let alone to on-camera self-flagellation. A game show was never meant to be anything more than what it had always sought to be: an easily assembled and cheaply produced means to help fill the maw of a content-ravenous entertainment medium. To be considered successful, all the shows had to do was draw a happy and loyal audience, and put lots of money into advertisers' pockets. It was this way in the 1950s; it was supposed to work the same way in the 1960s.

18. Future Dark, Future Bright

But America was entering a new era, fault lines were shifting, people were asking more from their entertainment providers just as they were asking more from their government, to which JFK felt compelled to disabuse them: "Ask not what your country can do for you...." By odd coincidence, *You're in the Picture* premiered on the very night of Kennedy's inauguration.

So decisively did the show fail that a hanging jury of viewers and critics delivered their verdict almost instantaneously. It was Gleason himself who, in the course of the following week's post-mortem broadcast, joked about the program's post-premiere party and his return to his hotel: "I opened the window to look out and see if it was still snowing, and they had the nets up."[2] In reporting on Gleason's follow-up apologia broadcast, *The New York Times* sniped, "Last night's performance, without panelist or game, was a good deal more entertaining than the first outing."[3]

Pat Carroll, when asked years later about the infamous game show debacle to which she was helpless participant, minced no words:

> Oh my God ... that *bomb*. It was the Hiroshima of television! And Johnny Carson was supposed to be on it. But he did one rehearsal and we never saw him again. He knew better than we did. Ha! ... I thought it was a very strange show, but I thought, "They know what they're doing. Jackie Gleason has *always* known what he is doing."[4]

She went on to talk about the following week's broadcast. Apparently it was a last-minute decision to scrap the show and have Gleason just talk with the audience:

> There was another gal there, wonderful performer, Jan Sterling. And [a week later] they had us both waiting to go on, holding chairs. Jackie had the only chair on the set ... and he did a national apology. When he ended his apology, we were still in the wings holding our chairs. I don't know why they even had us there. But there we were. We're standing with our chairs waiting to go on while Jackie is apologizing to the world. He was very funny doing it, I might add. I don't remember who was responsible for that show but it ... was ... *horrible*.[5]

Let history record that—in some kind of odd cosmic alignment—one of the five sequential appearances made by U.S. Marine Corps Major John Glenn and his young partner Eddie Hodges on *Name That Tune* fell on the very day—October 4, 1957—that the Soviet Union launched its first satellite, Sputnik 1. Eighteen months later, in direct response to this opening salvo fired in the U.S.-U.S.S.R. space race, the names of the "Mercury Seven" astronauts—America's first travelers into space—were announced.

John Glenn was among them, and proved himself to be an even better astronaut than TV game show contestant.

The space race received many a mention in the game shows of the late 1950s and early 1960s. Scientific projects related to the International Geophysical Year (actually 18 months: July 1, 1957, through December 31, 1958) also brought a cavalcade of scientists and explorers into TV's game show studios. James F. Calvert, commander of the USS *Skate*, appeared as a truth-teller on *To Tell the Truth* on June 11, 1957. *Skate* was the third commissioned nuclear submarine and the second to reach the North Pole. Two years after the broadcast, *Skate* became the first nuclear sub to surface at the Pole. The reason: to commit the ashes of polar explorer Hubert Wilkins to the arctic wilderness. Wilkins had, coincidentally, appeared as a challenger on *What's My Line?* on March 16, 1958, several months before his November 30 death.

Also in connection with the International Geophysical Year was an appearance by astronomer-astrophysicist Dr. John P. Hagen, who appeared on *To Tell the Truth* on June 4, 1957, in conjunction with Project Vanguard, America's early "earth satellite project." An attempted launch of the Vanguard TV3 rocket on December 7 (two months after the success of Sputnik 1) resulted in a dramatic launch pad explosion, a humiliating setback to the country's early efforts at space exploration. Explorer 1 was successfully launched several weeks later.

Incidentally, the popularity of science fiction in the 1950s cannot be understated. Two of the panelists on the *To Tell the Truth* panel, Hy Gardner and Kitty Carlisle, were keen to ask Dr. Hagen about flying saucers. A third panelist, Polly Bergen, confessed her own love of science fiction.

Such were the times.

One of the fastest ground travelers in history made his appearance on *To Tell the Truth* on September 3, 1957. Air Force Colonel John P. Stapp, a physician and biophysicist, as well as colleague and contemporary of the legendary Chuck Yeager, used rocket sleds to study the effects of acceleration and deceleration forces on the human body. The colonel demonstrated that a human can withstand at least 46.2 g in the forward position with adequate harnessing, and he set a record on December 10, 1954, by reaching a speed of 632 mph (which made him "the fastest man on earth"). Stapp is known for originating "Murphy's Law." The "Murphy" of reference was a real Air Force captain by that name who botched one of Stapp's experiments with painful results. Stapp has also given us "Stapp's

18. Future Dark, Future Bright

Ironic Paradox," which drolly states that "the universal aptitude for ineptitude makes any human accomplishment an incredible miracle."[6]

Missile technology and references to atomic science with all of its obvious implications, received multiple mentions on American game shows. There seemed in these waning months of the century's sixth decade, a passion for science, mathematics and technology, and with that came musings about the future and whether such knowledge would be harnessed for good rather than ill. The arms race and the space race were great motivators when it came to championing education among the American masses, so that the country wouldn't be bested astronomically, militarily or, God forbid, apocalyptically, by the Russians.

To Tell the Truth invited on its August 12, 1958, telecast the commander of the Air Force Missile Test Center at Cape Canaveral, Major General Donald N. Yates, who made reference to a first for the United States: the firing of an ICBM Atlas missile with all three engines. As a historical footnote, Yates had also been General Eisenhower's chief meteorologist during the Second World War. He was responsible for selecting June 6, 1944, for the Allied invasion of Europe—the only day that month, as it turned out, the English Channel could be successfully crossed.

Several weeks later, Air Force Captain Brandy Griffith appeared on the show. Griffith was working on the Pioneer project, with the goal of sending a satellite into orbit around the moon. Two previous attempts (on August 17 and October 11) had failed; Pioneer O (otherwise known as Thor-Able 1) experienced engine failure 77 seconds after launch. Pioneer 1 (Thor-Able 2) failed to achieve lunar orbit. Pioneer 2 was launched on November 8, 18 days after Captain Griffith's appearance before the *To Tell the Truth* panel. The lunar orbiter failed to ignite in its third stage, which kept the craft from achieving orbital velocity.

That same year, Airman First Class of the U.S. Air Force, Donald Farrell, came on *What's My Line?*, having just spent seven days (February 9–16) in a laboratory "space chamber," simulating a trip to the moon.

On January 29, 1958, Captain Ivan C. Kinchloe Jr.'s "secret" on *I've Got a Secret* was more brag than simple admission. The captain, nicknamed "America's Number One Spaceman," had at that point "gone higher into space than any other human being." Three months later, Paul Carpasack of Orlando, Florida, came on the show to tell folks, "I fired a Vanguard rocket Monday morning." Earlier, on November 6, 1955, viewers of *What's My Line?* had the chance to meet "America's First Space Pilot," rocket plane test pilot Major Arthur W. Murray, who, on August 26, 1954, piloted the

Bell X-1A research airplane, which had been launched from a B-29, to a new world's record altitude of 90,440 feet (or 17 miles), this feat making Major Murray the first human to see the curvature of the earth.

Spacemen need spacesuits, and the challenger on the October 25, 1959, *What's My Line?* made a living doing that very thing: developing spacesuits as head of NASA's Mercury project. R.S. Colley worked for the B.F. Goodrich Company and said that he'd been working in astronaut-wear since 1934. It would be over a year and a half before Alan Shepard would don a suit to pilot the Mercury-Redstone 3 mission that would make him the second person (after USSR cosmonaut Yuri Gagarin), and the first American, to go into space.

America's solar energy future got an early nod on *I've Got a Secret* on March 16, 1960, with an appearance by a gentleman named Charles Escoffery and his car "powered by sunlight," or more specifically, an early solar collector panel prototype, generating over 200 watts of energy from over 10,000 solar cells. The solar cell was beginning to get a lot more terrestrial attention after its use on Vanguard Satellite 1 two years earlier.

By February 13, 1955, the country was finally recognizing the increasing problem of air pollution in its cities and industrial towns. On this date, *What's My Line?* had on as one of its challengers Lou Fuller, the Director of Smog Control for the County of Los Angeles. In prior years, it had been other parts of the country and the world that had received attention for their dangerous air pollution events, which had taken severe tolls in terms of life and respiratory health: In October 1948, 20 people had died in Donora, Pennsylvania, during a temperature inversion which trapped dangerous industrial pollutants in the air. Another 50 succumbed over the following month. Four years later, 4000 (and by more recent estimates, as many as 12,000) Londoners perished in the infamous London Smog of December 1952.[7]

Los Angeles' smog problem, however, was largely related to an exponential increase of vehicular traffic. According to Chip Jacobs, author of *Smogtown: The Lung Burning History of Smog in Los Angeles*, throughout the '50s and '60s some parts of the City of Angels were getting dangerous amounts of smog as often as 200 days a year. It would take another 20 years for the state to put into place effective standards to reduce vehicular pollution.[8]

In the meantime, Mr. Fuller, having successfully stymied the *What's My Line?* panel, happened to mention to host John Charles Daly that New

Yorkers had their own air pollution issues, which they called "smaze" (smog plus haze). Daly, proud booster of New York City, had no response, except to usher Mr. Fuller expeditiously from the set. The fact of the matter was that New York City had undergone its own smog event in November 1953, resulting in an increased death rate for the city. In those days of a burgeoning number of cars and trucks on American highways, and with few regulations restricting what could be belched from America's smokestacks, the problem was one the whole country shared, and one that would take years to effectively address.[9]

By the end of the 1950s, America had started to wake up to problems arising from accelerated industrialization. They were beginning to exercise healthy skepticism over such industrial slogans as DuPont's "Better Living Through Chemistry." They had come to question if they really should "Stop worrying and love the Bomb."

A Portland Cement Association ad placed in home magazines in 1955 tried to set readers' minds at ease when it came to living in the Atomic Age. The association was pushing its "all-concrete blast-resistant house, based on principles learned at Hiroshima and Nagasaski":

> Here's a house with all the advantages of any concrete house—PLUS a protection from atomic blasts at minimum cost. A firesafe, attractive, *low-annual-cost* house, it provides comfortable living—PLUS a refuge for your family in this atomic age.[10]

Such a house wouldn't have helped the Gregg family of Mars Hill, South Carolina: On March 11, 1958, they were the victims of one of the most bizarre incidents of the nascent atomic age. Three weeks later, the family came on *I've Got a Secret* to talk about it. Their challenge to the show's celebrity panel was to guess what had been given no small amount of press coverage, in spite of the fact that it involved a mistake by the U.S. Air Force that could have resulted in massive loss of life.

On that day, a B-47E bomber, heading to Great Britain for a training mission, accidently dropped a 7600-pound, 10'8" atomic bomb on the Greggs' property near Florence, South Carolina, damaging their house, blowing up their children's playhouse and forming a crater on their land 35 feet deep and 70 feet wide. Fortunately, the Mark 6 30-kiloton fission bomb, which detonated on impact, had its nuclear core stored elsewhere on the plane, or else there would have been no Greggs available to answer questions about their experience.[11]

On October 6, 1955, Betty McAnally appeared on *You Bet Your Life* and discussed her avocation with Groucho. Considering what kinds of things fell from the skies in the 1950s, it was an apt job for the times: civil defense volunteer.

A *peaceful* application of nuclear technology came with the world's first operational nuclear-powered submarine, the USS *Nautilus*, whose executive officer, Lieutenant Dean Axene, appeared on the April 17, 1955, *What's My Line?*. Launched on January 21, 1954, and christened by First Lady Mamie Eisenhower, *Nautilus* became, on August 3, 1958, the first watercraft to reach the geographic North Pole.

In case one wonders about the degree to which workers and scientists in the atomic energy field were free to speak about the details of their employment, the son of *What's My Line?* contestant Dr. Robert M. Kloepper (who appeared on January 29, 1956) wrote to the TV.com website in 2005 to tell readers that his father, whose line was "tests atom bombs," "worked at the Los Alamos [New Mexico] Scientific Laboratory in J Division (testing) from 1952 to 1960. Potential questions had been reviewed in advance with the Lab, so my father was prepped to respond to them (e.g., 'Is it bigger than a breadbox?') without giving away nuclear secrets."[12]

It's appropriate in closing this chapter, which is largely about looking toward a future of great promise and accomplishment for the U.S., to note the guests on the September 17, 1962, *I've Got a Secret*. The secret disclosed to Garry Moore and the audience by a Mr. and Mrs. Armstrong of Wapakoneta, Ohio was: "Our son has been selected to be an astronaut." The name of the Armstrongs' son was Neil, and after the secret was revealed to the panel, Moore asked, "Now how would you feel, Mrs. Armstrong, if it turned out—of course nobody knows—but if it turned out that your son is the first man to land on the moon? ... How would you feel?"

Put somewhat on the spot, Mrs. Armstrong replied, "Well, I guess I'd say God bless him and I wish him the best of all good luck."

◈ 19 ◈

A Procession of Game Shows

On May 9, 1961, the newly appointed chairman of the FCC, Newton N. Minow, stood before a gathering of members of the National Association of Broadcasters, and in a speech which strongly encouraged the nation's TV programmers to do a better job of serving the public interest, he said,

> When television is good, nothing—not the theater, not the magazines or newspapers—nothing is better. But when television is bad, nothing is worse. I invite each of you to sit down in front of your television set when your station goes on the air and stay there, for a day.... Keep your eyes glued to that set until the station signs off. I can assure you that what you will observe is a vast wasteland.
>
> You will see a processsion of game shows, formula comedies about totally unbelievable families, blood and thunder, mayhem, violence, sadism, murder, western bad men, western good men, private eyes, gangsters, more violence and cartoons. And endlessly, commercials—many screaming, cajoling, and offending. And most of all, boredom.

The '50s had drawn to a close and a decade of exciting programming innovation and adventurous entertainment offerings had settled into vapidity and inanity. Minow singled out game shows as a genre of programming deserving of criticism. Were the quiz shows, the game shows and the audience participation programs (which have always defied clean categorization) deserving of such opprobrium—especially in a speech that has been heralded as one of the best of the 20th century in terms of its impact on a universal aspect of American culture?

Yes, American game shows of the '50s were often stupid—vapid and inane—as this book has clearly shown. But there was much more to them than simply the opportunity they provided for Americans to makes fools of themselves in pursuit of money and bling. A large number of the shows weren't about prizes at all. Some practiced and engaged in a form of intellectual gymnastics that was actually cerebrally stimulating. Others explored the warm corners of family and friendship. There were soldiers and sailors popping in to talk about their service to the country, mothers and fathers sharing with viewers their struggles to hold their families together. Some game shows gave their audience the feeling that they were flipping through the pages of a movie fan magazine or perusing the sports pages of their local newspaper. There were references to the nation's leaders, to current events, to things about which Americans needed to be halfway conversant. Because so many of these shows were broadcast live, there was always the sensation of shared experience, a rally-round-the-rabbit-ears feeling of community, a chance to laugh together and vicariously play together. Even when these programs were viewed alone, the sense of commonality they conveyed was inescapable.

People talked back to their sets. They shouted out the answers they knew. They cheered when someone they liked did well. They laughed when someone they saw each week said something funny and so deliciously in character.

Minow was right. There *was* a procession of game shows. A long procession. By this author's estimate, there were—beginning with the airing of the special stand-alone broadcasts of *Truth or Consequences* and *Uncle Jim's Question Bee* on July 1, 1941, and ending with Jackie Gleason's infamous *You're in the Picture* apology on the night of JFK's inauguration on January 20, 1961, 333 network game shows which insinuated themselves into America's homes and into the collective American consciousness morning after morning, afternoon after afternoon, night after night. America in those years, which largely embodied the "Fabulous '50s," was a vast quizland, the country deriving pleasure from the process of learning a great deal about itself.

In his famous speech, Minow doesn't qualify the phrase "procession of game shows." He simply allows them to *proceed*. Perhaps it's their number that is troubling, when too little of television in May 1961 was given over to programs intentionally broadcast in the public interest. Perhaps it's their number that is troubling when too few of them strived to be much more than what they were. But in an era in which there was so much bad in the world, and so much that was wrong, television game shows and the joyful community they created have to be classified as one of the good things.

In the 1950s, the "box" ended up being much bigger than a bread box. It was as big as America.

Chapter Notes

Introduction

1. Hugh Hart, "Feb. 1, 1951: TV Shows Atomic Blast Live," *Wired.com*, February 1, 2010, accessed February 21, 2017 via https://www.wired.com/2010/02/0201ktla-atomic-test. On April 22, 1952, KTLA set up the first live, national feed for a Nevada atomic bomb explosion, this one carried by the major networks. See Jeff Kisseloff, *The Box: An Oral History of Television, 1920–1961* (New York: Viking, 1995), 171–172.
2. Bruce Fretts, "The 60 Greatest Game Shows of All Time," *TV Guide*, June 12, 2013, accessed February 21, 2017, via www.tvguide.com/news/greatest-game-shows-1066568.
3. *You Bet Your Life* is one of only four radio and television game shows to win a George Foster Peabody Award. The other programs given nods by the apparently game show-averse Peabody board: *G.E. College Bowl, Wait Wait … Don't Tell Me*, and *Jeopardy!*
4. Farnsworth made his own game show appearance on July 3, 1957; he was a contestant on *I've Got a Secret*.
5. Christopher H. Sterling and John M. Kittross, *Stay Tuned: A History of American Broadcasting* (Mahway, NJ: Lawrence Erlbaum, 2002), p.147.
6. Stan Opotowky, *TV—The Big Picture* (New York: Collier Books, 1962), 9.
7. "Radio. Top Ten," *Time*, February 27, 1956. Accessed online through Time.com: TIME Vault.
8. Until live television transmuted into taped television with the embrace of video-tape technology in late 1956, watching quiz shows—both the old standbys and the newbie fillers—was a summer habit for American TV viewers.
9. *You Bet Your Life* took summers off and re-ran episodes from the season past. Many of the live quiz shows, like *What's My Line?* and *I've Got a Secret* worked right through the summer.
10. "Radio. Top Ten," *Time*, August 13, 1956. Accessed online through Time.com: TIME Vault.
11. James L. Baughman, *Same Time, Same Station* (Baltimore: The Johns Hopkins University Press, 2007), 285. The fall half of the 1959–60 season included twenty-nine westerns on the three networks compared to only three four years earlier.

Chapter 1

1. Johnny Carson. BrainyQuote.com, Xplore Inc, 2017, accessed February 22, 2017 via www.brainyquote.com/quotes/quotes/j/johnnycars100200.html.
2. Maxene Fabe, *TV Game Shows* (Garden City, NY: Dolphin, 1979), 102; 294–308.
3. *Radio Days*, directed by Woody Allen, produced by Robert Greenhut, distributed by Orion Pictures, released January 30, 1987.
4. Hart got into the game show act himself when he served as host of the 1950 NBC primetime offering *Answer Yes or No*.
5. Fabe, *TV Game Shows*, 117.

6. Robert Wernick, "Jackpot! Golden Rain of Motorcycles, Great Danes and Ermine Falls on West Philadelphia," *Life*, March 28, 1949, 103–104.

7. Erik Barnouw, *The Golden Web: A History of Broadcasting in the United States 1933–1953* (New York: Oxford University Press, 1968), 287.

8. Fabe, *TV Game Shows*, 117.

9. Ruth Duskin Feldman oral history interview on Archive of American Television, accessed February 22, 2017 via www.emmytvlegends.org/interviews/shows/game-shows#.

10. Fred Ferretti, "Fleeting Fame: When Quiz Kids Grow Up," *New York Times*, December 26, 1982. Accessed online through NewYorkTimes.com.

11. *Ibid*.

12. Thomas A. DeLong, *Quiz Craze: America's Infatuation with Game Shows* (New York: Praeger, 1991), 22–23.

13. *Ibid.*, 30.

14. *Ibid*.

15. *Ibid.*, 32.

16. *Ibid*.

17. Olaf Hoerschelmann, *Rules of the Game: Quiz Shows and American Culture* (Albany: State University of New York, 2006), 13.

18. DeLong, *Quiz Craze*, 29.

19. Not everyone enjoyed the fun and frivolity of Mr. Linkletter and company's stunts. A June 7, 1948, issue of *Life* magazine tells the sad tale of one Kathie Zahn, coincidentally running for Albany, California's city council, who had never even heard of Linkletter's show when she found herself in the middle of a *People Are Funny* stunt gone horribly wrong. After Mrs. Zahn's arrival one day at the San Francisco rail terminal, she was besieged by 2000 fans of *People Are Funny*, who had been instructed to look for the "Woman in the Red Hat," who would be passing out Raleigh cigarettes, and who, if properly identified, might help some lucky someone win a $20,000 jackpot award. Mrs. Zahn wasn't the "Woman in the Red Hat," but because her hat was red, she ended up having to be rescued by the "riot squad." Subsequently, she lost her election and filed a lawsuit against NBC, KNBC (the local NBC affiliated station), and the Brown and Williamson tobacco company. The author's research didn't turn up the outcome of her suit. See "People. Revenge on Radio," *Life*, June 7, 1948, 54.

20. "Daily NBC Show Will Be on Tape," *New York Times*, January 18, 1957, 31.

21. "New Mexico Legends. Hot Springs to Truth or Consequences," *Legends of America*, accessed February 22, 2017 via www.legendsofamerica.com/nm-truthconsequence.html; "Truth or Consequences—What's with That Crazy Name?" *Sierra County Is New Mexico True*, accessed February 22, 2017 via www.sierracountynewmexico.info/blog/a-town-named-after-a-game-show/. One would assume that some of those 295 Hot Springs residents who voted against the name change would make their displeasure known. One did. A pine coffin was left at the town cemetery filled with old bones and an envelope addressed to Hot Springs's "next of kin." Inside was a Joker from a pack of playing cards and a note that read, "Hot Springs, born December, 1916. Died March 31, 1950." The identity of the macabre prankster was never learned. See Sherry Fletcher and Cindy Carpenter, *Truth or Consequences (Images of America)* (Mount Pleasant, SC: Arcadia, 2010), 120.

22. "Radio Quiz Tells Guest Where $1000 Is, Holyoke Listeners Beat Train, Dig It Up," *New York Times*, November 6, 1944, 21.

23. Ralph Edwards oral history interview on Archive of American Television, accessed February 22, 2017 via www.emmytvlegends.org/interviews/shows/truth-or-consequences#.

24. Fabe, *TV Game Shows*, 117.

25. Ralph Edwards oral history interview.

26. *Ibid.*; "Radio Error Starts a Shower of Pennies That Turn to Mail Deluge in Staten Island," *New York Times*, January 26, 1943, 38; "Mail Flood Gives Radio Quiz Loser No Rest as Truckloads of Gifts Begin to Arrive," *New York Times*, January 28, 1943, 17; "Cause of It All Turns Up," *New York Times*, January 31, 1943, 26.

27. "Quiz Shows Blitz Actors," *Variety*, July 10, 1940, 1.

28. DeLong, *Quiz Craze*, 89–90.

29. *Ibid.*, 91–92.

30. *Ibid.*, 93.
31. *Ibid.*, 94.
32. *Ibid.*, 99.
33. *Vox Pop 1932–1945: The Story of "The Show That Travels America,"* promotional booklet, n.d., cited in Hoerschelmann, *Rules of the Game*, 33.
34. DeLong, *Quiz Craze*, 96.
35. *Ibid.*, 96.
36. *Ibid.*, 97–98.
37. *Ibid.*, 95.

Chapter 2

1. William S. Paley, *As It Happened: A Memoir* (Garden City, NY: Doubleday, 1979), 231.
2. James L. Baughman, *Same Time, Same Station* (Baltimore: The Johns Hopkins University Press, 2007), 63–64.
3. Lynn Spigel, *Make Room for TV: Television and the Family Ideal in Postwar America* (Chicago: University of Chicago Press, 1992), 32.
4. *Ibid.*
5. Comparative list of television receivers by name and model, tube size, and price, *Saturday Review*, February 26, 1949, accessed through Early Television Museum website, February 22, 2017, http://www.earlytelevision.org/pdf/sat_review_2-26-49.pdf.
6. There was a third charades-based game show during this period called *Tele Pun*, which ran for a few weeks in 1948 on NBC.
7. Networks liked to try to gussie and glam up game shows on occasion. It was suggested to Norm Blumenthal, producer of *Concentration*, that his show would benefit from opening "each telecast with a high-kicking chorus line of thirteen scantily clad female dancers. Just like French cancan dancers, each would turn their back to the camera, bend over, lift their skirts high above their heads, and reveal one of the letters in the title of our show on their backsides." See Norm Blumenthal, *When Game Shows Ruled Daytime TV* (Albany, GA: Bearmanor Media, 2010), 42.
8. Robert Dwan, *As Long As They're Laughing* (Baltimore: Midnight Marquee Press, Inc., 2000), 44–45.
9. Goodman Ace, column, *Saturday Review*, October 28, 1950, cited in Dwan, *As Long As They're Laughing*, 47.
10. Jason Mittell, *Television and American Culture* (New York: Oxford University Press, 2010), 245.
11. Even though experimentation in television technology was suspended during the war, advances in wartime radar were so beneficial to the development of TV, that some believe those five years weren't lost at all, and probably would have been needed to perfect signal delivery and reception even in the absence of world war. See Stan Opotowsky, *TV—The Big Picture* (New York: Collier Books, 1962), 30.

Chapter 3

1. Herta Herzog, "Professor Quiz—A Gratification Study," in *Radio and the Printed Page*, ed. Paul F. Lazarfeld (New York: Duell, Sloan & Pearce, 1940), 68–69.
2. Olaf Hoerschelmann, *Rules of the Game: Quiz Shows and American Culture* (Albany: State University of New York, 2006), 23.
3. Thomas A. DeLong, *Quiz Craze: America's Infatuation with Game Shows* (New York: Praeger, 1991), p 37.
4. The singular exception might have been the 1941 comedy-musical, which used the quiz show for its backdrop. *Pot o' Gold* starred Jimmy Stewart and Paulette Goddard, and had a strong tie-in with the radio series. (Stewart is alleged to have said it was his least favorite film from among all in which he'd appeared, but this author is unable to authenticate the statement.) *Pot o' Gold* was also the only movie produced by James Roosevelt, Franklin and Eleanor's oldest son. Both James and brother Elliott made appearances on *What's My Line?* in the 1950s, James as guest panelist and mystery guest, Elliot as mystery guest. (Their mother also appeared as a mystery guest). Nine years later, Stewart appeared in another movie related to a radio quiz show, *The Jackpot* (described in chapter 13). Another famous Democrat was tangentially associated with this film: Margaret Truman, who made

her debut as a radio actor by appearing in an adaptation of the movie on *Screen Director's Playhouse*, broadcast on April 26, 1951. (Margaret Truman's reviews were mixed, but she did mention that the president enjoyed her performance.)

5. DeLong, *Quiz Craze*, 38.

6. Jeff Kisseloff, *The Box: An Oral History of Television, 1920–1961* (New York: Viking, 1995), 126–127.

7. Maxene Fabe, *TV Game Shows* (Garden City, NY: Dolphin, 1979), 181–182; Kisseloff, *The Box*, 473–474.

8. Cited in Fabe, *TV Game Shows*, 181.

9. David Schwartz, Steve Ryan, and Fred Wostbrock, *The Encyclopedia of TV Game Shows* (New York: Facts on File, Inc., 1995), 6.

10. *Ibid.*, 224.

11. Robert Dwan, *As Long As They're Laughing* (Baltimore: Midnight Marquee Press, Inc., 2000), 63.

12. Fabe, *TV Game Shows*, 18.

13. David Halberstam, *The Fifties* (New York: Villard Books, 1993), 645.

Chapter 4

1. J. Ronald Oakley, *God's Country: America in the Fifties* (New York: Dembner Books, 1986), 228.

2. "Bride and Groom Coming Back on Television Soon," *Ellensburg Daily Record*, June 6, 1957, 2.

3. Robert Dwan, *As Long As They're Laughing* (Baltimore: Midnight Marquee Press, 2000), 118.

4. The Dorothy Dix Special Collection Research Guide. F.G. Woodward Library, Austin Peay State University, accessed February 23, 2017 via http://library.apsu.edu/Dix/research/guide.htm.

5. Harold Mehling, *The Great Time-Killer* (Cleveland: The World Publishing Co.), 45.

6. J. Fred MacDonald, *One Nation Under Television* (New York: Pantheon Books), 135–136.

7. "Advertising. Geritol's Bitter Pill," *Time*, February 5, 1973. Accessed online through Time.com: TIME Vault.

8. Pieter Cohen, and Nicolas Rasmussen, "A Nation of Kids on Speed," *Wall Street Journal*, June 16, 2013, accessed October 15, 2016 via https://www.wsj.com/articles/SB10001424127887323728204578513662248894162.

9. Alka-Seltzer, Arident Decongestant Tablets, Arrestin Cold Remedy, Banarin Cold Remedy, Bayer Aspirin, Bayer Nasal Spray, Bromo-Quinine, Bromo-Seltzer, Bufferin tablets, Carter's Little Pills, Colonaid Laxative, Coughlets, Count 4 Antacid, Delamine Antacid, Dondril Cough Tablets, Dr. Caldwell's Laxative, Driacol Cold Tablets, Dristan, Duplexin Headache Remedy, Eno Antacid, Excedrin Pain Reliever, Fortisun Cold Remedy, 4-Way Cold Tablets, Geritol, Haley's M-O, Heet Linament, Instantine Headache Remedy, Instil Stomach Remedy, the various Johnson & Johnson medicative products, Liquiprin for Children, Micrainin Headache Tablets, Musterole Chest rub, Nebs Pain Reliever, Nervine Liquid (and tablets!), Painquellizer Tablets, Pepto-Bismol, Pertussin Cough Remedy, Pine Bros. Cough Drops, Pinex Cough Syrup, Rem Cold Remedy, Sal Hepatica, Serutan, St. Joseph Aspirin, Super Anahist, Tabsin Cold Tablets, Thorexin Cough Syrup, Virisan Nasal Decongestant, and Zarumin Pain Reliever. This list leaves off mouth washes, sleep aids, and medicinal toothpastes, most of which contained the decade's most loudly touted but chemically nugatory ingredient: chlorophyll.

Chapter 5

1. Tom Clancy. BrainyQuote.com, Xplore Inc, 2017, accessed September 30, 2017 via www.brainyquote.com/quotes/quotes/t/tomclancy290229.html?src=t_news.

2. "The Defense of Staying Live," *Variety*, January 5, 1955, 92.

3. Interview of Mark Goodson by Thomas A. DeLong, April 24, 1984, cited in Thomas A. DeLong, *Quiz Craze* (New York: Praeger, 1991), 239.

4. James L. Baughman, *Same Time, Same Station* (Baltimore: The Johns Hopkins University Press, 2007), 41.

5. Jack Gould, column, *New York Times*, September 22, 1950, 54.

6. As a historical footnote, had he known that General Van Fleet was destined to become a centenarian, MacArthur might have been inclined to change his famous adage to "Some old soldiers actually do die, but first they get to live past the age of one hundred."

7. Multiple sources cited in *Wikipedia, The Free Encyclopedia*, s.v. "Anthony Herbert (lieutenant colonel)," accessed February 23, 2017 via https://en.wikipedia.org/wiki/Anthony_Herbert_(lieutenant_colonel). Coincidentally, General Westmoreland appeared as a challenger on *What's My Line?* on July 24, 1960 a few weeks after being appointed superintendent of West Point.

8. J.P. Shanley, "TV: A Grim Warning. 'I've Got a Secret' Drops Gags to Show Graphically Holiday Driving Perils," *New York Times*, August 29, 1957, 51.

9. Allan Sherman, *A Gift of Laughter* (New York: Atheneum, 1965), 134.

10. J. Ronald Oakley, *God's Country: America in the Fifties* (New York: Dembner Books, 1986), 241.

11. The Manchester, New Hampshire native is also remembered for his quote, "Don't glorify war. There's nothing glorious about it."

12. Norman Franks and Harry Dempsey, *American Aces of World War I* (Oxford, U.K.: Osprey Publishing, 2001), 49–50.

13. "It Could Be You!," *Ocala Star Banner*, September 25, 1960, 53.

14. Oakley, *God's Country*, 18.

15. DeLong, *Quiz Craze*, 242.

16. January 10, 2015 pinned post to Spindletop-Gladys City Boomtown Facebook page, accessed February 23, 2017 via https://www.facebook.com/GladysCity/posts/773112632753905.

17. With little doubt, one of Lambert's reasons for appearing on the show was to advocate for recognition of Dr. Roger Post Ames, without whom, contended Lambert, "there would have been no experiment." This oversight was corrected when Ames was posthumously awarded the Congressional Medal of Honor on September 2, 1958. Lambert's appearance on this very popular panel show was perhaps more than a little helpful in getting the bill that would give Ames the medal rescued from committee and brought to a vote by House and Senate.

18. For the challenge, the panel was blindfolded, since the uniform Shanafelt was wearing might be a giveaway; a bigger giveaway, however, which was missed by everyone except, perhaps, the correct guesser, Bill Cullen, was Shanafelt's entrance being accompanied by the playing of the Rough Riders' theme song (and Teddy Roosevelt's favorite ditty), "A Hot Time in the Old Town."

19. Jabara flew 108 combat missions, once suffering a mid-air collision with a German aircraft, both pilots bailing out and shaking hands after floating safely to the ground. In spite of cheating death on several occasions while participating in combat missions over Germany, Jabara died in Florida in 1966, at age forty-three in a vehicular roll-over. The vehicle was, with cruel irony, a German-made Volkswagen.

20. Oakley, *God's Country*, 155–156.

21. Gil Fates, *What's My Line? The History of America's Most Famous Panel Show* (Englewood Cliffs, NJ: Prentice Hall, 1978), viii.

22. Oakley, *God's Country*, 155–156.

Chapter 6

1. "Some Basic Statistical Data" insert in Margaret Mead, "She Has Strength Based in a Pioneer Past," *Life*, December 24, 1956, 26–27.

2. David Halberstam, *The Fifties* (New York: Villard Books, 1993), 648.

3. J. Ronald Oakley, *God's Country: America in the Fifties* (New York: Dembner Books, 1986), 234.

4. Terry-Thomas was a guest panelist on *What's My Line?* in May of 1964. Thirteen years earlier, he had been a celebrity challenger on the long-running British version of the show, which was broadcast on the BBC. There were versions of *What's My Line?* which aired throughout the world in the 1950s and 1960s. Here is a sampling of some of the literal translations of their titles: *Guess What He Does?* (Brazil), *To Each His Job* (French Canada), *What Am I?* (West Germany), *Guess Your*

Life (Spain), *Guess My Profession* (Sweden), and *My Job and I* (Venezuela).

5. Maxene Fabe, *TV Game Shows* (Garden City, NY: Dolphin, 1979), 37.
6. Fabe, *TV Game Shows*, 37–38.
7. Droodles were popular cartoons of the fifties whose humor was based on descriptions applied to an assembly of minimalist, often geometric shapes. For example, a long horizontal rectangle filled with five large X's could carry the caption "the Eiffel Tower seen through a mail slot."
8. Betty Friedan, "Television and the Feminine Mystique," in *Television: Selections from TV GUIDE Magazine*, Barry G. Cole, ed. (New York: The Free Press, 1970), 273.
9. Ibid., 275.
10. Halberstam, *The Fifties*, 590.
11. Martha F. Cassidy, *What Women Watched: Daytime Television in the 1950s* (Austin, TX: University of Texas, 2005), 26.
12. Fabe, *TV Game Shows*, 160.
13. "*The Big Payoff's* Third Anniversary," ad in *Variety*, January 5, 1955, 195.
14. Cassidy, *What Women Watched*, 208.
15. Thomas A. DeLong, *Quiz Craze: America's Infatuation with Game Shows* (New York: Praeger, 1991), 103–104.

Chapter 7

1. Stan Opotowsky, *TV—The Big Picture* (New York: Collier Books, 1962), 150.
2. Martha F. Cassidy, *What Women Watched: Daytime Television in the 1950s* (Austin, TX: University of Texas, 2005), 2. 130.
3. Harry Castleman, and Walter J. Podrazik, *Watching TV: Four Decades of American Television* (New York: McGraw-Hill, 1982), 85.
4. "Winning Ways," *Newsweek*, August 17, 1953, 61.
5. Cassidy, *What Women Watched*, 60.
6. Ibid., 61.
7. Thomas A. DeLong, *Quiz Craze* (New York: Praeger, 1991), 153.
8. Jack Gould, "A Look at 'Strike It Rich' as Video Entertainment: Human Emotions and Commercial Appeal," November 9, 1951, 34.
9. Ibid.
10. Ibid.
11. "Charity Vaunteth Not Itself," *Life*, August 17, 1953, 20.
12. "Letters to the Editors," *Life*, September 7, 1953, 8.
13. Ibid.
14. Alfred J. Barrett, "Stop the Misery!" *America*, March 13, 1954, 625–626.
15. Ibid.
16. Ibid.
17. "As We See It," *TV Guide*, January 8, 1954, 3; March 26, 1954, 2.
18. Barrett, "Stop the Misery!" 625–626.
19. "Ex-Convict Strikes It Rich Briefly on TV, but Fame Proves a Give-Away to Police," *New York Times*, January 27, 1954, 19.
20. "Charity Load Linked to Give-Away Shows," *New York Times*, February 5, 1954, 21.
21. "Giveaways ... Are Legal," *Business Week*, April 10, 1954, 128.
22. Cassidy, *What Women Watched*, 119.
23. Ibid., 118.
24. "NBC-TV's Major Daytime Advances; Forge Ahead on Sales, Ratings," *Variety*, February 6, 1957, 27.
25. Susan Murray and Laurie Ouellette, *Reality TV: Remaking Television Culture* (New York: NYC Press, 2008), 304.
26. "Queen for a Day: Housewives Schedule Wrecker," *Look*, April 1, 1958, 120.
27. Howard Blake, "An Apologia from the Man Who Produced the Worst Program in TV History," in *American Broadcasting: A Source Book on the History of Radio and Television*, edited by Lawrence W. Lichty and Malachi C. Topping (New York: Hasting House, 1975), 417.
28. "Reigns of Queens for a Day Span 15 Years with 3,921 Rulers, Mostly Crowned by Bailey," *Los Angeles Times*, May 1, 1960, 3.
29. Opotowski, *TV—The Big Picture*, 136.
30. "Reigns of Queens...," *Los Angeles Times*, 3.
31. Blake, "An Apologia," 417.
32. Murray, *Reality TV*, 303.

Chapter 8

1. Pearl Buck. Good Reads, accessed September 30, 2017 via www.goodreads.com/quotes/tag/new-york-city?page=3.

2. Teleplay writer Paddy Chayefsky plays an unintended role in the tumble into ignominy taken by the quiz show *Twenty-One*; the film version of Chayefsky's TV drama *Marty* was the answer to the question which contestant Herb Stempel was required to miss in taking his dive.

3. Gil Fates, *What's My Line? The History of America's Most Famous Panel Show* (Englewood Cliffs, NJ: Prentice Hall, 1978), 13.

4. During the run of the show, Rheingold was touted as the "official beer of New York," and commanded a large loyal following of city beer drinkers. The company stopped operating in 1976, three years after the opening of the World Trade Center. After the fall of the twin towers on 9–11, the rubble revealed numerous Rheingold beer cans, which had been stashed in the towers' beams by Rheingold-devoted construction workers, who had apparently taken quite a few beer breaks while on the job.

5. Fans of Hitchcock's *Rear Window*, released several months after this broadcast, will recall a scene in the film in which Grace Kelly personally caters an intimate lobster dinner for her apartment-bound boyfriend Jimmy Stewart, courtesy of 21.

6. Gordon Cotler, "That Strange TV Audience," *New York Times Magazine*, May 16, 1954, 19, 39.

7. Bennett Cerf, *At Random: Reminiscences of Bennett Cerf* (New York: Random House, 1977), 136.

8. Multiple sources cited in *Wikipedia, The Free Encyclopedia*, in "History of religion in the United States,": https://en.wikipedia.org/wiki/History_of_religion_in_the_the_United_States; "Jews in New York City,": https://en.wikipedia.org/wiki/Jews_in_New_York_City (both accessed February 24, 2017).

9. Susan Dworkin, *Miss America, 1945: Bess Myerson's Own Story* (New York: Newmarket Press, 1987), 182, 189.

10. Ibid., 189–190, 203.

11. Ibid., 196–197.

12. There was also a related problem unique to game and audience participation shows called "Plugola," in which contestants and other guests of the programs were paid in advance to "plug" certain products by working their mention into on-camera conversation.

13. Bernard Kalb, "Bennett Cerf: He Also Works in Video," *New York Times*, August 2, 1953, X9 (p. 222 @ timesmachine.nytimes.com).

14. Kliph Nesteroff, *Classic Television Showbiz* website, interview with Orson Bean, accessed February 25, 2017 via http://classicshowbiz.blogspot.com/2014/11/an-interview-with-orson-bean-part-three.html.

Chapter 9

1. Songwriters Hall of Fame website, 1992 Award and Induction Ceremony: Sammy Cahn Lifetime Achievement Award—Nat King Cole, accessed February 25, 2017 via http://www.songwritershalloffame.org/ceremony/entry/C3104/5044.

2. J. Fred MacDonald, *Blacks and White TV: African Americans in Television Since 1948* (Belmont, CA: Wadsworth Publishing, 1992), accessed through J. Fred MacDonald Presents website, February 25, 2017, http://www.jfredmacdonald.com/bawtv/bawtv1.htm.

3. James Arthur Von Schilling, *The Magic Window: American Television, 1939–1953* (Binghamton, NY: Haworth Press, 2003), 260.

4. James L. Baughman, *Same Time, Same Station* (Baltimore: The Johns Hopkins University Press, 2007), 164.

5. J.P. Shanley, "TV Boycott Asked on Network Job Bias," *New York Times*, February 21, 1955, 21. The problem of a lack of visibility for blacks on TV existed in the movie industry as well. As late as 1962, *Cape Fear*, which included a number of outdoor and other scenes of public congregation featured only white extras, there being only one black actor used in the entire film; he played a courthouse janitor. Many of these scenes were shot in Savannah, Georgia, a city with a historically

large African-American population. *Cape Fear* comes to mind because of the long association of one of its stars—Polly Bergen—with the panel show *To Tell the Truth*, but is nonetheless indicative of the mindset of the era.

6. Jeff Kisseloff, *The Box: An Oral History of Television, 1920–1961* (New York: Viking, 1995), 516.

7. Stan Opotowsky, *TV—The Big Picture* (New York: Collier Books, 1962), 110.

8. Kisseloff, *The Box*, 517.

9. Dick Hobson, "TV's Disastrous Brain Drain," in *Television: Selections from TV GUIDE Magazine*, Barry G. Cole, ed. (New York: The Free Press, 1970), 185.

10. Baughman, *Same Time, Same Station*, 163.

11. Ibid.

12. *The Billboard*, November 13, 1948, 19.

13. MacDonald, *Blacks and White TV*, accessed through J. Fred MacDonald Presents website, February 25, 2017, http://www.jfredmacdonald.com/bawtv/bawtv5.htm.

14. Ibid. In 1948, Howard hosted *The Bob Howard Show* on CBS, making him the first African-American with his own regularly broadcast TV show.

15. Cab Calloway and Bryant Rollins, *Minnie The Moocher and Me* (New York: Thomas Y. Crowell Co., 1976), 180.

16. Shanley, "TV Boycott Asked on Network Job Bias."

17. A.S. "Doc" Young, "The Black Athlete in the Golden Age of Sports, Part VI: The Black Athlete Makes His Mark," *Ebony*, May, 1969, 118.

18. Robert Dwan, *As Long As They're Laughing* (Baltimore: Midnight Marquee Press, Inc., 2000), 114.

19. Ibid., 114–116.

20. Harold Mehling, *The Great Time-Killer* (Cleveland: The World Publishing Co.), 65.

21. Ibid., 63.

22. Ibid., 62.

23. Ibid., 66.

24. Mark Goodson, "The Anatomy of a Game," Seminar, The Museum of Television and Radio, October 9, 1985.

25. Ibid.

Chapter 10

1. Jimmy Carter, BrainyQuote.com, Xplore Inc, 2017, accessed February 22, 2017 via www.brainyquote.com/quotes/quotes/j/jimmycarte158449.html.

2. Martha F. Cassidy, *What Women Watched: Daytime Television in the 1950s* (Austin, TX: University of Texas, 2005), 13.

3. Robert Dwan, *As Long As They're Laughing* (Baltimore: Midnight Marquee Press, Inc., 2000), 78.

Chapter 11

1. William S. Paley, "Broadcasting and American Society," *Annals of the American Academy of Political and Social Science*, January 1941, 63.

2. J. Ronald Oakley, *God's Country: America in the Fifties* (New York: Dembner Books, 1986), 230.

3. John Crosby, "Mr. Paley and the Critics," *New York Herald Tribune*, October 28, 1946.

4. Memo, Weaver to Joseph H. McConnell, November 12, 1951, in NBC Papers, Library of Congress, folder 586.

5. Jeff Kisseloff, *The Box: An Oral History of Television, 1920–1961* (New York: Viking, 1995), 375. Alcoa may have given Murrow and Friendly free rein over *See It Now*, but their liberality was selective. For a February 19, 1956 episode of their live drama anthology series *The Alcoa Hour*, the company forced Reginald Rose to rewrite his teleplay for "Tragedy in a Temporary Town," so that a lynching would take place in a shanty town of wooden shacks, rather than in a trailer camp, since most mobile homes are constructed of aluminum (and it's apparently not a great idea to associate aluminum with brutal lynchings). See J. Fred MacDonald, *One Nation Under Television* (New York: Pantheon Books), p.86.

6. It was *Mad Magazine* in its January, 1971 issue that put the whole tempest in perspective. It featured on the issue's back cover, four cemetery tombstones, with epitaphs reading, "Winston tasted good like a cigarette should've," "You mean *as a*

cigarette should've," "What did you want, good grammar or good taste?" and lastly, "I wanted to live a lot longer than this!" Another headache for the R.J. Reynolds Tobacco Company came with the aforementioned "modern stone-age family" Flintstones. As hard as it is for us of the enlightened 21st century to believe, a primetime children's cartoon program was actually sponsored by a cigarette company. Fred and Wilma Flintstone even did Winston commercials, enjoying an occasional Pleistocene smoke together. Winston stopped sponsoring *The Flintstones* when the couple became the proud parents of little Pebbles. (One hopes that Wilma had stopped smoking nine months before that.)

7. Henry Morgan, *Here's Morgan!* (New York: Barricade Books, 1994), 213.

8. *Ibid.*

9. Norm Blumenthal, *When Game Shows Ruled Daytime TV* (Albany, GA: Bearmanor Media, 2010), 185.

10. Erik Barnouw, *The Image Empire: A History of Broadcasting in the United States, Vol III—from 1953* (New York: Oxford University Press, 1970), 23.

11. Kisseloff, *The Box*, 365–366.

12. *Ibid.*, 366.

13. Harold Mehling, *The Great Time-Killer* (Cleveland: The World Publishing Co.), 57.

14. Marie Brenner, "The Man Who Knew Too Much," *Vanity Fair*, May, 1996, accessed February 25, 2017 via *Vanity Fair* website, http://www.vanityfair.com/magazine/1996/05/wigand199605.

15. Kisseloff, *The Box*, 521.

16. Opotowski, *TV—The Big Picture*, 110.

17. Sally Ashley, *F.P.A.: The Life and Times of Franklin Pearce Adams* (New York: Beaufort Books, 1986), 217.

18. *Printers Ink*, January 9, 1953, cited in Stephen Fox, *The Mirror Makers: A History of American Advertising and its Creators* (New York: Vintage Books/Random House, 1985), 212.

19. Thomas A. DeLong, *Quiz Craze: America's Infatuation with Game Shows* (New York: Praeger, 1991), 161.

20. William Clotworthy oral history interview on Archive of American Television, accessed February 25, 2017 via http://www.emmytvlegends.org/interviews/people/william-clotworthy.

21. Blumenthal, *When Game Shows Ruled...*, 185.

22. Allan Sherman, *A Gift of Laughter* (New York: Atheneum, 1965), 128–129.

23. *The Realist*, June, 1960, 3.

24. *Ibid.*, March, 1960, 5–6.

25. *Ibid.* June, 1960, 3–4.

26. *Ibid.*, 4.

27. *What's My Line?* on TV.com website, Episode 323—August 12, 1956, under Notes, accessed February 25, 2017 via http://www.tv.com/shows/whats-my-line/episode-323-95473/trivia/. President Truman relieved General MacArthur of his command of United Nations forces in Korea on April 10, 1951. MacArthur's bitterness over the sacking obviously remained intact.

28. Mehling, *The Great Time-Killer*, 59.

29. Andrew Tobias, *Fire and Ice: The Story of Charles Revson, the Man Who Built Revlon* (New York: William Morrow, 1976). Accessed October 2, 2016 via https://andrewtobias.com/fire-and-ice/.

30. *Ibid.*

31. Mehling, *The Great Time-Killer*, 26.

32. *Ibid.*, 26–27.

Chapter 12

1. Jeff Kisseloff, *The Box: An Oral History of Television, 1920–1961* (New York: Viking, 1995), 414.

2. Bennett Cerf interviewed by Robbin Hawkins, January 23, 1968, Interview #16, 732–733, for Columbia University Libraries Oral History Research Office Notable New Yorkers Series, accessed February 25, 2017 via http://www.columbia.edu/cu/lweb/digital/collections/nny/cerfb/transcripts/cerfb_1_16_710.html.

3. Jeff Kisseloff, *The Box: An Oral History of Television, 1920–1961* (New York: Viking, 1995), 476.

4. Letter from Louis Untermeyer to Lee Israel, 1977, cited in Lee Israel, *Kilgallen* (New York: Dell Publishing, 1979), 220.

5. "Red Visitors Cause Rumpus: Dupes

and Fellow Travelers Dress Up Communist Fronts," *Life*, April 4, 1949, 103–104.

6. "Death of a Salesman: Fine Tragedy Becomes a Critical and Box-office Sensation," *Life*, February 21, 1949, 115.

7. Arthur Miller, *Timebends: A Life* (New York: Grove Press, 1987), 263–264.

8. Val Adams, "Praise Pours in on Murrow Show," *New York Times*, March 11, 1954, 19.

9. J. Fred MacDonald, *Television and the Red Menace: The Video Road to Vietnam* (New York: Praeger, 1985), accessed through J. Fred MacDonald Presents website, February 26, 2017, http://www.jfredmacdonald.com/trm/11tvinpoticalcontext.htm.

10. *Ibid.*

11. Henry Morgan, *Here's Morgan!* (New York: Barricade Books, 1994), 204.

12. Coverage of all 187 hours cost ABC $600,000. See Martha F. Cassidy, *What Women Watched: Daytime Television in the 1950s* (Austin: University of Texas, 2005), 46.

13. Gil Fates, *What's My Line? The History of America's Most Famous Panel Show* (Englewood Cliffs, NJ: Prentice Hall, 1978), 11.

14. Erik Barnouw, *The Golden Web: A History of Broadcasting in the United States 1933–1953* (New York: Oxford University Press, 1968), 278.

15. According to Morgan in his autobiography *Here's Morgan!*, he was falsely accused of being a member of "something called Progressive Citizens of America," of having spoken by recording at a rally for the Stop Censorship Committee, and for participating in a different rally, this one for Veterans Against Discriminations. See Morgan, *Here's Morgan!*, 201.

16. Barnouw, *The Golden Web*, 257.

17. Former communist party member Harvey Matusow, who became a paid government informer and an aide to Senator Joseph McCarthy, told Jeff Kisseloff in his oral history of early television, *The Box*, "I worked for *Counterattack*. Besides the newsletter, for five thousand dollars we also set up security systems for companies. If a company bought our services, they would send us lists of names, and we would check them out in our files and let them know if they were acceptable or not. We had a humongous file. If a name appeared in an ad in the *New York Post* we put it on a card. We also had the Congressional testimony cross-indexed. We would go through the cards, and we would find out that so-and-so signed a petition in 1941 and we would tell the client. Lennon & Mitchell [ad agency] paid me $150 for a list of actors that we had indexed. It didn't take a lot of convincing. They were eager to have it because now they could just look at the file and—"Boom, we don't want him." See Kisseloff, *The Box*, 409–410.

18. Morgan, *Here's Morgan!*, 200.

19. *Ibid.*, 206.

20. *Ibid.*

21. *Ibid.*, 206–207.

22. MacDonald, *Television and the Red Menace*, http://www.jfredmacdonald.com/trm/11tvinpoticalcontext.htm.

23. *Red Channels: The Report of Communist Influence in Radio and Television* (New York: Counterattack, 1950), 3–4.

24. Wikipedia, The Free Encyclopedia, "The Hollywood Blacklist," accessed February 26, 2017 via https://en.wikipedia.org/wiki/Hollywood_blacklist#The_Red_Channels_list. The article includes a full listing of blacklisted individuals categorized by the lists on which their names appeared.

25. *Ibid.*

26. Groucho Marx, and Hector Arce, *The Secret Word is Groucho* (New York: G.P. Putnam's Sons, 1976), 85.

27. Robert Dwan, *As Long As They're Laughing* (Baltimore: Midnight Marquee Press, Inc., 2000), 125.

28. *Ibid.*, 127.

29. *Ibid.*

30. *Ibid.*

31. Leon Janney, biographical page, Allmovie website, accessed March 1, 2017, via http://www.allmovie.com/artist/leon-janney-p35207.

32. Barnouw, *The Golden Web*, 265–67.

33. Kliph Nesteroff, *Classic Television Showbiz* website, interview with Orson Bean, accessed February 26, 2017 via http://classicshowbiz.blogspot.com/2014/07/an-interview-with-orson-bean-part-two.html.

34. Morgan, *Here's Morgan!*, 202.

35. Thomas Doherty, *Cold War, Cool Medium: Television, McCarthyism, and American Culture* (New York: Columbia University Press, 2003), 32–33, 49–59.

36. Morgan, *Here's Morgan!*, 201.

37. Douglas made several TV game show appearances early in his centenarian's life: *The Name's the Same, Name That Tune,* and *What's My Line?*, as well as being bio-blindsided on Ralph Edwards' *This Is Your Life* at the ripe old age of forty-two.

38. Myrna Oliver, "Texas Humorist John Faulk Dies: Exposed and Beat Blacklisting," *Los Angeles Times*, April 11, 1990, accessed February 26, 2017 via http://articles.latimes.com/1990-04-11/news/mn-977_1_john-henry-faulk.

39. "John Henry Faulk, 76, Dies; Humorist Who Challenged Blacklist," *New York Times*, April 10, 1990, accessed via NYTimes.com.

40. "Elia Kazan Receiving an Honorary Oscar," video, accessed February 26, 2017 via YouTube, https://www.youtube.com/watch?v=3YziNNCZeNs.

41. Dean Kahn, "Ives-Seeger Rift Finally Ended with 'Blue-Tail Fly' Harmony: Skagitonians Ives, Murros Were on Opposite Side," *Knight Ridder Tribune Business News* [from *Bellingham Herald*, Washington], March 19, 2006, 1.

42. Cited in J. Ronald Oakley, *God's Country: America in the Fifties* (New York: Dembner Books, 1986), 184–185.

43. Oakley, *God's Country*, 74.

44. *Ibid.*, 184–185.

45. *Ibid.*, 185.

Chapter 13

1. "Radio. The Big Money," *Time*, September 3, 1956, accessed online through Time.com: TIME Vault.

2. James L. Baughman, *Same Time, Same Station* (Baltimore: The Johns Hopkins University Press, 2007), 147.

3. Martha F. Cassidy, *What Women Watched: Daytime Television in the 1950s* (Austin, TX: University of Texas, 2005), 208.

4. *Jefferson Drum* (also known as *The Pen and the Quill*) was the western TV series which convinced its producers, Mark Goodson and Bill Todman, that they ought to stick to game shows. It ran from April 25 until December 11 in 1958.

5. Maxene Fabe, *TV Game Shows* (Garden City, NY: Dolphin, 1979), 183.

6. Thomas A. DeLong, *Quiz Craze: America's Infatuation with Game Shows* (New York: Praeger, 1991), 103.

7. *Ibid.*, 104.

8. Bill Todman, "Freedom of the Dial," *Variety*, January 5, 1949, 105.

9. Elaine Tyler May, *Homeward Bound: American Families and the Cold War Era* (New York: Basic Books, 1988), 165.

10. Jeff Kisseloff, *The Box: An Oral History of Television, 1920–1961* (New York: Viking, 1995), 466.

11. Fabe, *TV Game Shows*, 194.

12. Harold Mehling, *The Great Time-Killer* (Cleveland: The World Publishing Co.), 43.

13. Richard A. R. Pinkham, address to NBC TV affiliates meeting, November 25, 1955, in NBC Papers, Library of Congress, folder 948.

14. David Schwartz, Steve Ryan, and Fred Wostbrock, *The Encyclopedia of TV Game Shows* (New York: Facts on File, Inc., 1995), 180.

15. "Prodigy Rings the Bell," *Life*, May 7, 1956, 59.

16. Maureen Dowd, "The Early Death of a Bedeviled Genius," *New York Times*, May 25, 1985, accessed via NYT.com.

17. "Interview with Leonard Ross," *The Mike Wallace Interview*, December 21, 1957, Harry Ransom Center, the University of Texas at Austin, accessed February 26, 2017, via http://www.hrc.utexas.edu/multimedia/video/2008/wallace/ross_leonard_t.html.

18. J. Fred MacDonald, *One Nation Under Television* (New York: Pantheon Books), 6.

19. See Chapter 3, Note 3 for discussion of Jimmy Stewart's other movie about a quiz show, *Pot o' Gold*.

Chapter 14

1. Attributed to Socrates by Plato.

2. Robert Dwan, *As Long As They're*

Laughing (Baltimore: Midnight Marquee Press, Inc., 2000), 113–114.
  3. J. Ronald Oakley, *God's Country: America in the Fifties* (New York: Dembner Books, 1986), 286–288.
  4. Allan Sherman, *A Gift of Laughter* (New York: Atheneum, 1965), 131.

Chapter 15

  1. Darwin Porter, *Merv Griffin: A Life in the Closet* (New York: Bloodmoon Productions, Ltd., 2009), ISBN 978-0-9786465-0-9.
  2. Robert Dwan, *As Long As They're Laughing* (Baltimore: Midnight Marquee Press, Inc., 2000), 118–119.

Chapter 16

  1. "Show Business. A Melancholy Business," *Time*, October 26, 1959, 54.
  2. James L. Baughman, *Same Time, Same Station* (Baltimore: The Johns Hopkins University Press, 2007), 148.
  3. Harold Mehling, *The Great Time-Killer* (Cleveland: The World Publishing Co.), 38.
  4. Winn is familiar to media critics as the author of the blistering critique of TV's addictive influence on young children, *The Plug-In Drug: Television, Children, and the Family* (1977).
  5. Redford's own association with game shows dates back to the 1950s. As a young actor waiting for his big break, he worked as a "demonstrator" on the game show *Play Your Hunch*.
  6. Thomas A. DeLong, *Quiz Craze: America's Infatuation with Game Shows* (New York: Praeger, 1991), 222.
  7. Russell Porter, "TV Inquiry Raises Perjury Question," *New York Times*, November 9, 1959, 27.
  8. DeLong, *Quiz Craze*, 226.
  9. *Ibid.*, 225.
  10. Baughman, *Same Time, Same Station*, 297.
  11. William Boddy, *Fifties Television: The Industry and Its Critics* (Urbana, IL: University of Illinois Press, 1990), 225.
  12. Mehling, *The Great Time Killer*, 52.
  13. Robert E. Lee, Catholic Apostolate of Radio-Television-Advertising, New York City, November 22, 1959, copy in Eisenhower Papers, General Files, box 380.
  14. This is known in the advertising industry as the "gratitude effect." A viewer who really enjoys a particular radio or television show is often motivated to buy the sponsor's product out of gratitude over the pleasure derived from the program.
  15. J. Fred MacDonald, *One Nation Under Television* (New York: Pantheon Books), 139.
  16. "As TV Scandal Stirs the Whole Nation, Views of the Viewers at One Quiz Show," *Life*, October 26, 1959, 32–33.
  17. Phil Meyer, "Miamians Debate Quiz Shows," *Miami Herald*, November 16, 1959.
  18. Russell Baker, "Do Them Yourself," *New York Times*, October 1, 1994.
  19. "Happy New Year," *Broadcasting*, December 28, 1959.
  20. Harry Castleman and Walter J. Podrazik, *Watching TV: Four Decades of American Television* (New York: McGraw-Hill, 1982), 135.
  21. "As TV Scandal Stirs the Whole Nation," *Life*, October 26, 1959, 32–33.
  22. "TV Quiz Business Is Itself Quizzed About Fix Charges," *Life*, September 15, 1958, 24.
  23. Robert Dwan, *As Long As They're Laughing* (Baltimore: Midnight Marquee Press, Inc., 2000), 90–92.
  24. Jeff Kisseloff, *The Box: An Oral History of Television, 1920–1961* (New York: Viking, 1995), 477.
  25. *Ibid.*
  26. Stan Opotowky, *TV—The Big Picture* (New York: Collier Books, 1962), 249.
  27. Mehling, *The Great Time Killer*, 51.
  28. Kisseloff, *The Box*, 477.
  29. *Ibid.*, 478.
  30. Glenn used his after-tax winnings to set up a college fund for his children. Hodges used his to pursue an acting career. Shortly after appearing on *Name That Tune*, he landed the role of Winthrop in the premier Broadway production of *The Music Man*. After leaving acting, Hodges went on to become a mental health counselor, working in the field of alcohol and drug-abuse prevention. See DeLong, *Quiz Craze*, 211.

31. Kisseloff, *The Box*, 478.
32. "A Big Quiz for Quizzes," *Life*, October 19, 1959, 52.
33. Kisseloff, *The Box*, 477.
34. Marx to Bergen Evans, February 27, 1959, Groucho Marx Papers, Library of Congress, box 1.
35. "As TV Scandal Stirs the Whole Nation," *Life*, October 26, 1959, 33.
36. Kisseloff, *The Box*, 498.

Chapter 17

1. "Radio. What Comes Naturally," *Time*, November 7, 1949, accessed through Time.com: TIME Vault.
2. Thomas A. DeLong, *Quiz Craze: America's Infatuation with Game Shows* (New York: Praeger, 1991), 105.
3. Ibid.
4. Ibid., 210.
5. One of the longer YouTube offerings was retrieved on February 27, 2017 via https://www.youtube.com/watch?v=EdZqUDUQ0Ro.
6. Allan Sherman, *A Gift of Laughter* (New York: Atheneum, 1965), 123.
7. Norm Blumenthal, *When Game Shows Ruled Daytime TV* (Albany, GA: Bearmanor Media, 2010), 121–122.
8. *How Products Are Made* website, Made How, Volume 6, "Hula Hoop," accessed February 27, 2017 via http://www.madehow.com/Volume-6/Hula-Hoop.html.
9. Scott Kirsner, *Inventing the Movies* (CinemaTech Books, 2008), 46.
10. Avery Gilbert, *What the Nose Knows* (New York: Crown, 2008), 159.; Jim Drobnick, *The Smell Culture Reader* (Oxford, New York: Berg, 2006), 360.

Chapter 18

1. Malala Yousafzai, BrainyQuote.com, Xplore Inc, 2017, accessed March 1, 2017 via https://www.brainyquote.com/quotes/quotes/m/malalayous569369.html.
2. "Television: Inspiring Post-Mortem," *Time*, February 3, 1961, accessed through Time.com: TIME Vault.
3. "Gleason Analyzes Last Week's Failure," *New York Times*, January 28, 1961, 39.
4. Kliph Nesteroff, *Classic Television Showbiz* website, interview with Pat Carroll, accessed February 27, 2017 via http://classicshowbiz.blogspot.com/2013/10/an-interview-with-pat-carroll-part-two.html.
5. Ibid.
6. "The Fastest Man on Earth," Part 1, *Improbable Research* website, accessed February 27, 2017 via http://www.improbable.com/airchives/paperair/volume9/v9i5/murphy/murphy1.html.; Graeme Philipson, "Technology Bites Back," *The Sydney Morning Herald*, April 9, 2005, accessed February 28, 2017 via http://www.smh.com.au/news/Icon/Technology-bites-back/2005/04/06/1112489536595.html.
7. Several articles reassess the numbers of fatalities from the Great Smog of 1952 (otherwise known as the "Big Smoke") footnoted in "Great Smog of London," *Wikipedia, The Free Encyclopedia*. See Footnote #2, accessed February 27, 2017 via https://en.wikipedia.org/wiki/Great_Smog_of_London.
8. Jess McNally, "July 26, 1943: L.A. Gets First Big Smog," *Wired.com*, July, 26, 2010, accessed February 27, 2017 via https://www.wired.com/2010/07/0726la-first-big-smog/.
9. "Brooklyn Doctors Ask Atom Curb, Sees Tests Far Away Peril to City," *New York Times*, June 19, 1954, 17.
10. Print advertisement for Portland Cement Association, in *50s All-American Ads*, Jim Heimann, ed. (Taschen, 2002), 155.
11. Anthony Bond, "The Day a Nuclear Bomb Fell on South Carolina: Extraordinary Story of How U.S. Air Force Accidentally Dropped Weapon of Mass Destruction onto Little Girl's Playhouse," *Daily Mail*, April 26, 2012; updated May 1, 2012, accessed February 27, 2016 via http://www.dailymail.co.uk/news/article-2135832/Boy-got-lucky-The-incredible-story-U-S-air-force-accidentally-dropped-nuclear-weapon-little-girls-playhouse-1958-South-Carolina.html. The Greggs' story comprises the 1958 entry for Mark Dunn's 100-short stories of the 20th century masterwork *American Decameron*, "Explosive in South Carolina."
12. *What's My Line?* on TV.com web-

site, Episode 295—January 29, 1956, under Notes, accessed February 27, 2017 via http://www.tv.com/shows/whats-my-line/episode-295–95445/trivia/. Not that it would take anyone but the most sophisticated nuclear scientist to make sense of the minutiae of atomic science that lived in the brilliant Dr. Kloepper's head. What follows is an abstract of an article he wrote with two other distinguished physicists for *Physical Review Letters*, published November 15, 1952. (A quick browse of the following is all that is required of the reader—accessed February 27, 2017 via http://journals.aps.org/pr/abstract/10.1103/PhysRev.88.695.)

Angular and Direction-Polarization Correlation for Co60, Cs134, and Sb124. Using the experimental techniques of Metzger and Deutsch the gamma-gamma angular and direction-polarization correlations have been measured for Co60, Cs134 and Sb124. The reliable results of previous investigations were confirmed for Co60 and served to check the instrument. The direction-polarization of Cs134 is consistent with a 4–2-0; EQ,EQ spin assignment. The absence of gamma-gamma angular and direction-polarization correlation in Sb124 requires a multipole mixture for the upper transition and a 3–2-0 spin assignment to the levels involved in the gamma-gamma transitions with no parity changes. The beta-gamma angular and direction-polarization correlation in Sb124 agrees with the 3–2-0 spin assignments for the levels of the beta-gamma transitions and with an EQ gamma.

Bibliography

Books

Ashley, Sally. *F.P.A.: The Life and Times of Franklin Pearce Adams.* New York: Beaufort Books, 1986.
Barnouw, Erik. *The Golden Web: A History of Broadcasting in the United States 1933–1953.* New York: Oxford University Press, 1968.
____. *The Image Empire: A History of Broadcasting in the United States, Vol III – from 1953.* New York: Oxford University Press, 1970.
Baughman, James L. *Same Time, Same Station.* Baltimore: The Johns Hopkins University Press, 2007.
Blumenthal, Norm. *When Game Shows Ruled Daytime TV.* Albany, GA: BearManor Media, 2010.
Boddy, William. *Fifties Television: The Industry and Its Critics.* Urbana, IL: University of Illinois Press, 1990.
Calloway, Cab, and Bryant Rollins. *Minnie The Moocher and Me.* New York: Thomas Y. Crowell Co., 1976.
Cassidy, Martha F. *What Women Watched: Daytime Television in the 1950s.* Austin, TX: University of Texas Press, 2005.
Castleman, Harry, and Walter J. Podrazik. *Watching TV: Four Decades of American Television* New York: McGraw-Hill, 1982.
Cerf, Bennett. *At Random: Reminiscences of Bennett Cerf.* New York: Random House, 1977.
DeLong, Thomas A. *Quiz Craze: America's Infatuation with Game Shows.* New York: Praeger, 1991.
Doherty, Thomas. *Cold War, Cool Medium: Television, McCarthyism, and American Culture.* New York: Columbia University Press, 2003.
Dwan, Robert. *As Long As They're Laughing.* Baltimore: Midnight Marquee Press, Inc., 2000.
Dworkin, Susan. *Miss America, 1945: Bess Myerson's Own Story.* New York: Newmarket Press, 1987.
Fabe, Maxene. *TV Game Shows.* Garden City, NY: Dolphin, 1979.
Fates, Gil. *What's My Line? The History of America's Most Famous Panel Show.* Englewood Cliffs, NJ: Prentice Hall, 1978.
Faulk, John Henry. *Fear on Trial.* New York: Simon and Schuster, 1964.
Fletcher, Sherry, and Cindy Carpenter. *Truth or Consequences (Images of America).* Mount Pleasant, SC: Arcadia, 2010.
Fox, Stephen. *The Mirror Makers: A History of American Advertising and its Creators.* New York: Vintage Books/Random House, 1985.

Francis, Arlene. *Arlene Francis: A Memoir.* New York: Simon and Schuster, 1978.
Halberstam, David. *The Fifties.* New York: Villard Books, 1993.
Hoerschelmann, Olaf. *Rules of the Game: Quiz Shows and American Culture.* Albany: State University of New York, 2006.
Israel, Lee. *Kilgallen.* New York: Dell Publishing, 1979.
Kisseloff, Jeff. *The Box: An Oral History of Television, 1920–1961.* New York: Viking, 1995.
MacDonald, J. Fred. *Blacks and White TV: African Americans in Television Since 1948.* Belmont, CA: Wadsworth Publishing, 1992.
_____. *One Nation Under Television.* New York: Pantheon Books, 1990.
_____. *Television and the Red Menace: The Video Road to Vietnam.* New York: Praeger, 1985.
Marx, Groucho, and Hector Arce. *The Secret Word Is Groucho.* New York: G.P. Putnam's Sons, 1976.
May, Elaine Tyler. *Homeward Bound: American Families and the Cold War Era.* New York: Basic Books, 1988.
Mehling, Harold. *The Great Time-Killer.* Cleveland: The World Publishing Company, 1962.
Miller, Arthur. *Timebends: A Life.* New York: Grove Press, 1987.
Mittell, Jason. *Television and American Culture.* New York: Oxford University Press, 2010.
Morgan, Henry. *Here's Morgan!* New York: Barricade Books, 1994.
Murray, Susan, and Laurie Ouellette. *Reality TV: Remaking Television Culture.* New York: NYC Press, 2008.
Oakley, J. Ronald. *God's Country: America in the Fifties.* New York: Dembner Books, 1986.
Opotowsky, Stan. *TV—The Big Picture.* New York: Collier Books, 1962.
Paley, William S. *As It Happened: A Memoir.* Garden City, NY: Doubleday, 1979.
Red Channels: The Report of Communist Influence in Radio and Television. New York: Counterattack, 1950.
Schwartz, David, Steve Ryan, and Fred Wostbrock. *The Encyclopedia of TV Game Shows.* New York: Facts on File, Inc., 1995.
Sherman, Allan. *A Gift of Laughter.* New York: Atheneum, 1965.
Spigel, Lynn. *Make Room for TV: Television and the Family Ideal in Postwar America.* Chicago: University of Chicago Press, 1992.
Sterling, Christopher H., and John M. Kittross. *Stay Tuned: A History of American Broadcasting.* Mahwah, NJ: Lawrence Erlbaum, 2002.
Tobias, Andrew. *Fire and Ice: The Story of Charles Revson, the Man Who Built Revlon.* New York: William Morrow, 1976.
Von Schilling, James Arthur. *The Magic Window: American Television, 1939–1953.* Binghamton, NY: Haworth Press, 2003.

Periodical Articles and Stand-Alone Book Chapters (including on-line articles)

Ace, Goodman. Column in *Saturday Review*, October 28, 1950.
Adams, Val. "Praise Pours in on Murrow Show." *New York Times*, March 11, 1954.
"Advertising. Geritol's Bitter Pill." *Time*, February 5, 1973.
"As TV Scandal Stirs the Whole Nation, Views of the Viewers at One Quiz Show." *Life*, October 26, 1959.
"As We See It." *TV Guide*, January 8, 1954.
_____. March 26, 1954.
Baker, Russell. "Do Them Yourself." *New York Times*, October 1, 1994.

Barrett, Alfred J. "Stop the Misery!" *America*, March 13, 1954.
"*The Big Payoff's* Third Anniversary." Ad in *Variety*, January 5, 1955.
"A Big Quiz for Quizzes." *Life*. October 19, 1959.
Blake, Howard. "An Apologia from the Man Who Produced the Worst Program in TV History." In *American Broadcasting: A Source Book on the History of Radio and Television*, edited by Lawrence W. Lichty and Malachi C. Topping. New York: Hasting House, 1975.
Brenner, Marie. "The Man Who Knew Too Much." *Vanity Fair*, May, 1996.
"Bride and Groom Coming Back on Television Soon." *Ellensburg Daily Record*, June 6, 1957.
"Cause of It All Turns Up." *New York Times*, January 31, 1943.
"Charity Load Linked to Give-Away Shows." *New York Times*, February 5, 1954.
"Charity Vaunteth Not Itself." *Life*, August 17, 1953.
Cohen, Pieter, and Nicolas Rasmussen. "A Nation of Kids on Speed." *Wall Street Journal*, June 16, 2013.
"Comparative list of television receivers by name and model, tube size, and price." *Saturday Review*, February 26, 1949.
Cotler, Gordon. "That Strange TV Audience." *New York Times Magazine*, May 16, 1954.
Crosby, John. "Mr. Paley and the Critics." *New York Herald Tribune*, October 28, 1946.
"Daily N.B.C. Show Will Be on Tape." *New York Times*, January 18, 1957.
"Death of a Salesman: Fine Tragedy Becomes a Critical and Box-office Sensation." *Life*, February 21, 1949.
"The Defense of Staying Live." *Variety*, January 5, 1955.
Dowd, Maureen. "The Early Death of a Bedeviled Genius." *New York Times*, May 25, 1985.
"Ex-Convict Strikes It Rich Briefly on TV, but Fame Proves a Give-Away to Police." *New York Times*, January 27, 1954.
Ferretti, Fred. "Fleeting Fame: When Quiz Kids Grow Up." *New York Times*, December 26, 1982.
Fretts, Bruce. "The 60 Greatest Game Shows of All Time." *TV Guide*, June 12, 2013.
Friedan, Betty. "Television and the Feminine Mystique." In *Television: Selections from TV GUIDE Magazine*, edited by Barry G. Cole. New York: The Free Press, 1970.
"Giveaways ... Are Legal." *Business Week*, April 10, 1954.
"Gleason Analyzes Last Week's Failure." *New York Times*, January 28, 1961.
Gould, Jack Gould. Column. *New York Times*, September 22, 1950.
_____. "A Look at 'Strike It Rich' as Video Entertainment: Human Emotions and Commercial Appeal." *New York Times*, November 9, 1951.
"Happy New Year." *Broadcasting*, December 28, 1959.
Hart, Hugh. "Feb. 1, 1951: TV Shows Atomic Blast Live." Wiredwww, February 1, 2010.
Herzog, Herta. "Professor Quiz – A Gratification Study." In *Radio and the Printed Page*, edited by Paul F. Lazarfeld. New York: Duell, Sloan & Pearce, 1940.
Hobson, Dick. "TV's Disastrous Brain Drain." In *Television: Selections from TV GUIDE Magazine*, edited by Barry G. Cole. New York: The Free Press, 1970.
"It Could Be You!" *Ocala Star Banner*, September 25, 1960.
"John Henry Faulk, 76, Dies; Humorist Who Challenged Blacklist." *New York Times*, April 10, 1990.
Kalb, Bernard. "Bennett Cerf: He Also Works in Video." *New York Times*, August 2, 1953.
Krassner, Paul. "Case History of a TV Hoax." *The Realist*, June, 1960.
_____. "A Stereophonic Hoax." *The Realist*. March, 1960.
"Letters to the Editors." *Life*, September 7, 1953.
"Mail Flood Gives Radio Quiz Loser No Rest as Truckloads of Gifts Begin to Arrive." *New York Times*, January 28, 1943.
Meyer, Phil. "Miamians Debate Quiz Shows." *Miami Herald*, November 16, 1959.
"NBC-TV's Major Daytime Advances; Forge Ahead on Sales, Ratings." *Variety*, February 6, 1957.

"New Mexico Legends. Hot Springs to Truth or Consequences." *Legends of America.* (Online: www.legendsofamerica.com.)
Oliver, Myrna. "Texas Humorist John Faulk Dies: Exposed and Beat Blacklisting." *Los Angeles Times*, April 11, 1990.
Paley, William S. "Broadcasting and American Society." In *Annals of the American Academy of Political and Social Science*, January 1941.
Porter, Russell. "TV Inquiry Raises Perjury Question." *New York Times*, November 9, 1959.
"Prodigy Rings the Bell." *Life*, May 7, 1956.
"Queen for a Day: Housewives Schedule Wrecker." *Look*, April 1, 1958.
"Quiz Shows Blitz Actors." *Variety*, July 10, 1940.
"Radio Error Starts a Shower of Pennies That Turn to Mail Deluge in Staten Island." *New York Times*, January 26, 1943.
"Radio Quiz Tells Guest Where $1000 Is, Holyoke Listeners Beat Train, Dig It Up." *New York Times*, November 6, 1944.
"Radio. The Big Money." *Time*, September 3, 1956.
"Radio. Top Ten." *Time*, February 27, 1956.
_____. August 13, 1956.
"Radio. What Comes Naturally." *Time*, November 7, 1949.
"Red Visitors Cause Rumpus: Dupes and Fellow Travelers Dress Up Communist Fronts." *Life*, April 4, 1949.
"Reigns of Queens for a Day Span 15 Years with 3,921 Rulers, Mostly Crowned by Bailey." *Los Angeles Times*, May 1, 1960.
Shanley, J.P. "TV Boycott Asked on Network Job Bias," *New York Times*, February 21, 1955.
_____. "TV: A Grim Warning. 'I've Got a Secret' Drops Gags to Show Graphically Holiday Driving Perils." *New York Times*, August 29, 1957.
"Show Business. A Melancholy Business." *Time*, October 26, 1959.
"Some Basic Statistical Data." Insert in Mead, Margaret. "She Has Strength Based in a Pioneer Past. *Life*, December 24, 1956.
"Television: Inspiring Post-Mortem." *Time*, February 3, 1961.
Todman, Bill. "Freedom of the Dial," *Variety*, January 5, 1949.
"Truth or Consequences—What's with That Crazy Name?" *Sierra County Is New Mexico True.* (Online: www. sierracountynewmexico.info/blog/a-town-named-after-a-game-show/.)
"TV Quiz Business Is Itself Quizzed About Fix Charges." *Life*, September 15, 1958.
Wernick, Robert. "Jackpot! Golden Rain of Motorcycles, Great Danes and Ermine Falls on West Philadelphia." *Life*, March 28, 1949.
"Winning Ways." *Newsweek*, August 17, 1953.
Young, A.S. "Doc." "The Black Athlete in the Golden Age of Sports, Part VI: The Black Athlete Makes His Mark." *Ebony*, May, 1969.

General Web Sources*

Archive of American Television. Oral history interviews. www.emmytvlegends.org/interviews/shows/.
Early Television Museum. www.earlytelevision.org/.
I've Got a Secret Episode Guide. http://carsonscrafts.com/igas/igas_1959.htm.
Nesteroff, Kliph. *Classic Television Showbiz* website. www.classicshowbiz.blogspot.com/.
1956–67 Episode Guide. *To Tell the Truth.* CBS Nightime Series. http://www.ttttontheweb.com/ttttnighttimeguide.html.
TV.com website, for complete *What's My Line?* episode guide. www.tv.com/shows/whats-my-line/.

Miscellaneous Sources

Cerf, Bennett. Interview with Robbin Hawkins, January 23, 1968. Columbia University Libraries Oral History Research Office Notable New Yorkers Series.
Goodson, Mark. "The Anatomy of a Game." Seminar, The Museum of Television and Radio, October 9, 1985.
Marx, Groucho. Marx to Bergen Evans, February 27, 1959, Groucho Marx Papers, Library of Congress.
Pinkham, Richard A. R. Address to NBC TV affiliates meeting, November 25, 1955. In NBC Papers, Library of Congress.
Ross, Leonard. "Interview with Leonard Ross." *The Mike Wallace Interview*, December 21, 1957, Harry Ransom Center, the University of Texas at Austin. http://www.hrc.utexas.edu/multimedia/video/2008/wallace/ross_leonard_t.html.
Weaver, Pat. Memo from Weaver to Joseph H. McConnell, November 12, 1951. In NBC Papers, Library of Congress.

* See *Periodicals* for periodical articles published on-line. Video recordings of many of the programs referenced in this book were viewed by the author via such internet sites as YouTube.com and Internet Archive (archive.org), where, over the last ten years, hundreds of these recordings have been uploaded by individuals under terms of fair-use access (thus obviating the need for contemporary and future researchers to make arrangements for use via custodians of traditional institutional media holdings—a boon to media history scholars). The recordings are largely accessible by title and date or, in the case of YouTube, as part of collections and subscriptions. Shows from the Goodson/Todman stable are, for example, easily accessible on YouTube.com via subscription-channels expressly related to those programs.

Index

Abel, Hazel 69
Abel, Rudolf 126
AFTRA (labor union) 135–136
Alaska statehood 52
The Alcoa Hour see "Tragedy in a Temporary Town" (*The Alcoa Hour*)
Allen, Fred 12–13
Allen, Steve 128; *see also What's My Line?*
Allen, Woody 10
Am Plus 43; *see also* Charles Pfizer (pharmaceutical company)
American Gas Association 121
Americana 149
Amos 'n' Andy 93
Andrews, Julie 85–86
Anka, Paul 148
Anybody Can Play 32
Anybody Can Win 32
Armstrong, Neil 180
Army-McCarthy hearings *see* Senate Subcommittee on Investigations
AromaRama 172
The Art Ford Show 26
AWARE (organization) 130, 135–136

Bailey, Jack 78, 140; *see also Queen for a Day*
Balestrero, Manny 52
Banzhaf, Max 123
Barrett, Alfred J. 75–76
Barry, Jack 10, 42, 162–163
Beale, Al 53
Bean, Orson 91, 133–134
Beat the Clock 3, 24, 61, 150
beatniks 170–171
Belafonte, Harry 102–103
Belcher, Jerry 29; *see also Vox Pop*
A Bell for Adano (book) 48

Bennett, Harve 13
Bergen, Polly 146; *see also To Tell the Truth*
Beulah 92–93
Bid 'n' Buy 139
The Big Payoff 66–67, 90, 139
The Big Surprise 107
Billingsley, Sherman 84
Blake, Howard 78–79; *see also Queen for a Day*
Blatty, William Peter 34
Blind Date 21
Blue Denim (play) 148
Blumenthal, Norm 117
Boyington, Pappy 48
Bride and Groom 37–38, 139
Bridge of Spies (film) 126
Bromo-Seltzer 42–43
Brothers, Joyce 58–59
Brown, Vanessa 13
Bunche, Ralph 103

Cadore, Leon 41
Calloway, Cab 97
Calvert, James F. 176
Camel cigarettes 114–115
The Camel News Caravan 114–15
Cape Fear (film) 189–190*ch*9*n*5
Carlisle, Kitty 11, 106; *see also To Tell the Truth*
Carroll, Pat 175
Carson, Johnny 65–66; *see also Who Do You Trust?*
Caruso, Enrico (hair stylist) 170
Cash and Carry 27, 31
Cates, Joseph 161
The CBS Television Quiz 27
Cerf, Bennett 83–84, 87, 90–91; *see also What's My Line?*

203

Index

Chance for Romance 37
Charles Pfizer (pharmaceutical company) 43; *see also* Am Plus
Chen, Maisie 107
Chesley, Harry W. 123
Choose Up Sides 104
Clark, Odelle 98
Cobb, Ty 41
Cole, Nat King 95–96
Collette, Buddy 101
Collyer, Bud 106, 136; *see also Beat the Clock*; *To Tell the Truth*
Concentration 117, 185n7
coonskin caps 171–172
Corrigan, "Wrong Way" 54–55
Counterattack (newsletter, publisher) 129–130, 192n17
Cowan, Louis G. 155–156
The Cuban Revolution (1953–59) 52
Cullen, Bill 53, 166
Cultural and Scientific Conference for World Peace *see* 1949 Cultural and Scientific Conference for World Peace

Dagmar 59
Daly, John Charles 59, 146, 153; *see also What's My Line?*
DeSoto Plymouth automobiles 117
Dingell, John 52
Dix, Dorothy 40
Do You Trust Your Wife? 115
Dr. I.Q., the Mental Banker 14
The Doom Pussy (book) 70
Doss, Karl 99
Dotto 156
Double or Nothing 165–166
Douglas, Kirk 134–135
Downs, Hugh 117
DuMont Television Network 27, 83, 95
Dwan, Robert 25, 33, 100, 132–133, 145; *see also You Bet Your Life*

Edwards, Ralph 16–19, 76; *see also Truth or Consequences*
Eisenhower, Dwight D. 50, 57, 69, 126, 151, 158, 160, 177
Eisenhower, Mamie 57, 180
Ellison, Ralph 92
Everything You Always Wanted to Know About Sex (*But Were Afraid to Ask)* (film) 10

Faragó, Ladislas 48
Fates, Gil 129

Faulk, John Henry 135–136
Feldman, Ruth Duskin 13
Fielding, Jerry 100, 132–133; *see also You Bet Your Life*
Fischer, Bobby 148
Fitzgerald, Ella 102
Forever Amber (book) 169
The Four Horsemen of Notre Dame (football team backfield) 51
Framer, Walt 73, 90; *see also The Big Payoff*; *Strike It Rich*
Francis, Arlene 21, 38, 60, 86, 91, 102; *see also Blind Date*; *What's My Line?*
Freed, Allen 146
Freedman, Albert 159, 161–164
Freedom Rings 61
Friedan, Betty 63–64
Friedkin, William 102
Fuller, Lou 178–179

Gabel, Martin 86, 91, 132; *see also What's My Line?*
Gagnon, Rene 49
Geritol 41–42; *see also* Pharmaceuticals, Inc.
Glamour Girl 72–74, 77
Gleason, Jackie 60, 173–175; *see also You're in the Picture*
Glenn, John 162, 175–176
Golenpaul, Dan 117
Gonzales, Pancho 108
Gonzalez Gonzalez, Pedro 108
Goodson, Mark 60–61; *see also* Goodson-Todman Productions; *I've Got a Secret*; *The Price Is Right*; *To Tell the Truth*; *What's My Line?*
Goodson-Todman Productions 31, 110; *see also* Goodson, Mark
Gould, Jack 46, 73–74
Griffin, Merv 152, 170
Griffith, Brandy 177
Guedel, John 25; *see also You Bet Your Life*

Hagedorn, Connie 171
Hagen, John P. 176
Hair, Warren 50
Harris, Oren 157
Hartnett, Vincent 130–131
Hawaii statehood 52
Heller, Franklin 124
Herbert, Anthony 46–47
High Finance 80
Hilgemeier, Edward, Jr. 156

Index

Hit the Jackpot 140
Hodges, Eddie 162, 175, 194*n*30
House Subcommittee on Legislative Oversight 121, 157
House Un-American Activities Committee 127
Hubert, Julia 12
hula hoop 171
The Hungarian Uprising (1956) 50

Information Please 14–16, 117, 161
International Geophysical Year 176
Invisible Man (book) 92
It Could Be You 49–50, 107
It Pays to Be Ignorant 16
It's a Mad, Mad, Mad, Mad World (film) 60
I've Got a Secret 40–41, 46–47, 49–50, 52, 54–56, 60, 83, 85, 88, 90, 98, 107, 113, 117–118, 148, 150, 170–172, 177, 179–180

The Jackpot (film) 144
Janney, Leon 133
Johnson, Parks 29; see also *Vox Pop*
Jones, Daniel "Chappie," Jr. 103
"Judgment at Nuremberg" (*Playhouse 90*) 120–121
Juvenile Jury 162

Katz, Oscar 162
Kay Kyser's Kollege of Musical Knowledge 20–21
Keep It in the Family 150
Kefauver, Estes 53, 171–172
Kennedy, John F. 106, 158, 170, 175
Kilgallen, Dorothy 86, 91, 127–128, 146, 168; see also *What's My Line?*
Kitt, Eartha 94
Kloepper, Robert M. 180
Kollege of Musical Knowledge see *Kay Kyser's Kollege of Musical Knowledge*
Krassner, Paul 118–119
Kupperman, Joel 13
Kyser, Kay 20

"Lavender Scare" 151
A League of Their Own (film) 68–69
Lee, Gypsy Rose 133
Leiber, Jerry 146
Leyden, Bill 49; see also *It Could Be You*
USS *Leyte* (CV-32) 55
Liberace 152
Lincoln, Abraham: assassination 54

Lockerman, Gloria 96–97
Loeb, Philip 130–131
Lorayne, Harry 88
Louis, Joe 80
Lynley, Carol 148

MacArthur, Douglas 120
"Madison" (dance) 171
Man Against Crime 114
Marx, Groucho 5, 25, 32–34, 64, 99–100, 108, 117, 132–133 146–147, 153–154, 161, 163, 166–168, 170–171; see also *You Bet Your Life*
Masquerade Party 5, 84, 118–119
McCarthy, Joseph 126–128
McCoy, Jack 77; see also *Glamour Girl*
Merrill, Howard 169
Miller, Arthur 37, 125–126
Minow, Newton N. 181
Modern Women: The Lost Sex (book) 64–65
Monroe, Marilyn 37, 172
Montenier, Jules 119–120
Moore, Garry 113, 148; see also *I've Got a Secret*
Morgan, Henry 113, 128–131, 134, 170; see also *I've Got a Secret*
Morton, H.G. 64
Mother's Day 62
The Mrs. America Pageant 67
Murray, Jan 88
Murrow, Edward R. 96, 112, 126–127
Myerson, Bess 66–67, 89–90; see also *The Big Payoff*

Nadler, Terry 143
Name That Tune 97, 162, 166, 175
The Nat King Cole Show 95
USS *Nautilus* 180
1949 Cultural and Scientific Conference for World Peace 125

O'Brian, Jack 127–128
O'Keefe, Walter 165–166
Old Gold cigarettes 114
Omnibus 94
One in a Million 33

Paley, William S. 94
Palmer, Betsy 2; see also *I've Got a Secret*
Papp, Joseph 85
Parks, Bert 68
Parliament cigarettes 116

206 Index

People Are Funny 184*n*19
Person to Person 96
Pharmaceuticals, Inc. 41–42; see also Geritol
Philbin, Regis 10–11
Place the Face 74–75
Playhouse 90 see "Judgment at Nuremberg" (*Playhouse 90*)
Poitier, Sidney 94
polio 52–53
Pot o' Gold 29–30
Pot o' Gold (film) 185*ch*3*n*4
Pot o' Gold (radio play) 185–186*ch*3*n*4
Powers, Francis Gary 126, 160
Presley, Elvis 146–147, 172
The Price Is Right 31–32, 139
Procter and Gamble 101–102
Project Vanguard 176
Purvis, Melvin 55

Queen for a Day 3, 73, 77–81, 140–141
Quiz Kids 13–14
Quizzical 97–98

Radio Days (film) 11, 13–14
The Realist (magazine) 118–119
Red Channels 129–132, 136
Remington Rand (company) 120
Rene, Roberta 146–147
Revson, Charles 121–123
Revson, Martin 122
Rheingold Beer 189*ch*8*n*4
RICO Act 53
R.J. Reynolds (tobacco company) 113–114
Robertson, Oscar 148
Robinson, Jackie 98
Rogers, Walter 122
Roosevelt family (Eleanor, Elliot, James) 185*ch*3*n*4
Ross, Lenny 142–143
Roxanne (Dolores Rosedale) 61; see also Beat the Clock
Rudolph, Amanda 95

Sarnoff, David 127
Schell, Ronnie 170–171
Schisler, John 52
Schweitzer, Mitchell D. 156
Second Honeymoon 68, 139–140
See It Now 112
Senate Subcommittee on Investigations 128–129
Seneca, Cornelius Vanderbilt 105–106

Serutan 42
Seymour, Samuel L. 54
Shepard, Elaine 69–70
Sherman, Allan 117–118, 150, 169; see also I've Got a Secret
The $64,000 Question 58, 96–97, 107, 142, 155
Sixty Minutes 115
USS *Skate* 176
Smell-O-Vision 172
Spindletop (Texas) Oil Field 55
Springs, Elliot White 49
Sputnik 1 50, 175
Stapp, John Paul 176–177
Stempel, Herb 156–157
Stoller, Mike 146
Stop the Music 11–12
The Stork Club 84
Strike It Rich 71–76
The Suez Crisis (1956) 53
Susann, Jacqueline 90

Talmadge, Herman 92
television station license freeze 23
Terry-Thomas 60
Think Fast 133
This Is Your Life 76
Thomas, John Charles 147
To Tell the Truth 37, 40–42, 48, 50–52, 54–55, 57, 68–69, 97–98, 105–106, 111–112, 116, 126, 146, 152, 170–172, 176–177
Todman, Bill see Goodson-Todman Productions
Tombaugh, Clyde 56–57
Tomkins, William F. 126
Toscani, Frank E. 48
"Tragedy in a Temporary Town" (*The Alcoa Hour*) 190*n*5
Treasure Hunt 160
Truman, Harry S. 120
Truman, Margaret 185–186*ch*3*n*4
Trumbo, Dalton 135
Truth or Consequences 16–19, 46, 184*n*21
Truth or Consequences, New Mexico 17–18, 184*n*21
Twenty-One 41, 155–157, 159–161

Untermeyer, Louis 124–126

Vander Meer, Johnny 41
Van Doren, Charles 155, 157, 159–161
Van Dyke, Dick 38

Index

Vanguard rocket *see* Project Vanguard
"Vast Wasteland" speech (Minow) 181
Vox Pop 29

Wallace, Mike 115–116, 143
Washington, Kenny 99
Watson, James 14
Weaver, Pat 45, 110–112
Whatever Happened to the Quiz Kids? (book) 13
What's My Line? 2, 35–36, 38–40, 49, 52–53, 57, 59, 67–69, 83–86, 97–98, 119–120, 124, 126–129, 146, 153, 168–169, 171–172, 176–180, 187*n*4
Who Do You Trust? 65–66
Wigand, Jeffrey 115

Wilkins, Hubert 176
Williams, Richard L. 13
Winchell, Paul 88
Winn, Marie 156
Winsor, Kathleen 169
With This Ring 37
Word for Word 170
The Wrong Man (film) 52

Yates, Donald N. 177
You Bet Your Life 5, 25, 32–34, 46, 64, 98–101, 108, 117, 132–133, 145–146, 153–154, 161, 166–168, 170, 179–180
You're in the Picture 173–175

Zarumin 42

www.ingramcontent.com/pod-product-compliance
Ingram Content Group UK Ltd.
Pitfield, Milton Keynes, MK11 3LW, UK
UKHW042002140426
5217IPUK00015B/947